Bob Church

THIS *Fishing* LIFE

The Crowood Press

First published in 2003 by
The Crowood Press Ltd
Ramsbury, Marlborough
Wiltshire SN8 2HR

www.crowood.com

British Library Cataloguing-in-Publication Data
A catalogue record for this book is available from the British Library.

ISBN 1 86126 622 7

Dedication
I dedicate this book to my lovely wife Jeanette. I am very proud of what
she has achieved, in fly fishing and fly tying, although she will never
accept any praise. In twenty-five years she has never stopped me from
consistently pushing my selfish pursuits, fishing and football. I could not
have done all these fishing stories without her help and support.

Acknowledgements
Quite a lot of people to thank, certainly Donna for typing the
manuscript and Julie for the poem. Thanks must go to EMAP who
allowed me to run my trout page in the *Angling Times* for twenty-eight
years. Also under the EMAP banner is *Trout Fisherman Magazine*,
created by Bob Feetham, John Wilshaw and myself, it's been a success
story. It has been the two editors, Chris Dawn and John Wilshaw, with
whom I have worked closely. From my publishers, Crowood, I have
always had an understanding relationship and we have six other
successful books to our partnership. Thanks to the other recent editors,
for instance, Kevin Clifford, of *Coarse Angling Today* and Stu Dexter of
Coarse Fisherman Magazine, for whom I am currently writing. I must
also thank my old competitive partner for his very kind words in the
foreword.

Typeset by Textype, Cambridge

Printed and bound in Great Britain by The Bath Press

Contents

A Lifetime of Fishing

Locked in the memory of every man
Is the tale of his fishing and how it began.
No longer a boy with his youthful ways
But a man who has fished 'til the end of his days.

Once was a time when he never saw age,
When rods were split cane and silk lines all the rage.
Those seemingly endless, carefree times
When wild trout would tug at the end of the lines.

Times moved so fast, still waters began
To capture the heart of the fisherman.
Loch style was invented, drifting with ease,
Casting at fish who always would tease.

Drogues were the new thing to slow the drift down,
Sunk lines were considered the best thing in town.
Mini lures replaced the old claret and teals
With marabou feathers and fur from the seals.

By now rods are so light and so easy to cast
Aching shoulders are a pain of the past.
Motorised boats with no need to row
Taking the angler where he wants to go.

As years come and go so much has changed,
But the love of our sport will always remain.
Armed with all the new inventions of the fishing trade
That first-caught trout is an angler made.

Look back over the years to your very first cast,
Remember that moment way back in your past.
The thrill of the take, the scream of your reel,
That very first fish and how it made you feel.

Julie Emerson

Forewords

When the England team won their third World Championship gold in Canada, present at the final dinner by chance was the late Norman Lumsden, alias J.R. Hartley of TV fame. Sitting at the table next to the Japanese team I found it difficult to explain to them why someone who could not fish had briefly become the best-known angler in the country.

However, there is no problem for me in justifying the overwhelming vote in *Trout Fisherman* of April 2000 nominating Bob as the Angler of the Millennium. Izaak Walton's effigy on the Great Screen at Winchester Cathedral might have raised an eyebrow at his omission, but no angler of the last century has any reason to gripe at the choice. Indeed it underplays Bob's many contributions to the sport that the vote was confined to trout and fly fishermen when a main part of his achievements is his all-round skills. His coarse-fishing record is also outstanding, as is his specimen hunting. He was a founder member in 1963 of the Northampton Specimen Group, which is currently rated the best in the UK.

Northampton figures prominently in Bob's all-round sporting interests, which extend to cricket, rugby and soccer. Being a director of Northampton Football Club has given him much pleasure, together with some emotional suffering and much financial loss, without ever denting his eternal optimism!

There are other more important aspects justifying his reputation as being, like Walton, a Complete Angler. There is his success as TV and media personality. This is, for instance, his tenth book. Editors don't accept so many unless the earlier ones are successful. Nor do they continue to endorse a column like Bob's in *Angling Times* which has appeared without a break for thirty years. As a writer I know what an extraordinary feat it is to writes as many articles without slumping to boring repetition.

There is, too, his readiness to help as wide a range of anglers as possible to share his pleasure and his discoveries. Many would have kept to themselves his developments like new flies, or slow sink lines being better than floating on reservoirs, followed by even greater success with Hi D and the deadly 'lift and hang' technique. Instead, Bob publicized them at once.

I also find particularly admirable his massive competition success. There are several pontificating pundits whose practical ability does not match their writing or research skills. Bob has never shirked putting his reputation on the line. Lord Grey wrote that the final stage in an angler's development is a desire to test your skill against others. Walton wrote 'I envy not him that is richer than I. I envy him, and him only, who catches more fish.' Bob has passed Grey's test triumphantly. His catch rate, and the size of his varied specimen fish, would have turned Walton green.

There is no space to list the catalogue of his success in national or international competition up to the highest level in European, Commonwealth and World events. One example will suffice. Bob has a complete set of World Championship medals with two golds, a silver and a bronze (and a fourth as well).

Bob was a mainstay of several of the teams in the ten years when England dominated the championship with five individual and four team golds, plus a clutch of silvers and bronzes. Part of this success was due to six or seven remarkable anglers like himself including all those in the 1987 team. They won the team event on Rutland and Grafham with more than double the points of the next place of the twenty other countries. In the individual event, extended to stillwater and river to test all-round skills, they were 1st, 2nd, 3rd, 4th and 6th. Compare that with the recent humiliating 12th place the next time the championship was staged in England, with very similar venues and number of countries involved.

Much of the ten years of success was also down to Geoff Clarkson's managership and virtual control of selection, and to the members' total commitment to doing well, pride in performance and the best teamwork I have witnessed in any sport. In that, too, Bob was outstanding.

A change to more 'democratic' selection (as I warned at the time), coupled with failure to maintain previous standards in the basics of preparations, teamwork and individual commitment have led inevitably to failure to win a single medal since. But in part it must be due to inability to find replacements with the all-round skill of Bob and the 1987 team, and a few others like Jeremy Herrmann.

With his wide-ranging experiences and knowledge we are lucky to benefit from Bob's ever-present desire to share them with others. Enjoy his book. I have.

Tony Pawson OBE

We all owe Bob Church a debt of gratitude, and me probably more than most. I'll explain.

I first met Bob thirty years ago when he suggested we share a boat on Ravensthorpe. He had an idea he wanted to discuss. Would there be room for a magazine devoted to stillwater trout fishing? A year later, *Trout Fisherman* was born and the rest is history.

What isn't so well known is that all of those early contributors – the likes of Dick Shrive, Frank Cutler and Arthur Cove, all giants in their own special ways – only agreed to reveal their secrets to me purely on his recommendation. Without Bob's help those early magazines would have been pretty dull affairs.

In forty-odd years of angling journalism, I have yet to meet anyone who has put so much back into the sport. Others who later enjoyed quicksilver fame served only to prove the rule that Tuesday's roosters often become Wednesday's feather dusters. Bob was at the cutting edge of stillwater fishing back then, and that's where he has remained. Why? Simply because the next fish is the one he wants to catch, be it bearing spots or stripes, or living in a crystal stream or a murky river. And if he fails to catch, then he wants to know why. Competition, be it against a host of others or just himself, this is what makes Bob Church tick. On those early days at Graham and Draycote, where he pioneered many of the methods and flies regarded today as standards, he was the closest thing to perpetual motion. The new generation of high-speed competition lure pullers would have had their work cut out to keep up with a 1970s Bob Church at Muddler time. Remember, too, that the rods were chopped-down glassfibre carp rods and fly-lines thick enough to support a decent line of washing.

Bob and I are of an age. But while my fishing is a now pretty relaxed affair, done as much for the company and the pleasant places we get to fish, Bob is still going at it full tilt and I take my hat off to him.

John Wilshaw

At 17lb 3oz, this wild ferox brown trout from Ireland's Lough Corrib is Bob Church's favourite ever capture. It was returned alive and well to the depths.

Introduction

I was born in Northampton on 26 December 1935 and I have lived there ever since. Why would I wish to move, when the fishing hereabouts is some of the very best in Europe? There were never any anglers in my family before, although they did enjoy other sports. I too love all, or nearly all, other sports such as football, cricket, bowls and rugby union. However, I was destined to become a fanatical fisherman. Every trip to the waterside, from a young boy to a senior citizen, has always been a new adventure for me. I never tire or get bored no matter what species I am fishing for, or at any venue.

With my father volunteering for the Army in 1939, my mother moved to live with her mother in the country, at a tiny Northants village called Eastcote. It was here that I discovered my Grandma Burgess was a very tough lady. She was good at everything: she was a great cook, she ran the village pub (Rose & Crown) and I learned a lot of early lessons from her, including discipline.

The lovely country way of life had its drawbacks, such as a bucket loo at the top of the garden; water was by way of the village-green pump, which was some quarter of a mile away. Baths were pretty rare, but I did discover my first pond and I was fascinated by the creatures that lived in it.

In late-1943 we moved back to Northampton on the northern outskirts, at Kingsthorpe. It was a good place for me because the upper reaches of the River Nene ran through it. My new friends were Terry Inwood, Keith Denton and Arnold Haddon and we all loved fishing. Northampton has one of the largest open markets in England; it is right in the very centre of town. In those latter war-years the population was around 90,000 and it was primarily a shoe-making town.

Arnold's family of uncles and aunties, and so on, was big and they all had fruit and vegetable stalls on the market. Most Saturdays we boys would get on a bus to the town centre and visit all Arnold's relatives for his pocket money. We then went to Elmer's tackle shop to buy our tackle, which Arnold would share with us. Even in those days, eight to ten years old, I was businesslike. I remember we used to dig people's gardens for them, as most men were in the Armed Services. I also had a good sideline of collecting empty lemonade bottles, for which I would get tuppence each on their return.

My new school was Bective, first the juniors and then the secondary modern (after eleven years of age). It was a sporting school and I couldn't have landed in a better place. Most of the teachers were keen sportsmen too, so they pushed us to be good at athletics, football, rugby union, and swimming and we also boxed. Mr Gill Sibley was ex-RAF boxing champion and, although he was primarily a woodwork teacher, boxing tuition was a regular treat for us.

I was keen on all sports and participated well. My academic side remained very average until I was about thirteen, when I took a lot more interest. I began Comprehension, which really was English and essay writing. From then on I was always top of the class at Geography, History and, always for the four years at this school, top at Woodwork. This included technical drawing and practical. Do you know that, since leaving school, I have never made anything out of wood?

I did represent the school for hurdles, hop-step-and-jump, high jump, swimming, football and rugby. By the way, rugby was introduced into Northampton schools by our teacher at the time, Mr Les Barnes, who was on the committee at Northampton Saints Rugby Club. Naturally I had to have a go at this new sport as well. Another social and sporting club I had joined was the Boys Brigade. I was in the third company, who had a great football team. My first proper holidays were, in fact, with the Boys Brigade. A fortnight's camping at Skegness at fourteen and at Weston-super-Mare the following year were big time events for me. Of course, during the schoolday years I was wandering off to the banks of the River Nene to catch gudgeon, roach, perch, dace and even sometimes a small jack pike.

I had a very bad accident with just one week to go of my school days, just before my fifteenth birthday. It was during one of Mr Sibley's boxing matches. I had cut my opponent's lip – I remember him well, Edwin Winfield. I was concentrating on Mr Sibley's instructions of short straight punches. Edwin in the meantime had been throwing a series of 'haymaker' punches (wild swings) that I was brushing off with my arms. However, one such punch caught me exactly on my left elbow joint as I went to push it away. The result, as my arm went back the wrong way, was a massive dislocation with many fractures. I was rushed off to hospital in an ambulance where I stayed for a week following an emergency operation. Later, the results of the injury kept me out of the RAF, which I so wanted to join.

My new friends in my later teens were 'Nobby' Prigmore and Dave Smith. It was Dave who loved fishing. Dave was also an apprentice motor mechanic and he was the first of us to have a motor car, an old 1934 Ford 8. We used to go fishing all over in this, but mostly on the Great Ouse around Turvey, Lavendon and Newton Blossomville. One of the lakes we fished at was Horton. This was the scene for our early specimen tench, roach, perch and pike.

In between the fishing we had a great social life, with various village dances on a Saturday night. Amazingly there were no such things as drinking-and-driving bans, however, even in the fifties there wasn't a massive amount of traffic on the roads. We all had several holidays together at Blackpool, of which I still have great memories. It was the days of the big bands at the Tower Ballroom and the Winter Gardens. We danced (proper Ballroom dancing including Jive) to Ted Heath, Ken Mackintosh, Geraldo, Johnny Dankworth and others.

Throughout these years I had worked, firstly in the shoe trade and then on a large farm. I learned to drive on a Fordson tractor. Then back to the shoe trade with the highly respected worldwide firm Crockett and Jones of Northampton. I went to college to get my City and Guilds in shoe making and, yes, if I had to I could still make a pair of men's shoes right through.

I worked for Crockett's for twenty-two years on the manufacturing side and thus learned stock control on materials and so on. During my time there, at our peak we were making 1,400 pairs of men's shoes per day and also up to 600 pairs of ladies'. My boss, John Eyton Jones, was a sporting man – a good golfer and he loved his fishing. When he learned of my successes in the angling world, he helped me by allowing me time off to do television angling films and the like. But I am jumping ahead too far!

I had met Betty Jones from Dunstable and we had been going out together for a year or more. We bravely decided to get married on 27 March 1957. She was twenty and I was twenty-one. Eventually we lived in a terraced house in Abington, Northampton and although I continued my rather selfish pursuit of fishing with Dave, he had also got married.

During this period I was also watching a lot of football, as well as Northampton 'Cobblers'. I used to love going on the steam train to watch West Bromwich Albion, who then had a great side. The Crockett and Jones Bowls Team played under the name of 'Health' and I also played in the evening Leather Trades Bowls League for them. This was a great team of old boys, with me the only young fellow. In short, we won the Leather Trades League many times, also the Racecourse League, the Mansfield Cup and the All-County Crockett Cup.

Dave and I also got to the pairs final of the whole-town leagues at Darts, when there were several hundred entries. All this and we both found time to play some cricket. But it was always the fishing that had this great romantic pull, perhaps more so for me as I now was becoming quite good and, I have to say it, a bit of a fanatic.

Betty and I were married for seven years; we had a son, Stephen, who stayed with me and a daughter, Sharon, who went to live in Australia with her mother when she re-married. I shall never forget Betty's classic comment on why she left: 'Nothing any good will ever come out of fishing.' If ever I needed any further motivation in my angling career that was it.

Introduction

I had a series of pleasant love affairs, which wasn't really the answer because it affected the fishing time. I met Beryl, who was divorced. She never moaned about me fishing all the while and she was a good cook and more. What more could a man want; we got on fine. Eventually we got married and had a daughter, Nicola, who runs the financial side of the Bob Church & Co. tackle business today, together with my son Stephen.

Beryl could fish quite well, catching on one occasion a brace of roach of 2lb 4oz and 2lb 1oz, also tench to 5lb 4oz, pike to 15lb and plenty of trout. Our marriage ended because of continuous arguments; I was in a no-win situation, so I left. But we did set up the business together, in which Beryl was a skilled pattern-maker and machinist. Beryl is now re-married and lives in Las Vegas, America, where she is quite a professional gambler. I am not kidding. I could never understand why my ex-wives go and live on the opposite side of the world after our divorce.

Jeanette and I have been together for twenty-five years. We actually dared to get married again after twenty-one years, which meant that I gained a stepdaughter, Donna, and a stepson Adam, and everything has worked out just fine. Under her previous name, Taylor, Jeanette became a top international fly-fisher and also an extremely talented professional fly-tyer, going under the name of 'Genies Flies'.

Jeanette comes from Ely, in the heart of the Fenland, a place that I was drawn to for my winter pike and zander fishing, and that is how we met. She soon became very good at trout fishing and fished for England Ladies eight times before retiring. Of those eight internationals she was outright Four Home Counties Champion twice, once at Rutland and again on Grafham. She has also been European Grand Slam Champion over three legs fished at Grafham, Dreux and Ghent, and the winner of many other competitions, including the Leeda Pairs with Nicola (my daughter) and the Mid-Northants Fly Fishers Championship Angler of the Year. Another great honour was coming runner-up in the World Open Fly Tying Championships held at Mount Juliet House in Waterford, Ireland.

Today she does less fishing and ties flies only for pleasure, but she is still a great cook, also the garden is kept in magnificent condition. I am not allowed to touch it – which suits me. She is very artistic, an excellent flower arranger, oil painter, football pundit and more. All of which means we get on great and I can go fishing anytime, any day. When I look at some of the problems fishing can cause to marriages I consider myself to be very, very lucky!

I left Crockett and Jones thirty years ago, to start my fishing tackle and outdoor clothing business. A good friend, Peter Dobbs, encouraged me to do this and really helped in getting me started full-time. Bob Church and Company has been at the forefront of development and design of many of today's clothing and fly-fishing tackle items. For example, the first ever large arbour fly reel, the Line Shooter, the first fly-fishing waistcoat made in green gabardine (such was the popularity we had eight machinists working full-time, stitching them every day for about ten years), the first one-piece suit and the first bib-and-brace suit.

During the eighties and early nineties we had massive sales on fly rods as, during that time, the only other serious opposition was Hardy, and Bruce and Walker. The Boron range of fly rods was a dramatic success, with the flagship, the Alan Pearson ten-and-a-half footer, selling around 24,000 over ten years. Nowadays, with so much competition, fly rod sales are fewer.

We have always taken pride in being able to supply the 1,000-customer base of retail tackle shops with a very modern catalogue. This helps generate our sales, of everything you would ever need to go fly or coarse fishing. So this is where we are today; I am semi-retired, we are in a lovely new warehouse and things look OK. Now to another interesting part of my life!

In 1985 the new chairman of Northampton Town Football Club, Derek Banks, invited me to join the board of directors. As I knew the new manager, Graham Carr, well, I signed up. Although the whole experience has cost me quite a lot of money, I have enjoyed it so much. I have met all the big names in football, past and present, and visited three quarters of all the league grounds in the four divisions.

Graham's exciting 'Cobblers' team of 1987 won Division Four quite easily, scoring 103 goals on the way. When Dave Bowen, club president, died in 1995, I was in for the position, as I had been a friend of Dave's and was the oldest on the current board. So I retired as a director and have been president ever since.

We did get to the play-off final at Wembley Stadium twice in successive years, winning 1-0 against Swansea and then gaining promotion to Division Two, and just missing out the following year, 1-0 to Grimsby Town, which took them into Division One.

Since then we dropped back to Division Three, but had direct promotion back to Division Two and that is where we are now. Football is my escape from too much fishing and I do enjoy the high drama of it all. I also occasionally get invited, by my dear friend Graham Smith, to Northampton Saints, who are a top premiership club in Rugby Union. It is always a great day out; as I mentioned before, I just love all sports.

1
Looking Back

My Sixty-Sixth Year

I am starting my story in my so-called retirement year (it never happened) following my sixty-fifth birthday, 26 December 2001. The year began quite disastrously for everyone connected with fishing and the countryside. Foot-and-mouth disease struck the farming community very seriously and this had the knock-on effect of stopping virtually all fishing until, slowly, it began to recover in May.

It was 19 June that a small party of fishing friends gathered at Basil Shields, Ardnasillagh Lodge guest house on the lakeside of mighty Lough Corrib. It was intended that we concentrate not on Corrib, but Kylemore Abbey Lough, along the beautiful Connemara mountain pass. Basil had taken us here two years earlier, when we had caught salmon (grilse), and sea trout to 4½lb, from a traditional drifting boat. Now, I would make the point here that salmon fishing on the fly is difficult enough these days while wading a river. So there are not too many fly fishers who deliberately set out to catch them on a dibbled top-dropper fly from the boat. A little bit elitist I suppose, but I like it.

Our party consisted of my wife Jeanette, her close friend Carol Neal and her husband Dave, also Carol's mother Flossie, a young seventy-six-year-old who fishes well. My two close fly-fishing mates, John Emerson and Graham Smith, were also there and I had built up their hopes so high about the salmon we would catch.

I had checked everything thoroughly, picking with Basil the best week on average performance over the previous two years, beginning 29 June. Let me first say that the west of Ireland, in counties Mayo and Galway, is my all-time favourite place to escape to for holidays. There is so much variety of fishing there in rivers, small loughs and four major limestone giant loughs – in order of size: Carra 3,300 acres, Conn 12,500 acres, Mask 21,000 acres and the mighty Corrib 44,000 acres. All have very good, testing, brown trout fishing and there is also pike fishing on all four loughs, but if you fancied a go for the ferox you would need to concentrate on Mask or Corrib – this time I chose Corrib.

It was pure chance that my red letter day, never to be forgotten, came about. A party of friends were staying at Basil Shields' guest house on the shores of Corrib and during the week we were to mix some salmon and trout fishing at various near-by locations. It was day two and the salmon were once again not playing to the rules, for there were few fish in Kylemore Lough where we fished on day one.

Day two was scorching hot and, as we ate our breakfast overlooking Corrib, we wondered what we could do today, the lough being completely flat calm. John Emerson and Dave Neal opted to go out on Corrib wet fly fishing even though conditions were the worst they could possibly be. It was here that my luck changed, as Basil's number-one ghillie, Stephen Greaney, said, 'Bob, why don't I take you out trolling for one of the big fellas? I never fail in these conditions.'

Although this sounded very encouraging I thought to myself, I've heard that before. I quickly agreed to go out with Stephen and while John motored off into the distance muttering, 'You wouldn't catch me trolling, I would sooner catch nothing using a fly rod,' Stephen said 'Don't put any fly gear in the boat, then you will not be tempted to use it.'

'Today we will be trolling slowly with our baits on the twenty-five-feet-deep mark and we shall be using a ten-inch roach dead-bait. The flat calm conditions enable the boat to be motored at a constant trolling speed, much better than if it was a good wave.' Steve showed me his special weighted rig, with two barbless trebles to mount the roach on. The bait spins and wobbles very enticingly and, of course, it looks just like a live swimming fish.

I used a 10ft Bob Church spinning rod, with 15lb breaking-strain line on a multiplying reel. Under Steve's instruction I let out about 100yd of line, put the rod in the special rod-rest provided on the side of the boat and sat back and sunbathed while I waited for a take. At this point the vibes were good and I did feel I would catch one.

In all my trout-fishing years I had caught many double-figure rainbows, but in the main these were all stocked fish, the best being 27lb 2oz. My best brown was 8lb 2oz and it was a long-held ambition to catch a double-figure brownie. After only one and a half hours of trolling the rod arched round and I was into a very powerful fish. After about ten anxious minutes, Steve netted my first ever 'double', a ferox brown of 10½lb.

I was over the moon; a few quick photographs and weighing, and we returned this magnificent fish to the depths of his home – I see no reason whatsoever for killing such a wild creature. I thanked Stephen for helping me to realize my ambition; at last my double-figure brownie. Shortly before going in to one of Corrib's 365 islands for lunch and a brew I hooked another decent ferox of 5½lb.

Some anglers say trolling is boring, but let me tell you, once you have tasted the success of catching one of these big boys the anticipation is incredible – it certainly is far from boring.

It was now 6.25pm and we were to pack up at 7pm, when once more the familiar tap tap tap on my rod top. Twenty-five feet down a giant ferox trout was head butting my roach dead-bait to try and knock it off its course. I sat ready and, as it engulfed the roach, I lifted the rod at just the right moment. About 100yd or more behind the boat the huge fish surfaced and the long battle began.

First it dived and ran off a couple of times making the reel's clutch sing. Then I was reeling in with no resistance at all. 'It's off,' I said to Stephen and reeled in about 90yd of line. But this big old fish was clever; it had slack lined me at terrific speed, swimming straight back towards the boat.

Fortunately the barbless hook held and I re-engaged the fight; some twenty minutes went by with just steady strong pressure being applied and now it was close to the boat's side. In the gin-clear water we could see it was hooked by just one hook of one of the trebles. So, with my heart in my mouth, I took great care in playing this obvious once in a lifetime fish for the next few minutes while Stephen slid the net under her.

It was now 7.10pm. I was on such a shot of adrenalin because we could both see the fish was not only massive but a most perfect conditioned specimen. We let it rest in the deep landing net, giving it time to recover; then the weighing and photographing and away back to the depths. Oh yes, the weight was 17lb 3oz. I had gone over forty years without catching a double-figure brown and now I had a brace of them in one day. The west of Ireland can make your fishing ambitions come true alright.

That evening at dinner I was full of it as I recalled my dramatic day's moments. Just as we were about to go to bed John said, 'Bob do you think I could come out trolling with you tomorrow?' This was, of course, a big climb down for John after his earlier bold statement. I was so elated that I never said pee off. I told him I wouldn't fish and that he could have both trolled rods. See, I *am* a nice man. The result was that John caught an 8½lb ferox the next day. He then went out once more with Dave Neal the following day. John had another fine fish of 9lb 2oz and Dave had an eight and a half pounder at his first attempt.

A pretty good three days fishing with a red-hot ghillie; he was young and confident and knew the lough's 'hotspots'. He had studied the ferox species in great detail. The ferox is a separate strain cousin of our normal brown trout and its genes date back to the ice age. There are ferox in our Lake Windermere and in some lochs in Scotland, like the record-breaking Loch Awe. They are also found in a few big lakes in Sweden, Norway and Finland as well as, of course, Ireland. Ferox are known to feed deep down on char in many of these waters. However, on Corrib, the roach explosion over the past fifteen years has meant that the ferox has a new plentiful food source. It has given this most efficient predator a new lease of life and I expect the fishing there to remain very good for the years ahead, as long as the ghillies advise their clients to fish catch and release. Now we must get back to Kylemore Abbey Lake and the salmon fishing – but that's another story.

Arriving back home from Ireland and catching up with work soon saw me fishing locally again. I put in a few trips to the reservoirs where my team Bob Church Tackle won the Midland Hardy heat as they usually do, putting us through to the English final at Bewl Water in Sussex.

Now I began to concentrate on the river Great Ouse at Adams Mill where the big barbel was my aim. I have gone full circle, because these days I spend just as much time fishing for big barbel and other specimen coarse fish as I do trout. Ask any barbel angler what weight of fish he is trying to catch and he would probably say, 'Over 10lb'. Then what would the fish of a lifetime be and he would say, 'If I was very lucky a thirteen pounder'.

It's now that my lucky sixty-sixth year continues, because I was about to have a golden run that even I thought very unlikely. I was into my third season and I had caught several good barbel up to 14lb 4oz in that time. My new caramel boilie bait, commissioned to John Baker to roll for me, was beginning to work well and it had accounted for some good sport. My young neighbour, Gareth Hancock, had landed the heaviest ever summer barbel on it the September before, its weight 17lb 5½oz – this fish is known as the 'Pope'. Gareth had gone twenty-eight times to Adams without a barbel before hooking this, his first fish there. The Adams stretch is only twenty minutes drive for me and I love the place. Why? Right from the very first visit, as I walked the quarter-mile length, I was so excited. I spotted a 16lb-plus barbel in less than 2ft of gin-clear water and I watched this fish for several minutes before it swam under the boundary wire and off in the direction of Kickles Farm. My instant reaction was, I have got to have some of that! Well what would you have done?

In my first season I did not find it easy to catch barbel at Adams. I had plenty of good chub, but only a few barbel – to a personal best 12lb 12oz. I was really enjoying the challenge and the social side was good with the regulars. I have always found the anglers at Adams very friendly and two I met put me on the right path. They were Graham Attwood and Trevor Wilson from London. They are both excellent barbel fishers and Trevor has an uncanny knack of catching big barbel from rivers all over the country.

These two made me realize the importance of finding a good barbel bait and then, once found, sticking to it. I had ten kilos of small caramel boilies and enough of the same mixture to make plenty of fresh paste for the rest of the season. The only other bait I found excellent was simple trout-pellet dust mixed with eggs, a tiny drop of olive oil and clear gelatine. It is very effective in summer and autumn, your actual soft boilie.

Using these two baits my next six fish went like this 13½lb, 13lb 6oz, 13lb, 14lb 2oz, 14½lb, 10lb 12oz, and a 5lb 4oz chub was thrown in. Now I know six fish from twelve trips is not many, but each of these barbel over 13lb was the fish of a lifetime up to two or three seasons back, and probably still is. After this a couple of fish at 8¾lb and 8¼lb in early November when the temperature dropped to 42°F and under, until the end of February when, at 46°, the fish came back on feed and I finished off in style with my personal best barbel at 15lb 2oz from 'The Bend' swim. It took one and a half of my caramel boilies, hair-rigged with a No. 10 hook, and my Bob Church/Stef Horak 11ft Great Ouse Barbel rod. A perfect end to a fabulous season.

There was the national final of the Hardy at Bewl. I did quite well on a difficult windy day to get five rainbows for nearly 12lb weight and was top rod in our team and overall tenth in the individuals. But we won nothing this time.

Not so though in the other big event I entered. It was the British Open Pike Championships on Fly, held at Grafham Water, which if I say so myself I do know a little about. Most of the county's top pike-men had entered, but I did have a slight advantage as I know the pike 'hotspots' from all my trout fishing at Grafham, which dates back to its opening in 1966.

In the last few years, pike fishing with fly tackle has caught on more with trout fishers, and even coarse-bait fishers have learnt how to cast a fly, especially to have a go at this short and effective approach.

It had always felt criminal when big pike culls were made on the trout reservoirs. However, that is the way it had always been until more recently. It must have been twenty-five years ago that my old friend, Dr Barrie Rickards, made this statement. 'If you kill off, or remove by netting and the like, the larger pike from any fishery it only results in an explosion in the species.' Then after two or three years the water concerned is overrun by too many nuisance pike in the three to six pounds bracket. Where trout fisheries are concerned I can tell you for certain that it is far better to have fewer but larger pike in the water than hoards of smaller pike, which are forever aggressively harassing the trout and biting off fly fishers' lures and nymphs. For a trout fisher they are a pain in the you-know-what.

I had always supported Barrie's findings and backed them up at every available opportunity. Gradually, I am pleased to say, the thinking is being adopted. In realistic terms I am sure this helps all concerned. The pike fishers are catching larger trout-fed fish than they ever dreamed of. The fishery owners are taking extra cash from the pike fishers at a time when the trout season is traditionally at an end. The trout fishers themselves get the final spin off – with the extra revenue they get the extra trout stocking the following spring. Everyone is happy.

Still being carried on at a number of water authority patrolled reservoirs is the removal of pike by either netting or allowing anglers to fish and then to remove their catch alive. These fish are then sold with the idea of making some other lake into a good pike water. Sadly this is not what happens, as the pike rapidly lose weight and condition in their new homes. The truth is that there just isn't the same food there for them. It really is quite cruel to move such big pike, but some say it is better than just the old fashioned way of thinking. I'm not so sure. Far better if all the pike anglers get on the same wavelength and preach the Barrie Rickards Gospel – at least this is a winning formula for the pike.

Now I have got that off my chest, back to the pike competition. I was drawn to fish with Stuart Whybrow, from St Neots; we both knew each other from fishing together before in the fens. I took one look at Grafham Water, which was the colour of green pea soup, and I knew where we had to go.

Motoring over in the boat to the aeration tower on the north shore, I said to Stuart that, in such low visibility, the only chance we had was in the clear area of the fizz bubbles from the aeration pipe. This stretches along the bottom for 100m or more and in 30ft of water. This is traditionally a 'hotspot' when the water is normal, today in this soup, it would be the only chance. Within half an hour I boated a ten and a half pounder and there and then I felt this would be enough to pick up the first place. I was right, for only one other pike was caught and this only weighed 4lb. The winner's trophy was a magnificent bronze of a pike and I won quite a lot of tackle, which I shared with Stuart.

Was I becoming a better angler with age? The results seem to indicate yes. Now I think we can return to the beginning of my fishing career, so you can judge my progress over the years.

The Early Years

Let's now go back to those early years. My coarse fishing mentors were the late Dick Walker and the master river angler Dave Stuart. I became a natural specimen hunter, always fishing for the bigger fish. The species that really interested me at first were, in order, tench, chub, pike and eels. It was Dave Smith who became a good fishing friend and each Sunday we would go in his old Ford 8 car to nearby Horton. Here we fished the dammed stream, which had created a superb, long, overgrown lake. When tench fishing there in summer we would go over the day before to rake drag the swim. This always paid dividends and for me still does at every water I have ever fished since. The tench we caught went up to 4½lb.

On frosty, still, winter Sunday mornings, we used to take our buckets of live baits and fish there for pike. Fish in the 10–15lb weight bracket were often caught and, to us at the time, these were very good specimen size. For some reason I have always associated white frosty mornings with good pike fishing ever since – but it had to be a live bait. Dead bait and artificials were never in the same league, as pike catchers then and later.

In 1963 I noticed in my local Saturday sports paper, the *Chronicle and Echo*, that the angling columnist who wrote under the pen name of 'Ground bait' was retiring. This was to be his last column. Well, I thought to myself,

I could do that, so I promptly wrote a letter to the paper's sports editor and I got the job. Although only a short weekly piece, it gave me experience of what was to come in my angling writing career. Oh, by the way, I wrote under the pen name of 'Streamer fly'. Later they gave me much more space; I then used photographs and my own name, which was becoming much more known. I kept that column going for over twenty years and it was always a pleasure to write it.

A very big year for me was 1963, because it was in that year that a few of us local anglers set up the now very famous Northampton Specimen Group. As a founder member now forty years on, a lot of water has flowed under the bridge, as regards membership. From the early days until now, we have had some really famous anglers and characters as members. Men like Fred Wagstaffe, who I always rated highly as an angler; all those years ago, he was one of the very first to catch winter carp and write on the subject in the national angling press.

Many a big name passed through our ranks, Ray Clay, Cyril Inwood, Frank Cutler, Keith Saunders, Jim Gibbinson, Alan Smith, Frank Wright, Matt Hayes, Andy Barker, Duncan Kay, Dick Shrive and so on, right up to today's top men like Eric Kyte, Tony Gibson and Chris Berry. The NSG was created for local anglers who liked to target big fish of any species, be it coarse or game. Membership is by invitation only, following a letter to join the group read out at our monthly meeting so all members can get a vote. This has been our successful formula for over forty years.

I used to dabble at fly fishing, being encouraged to begin by Reg Smith, who owned the local tackle shop. I remember his words, 'Trouble is Bob, if you get into trout fishing it takes over from your coarse.' There was a lot of truth in what he said.

Pitsford opened on 1 April 1963 and I was there nice and early and keen to go. By pure coincidence I fished the bank spot alongside Cyril Inwood, who was probably the best known expert fly fisher in the Northampton area.

At this stage it was still split-cane fly rods and silk fly-lines named Kingfisher. These you needed to grease up every couple of hours to ensure they remained floating. Flies were merely traditional wets like Zulu, Invicta, Black Pennel, Mallard and Claret, Greenwells Glory and the rest. We caught a lot of fish, all rainbows of a pound or so, and we were fishing catch and release even in those days, although the rules never really allowed it.

On Friday evenings I used to go for a pint in the White Elephant pub and often I would talk to Norman Bryan. Norman was a very good local match angler and fly fisherman and we began to share a boat at Ravensthorpe Reservoir on Sundays. I learnt a lot from Norman and by the end of the 1964 season I had become quite expert, and good enough to take on anybody. My trout trips would be to Ravensthorpe, Eyebrook and Pitsford reservoirs with an occasional visit to Chew Valley near Bristol.

Another very big year was 1966, for on 1 June it was the opening of Grafham Reservoir near Huntingdon. At 1,500 acres it was the largest reservoir at that time and it produced the most marvellous sport that any trout fisher had ever dreamed of. Wild, super-fit rainbows up to 6lb and browns to 4lb were there in plenty for everyone to catch from the bank – the average weight of the rainbows was around 3½lb. I shall never forget it.

What this all did, of course, was to trigger a situation of lots more coarse fisherman wanting to take up fly fishing and so the numbers began to rise quite rapidly. I was in a strong position, because having those half-a-dozen years of fly-fishing experience behind me I soon became a Grafham top rod and a regular there.

I was now mixing my fishing between Grafham for trout, Sywell for tench and the Grand Union Canal for eels. I will give you more details on all three in separate chapters later in my book. My winter fishing was chub from the Great Ouse and pike from anywhere.

There were a few luxury fishing sessions, like weekends on the Broads for pike, weekends in north Wales for sea trout and salmon, to the Test and Itchen rivers for trout, sea trout and salmon and so on and so forth. I had broadened my writing and was doing regular features for *Fishing* magazine and *Angling* magazine, edited by Roy Eaton and Brian Harris. I also contributed to *Anglers Mail* and *Angling Times* with features and news stories. But if this wasn't enough I had become good friends with Peter Wheat of Poole in Dorset and he was editor of a magazine called *Anglers World*. We did some good features in those early days.

A species not available locally at the time of the mid-sixties, was the barbel. Each year I would spend a week's holiday in the Bournemouth area, so I could fish the famous Royalty stretch of the River Avon for this exciting hard-fighting species. I seem to be racing on somewhat and not giving enough detail, so I am going to give you a more precise picture of my fishing, species by species.

2
Eels and Tench

Fishing for Big Eels

The eel and all its mysteries began to capture my imagination in the early sixties. As an early member of the National Anguilla Club, along with such noted eel anglers as Arthur Sutton and Dr Terrence Coulson, I had a passion for catching big eels. We were trail blazers in making fishing for specimen eels accepted. Prior to this no one really fished for eels as a sport, only for the pot.

Our aim at the time was to pool our knowledge of where and how to catch big eels; we did this through the club's in-house regular bulletins. We used to have social fishing get-togethers and I remember we chose the Grand Union Canal at Weedon one Whitsun bank holiday. Bob Rolph had a fine eel of 5lb 5oz on this occasion. We publicized our catches in the *Angling Times* and wrote articles for the old *Fishing* magazine. The eel with all its mysteries became respectable and eel anglers became a normal part of the then specimen-hunting boom period.

The year was 1965 and I dearly wanted to catch a big eel – a four pounder would be nice, but I had my sights set on a 5lb-plus fish. I might add that a 5lb eel is rare still today and very few anglers ever catch or even see such an eel in their lifetime of fishing.

I had been catching plenty of eels to 3lb from the Great Ouse, sometimes as many as six per night, but it seemed I was struggling to better that weight. A friend of mine from work, who was just a casual daytime eel angler, came in one Monday morning with a story to tell me. 'Been up the cut,' he said. 'Had an eel of over 4lb.' The cut, of course, was the local Grand Union Canal near Northampton. I congratulated him on his fish, especially as he had caught it in the daytime.

He had another story to tell me as well. Apparently the resident lock-keeper had been riding his cycle along the towpath when he came across a big dead eel. It was freshly killed with a large portion of flesh bitten away from the back of its head. We agreed that an otter must have been responsible, but the weight was over 6lb. Now this set me really bubbling; I would obviously have to fish the canal. I confided the story to Fred Wagstaffe, who had also become interested in catching a big eel. The summer of 1965 was nearly over, so it was to be a serious assault in 1966.

It was Fred who suggested that the National Anguilla Club have a closed season fish-in, with fifteen members taking part. Closed season eel fishing was allowed under old River Nene board rules. The date was 31 May, a memorable occasion, as Bob Rolph's 5lb 5oz eel was shown to everyone at first light. It was the first 5lb eel I had ever seen; it looked so impressive. Two more eels of 2½lb were landed, although the majority blanked. Bob stayed an extra night, had another good eel of 4lb 2oz and lost what he estimated to be a much bigger one. It was now certain that the canal held few eels, but what were there were big and well worth catching.

Phil Shatford, who was mainly a Billing carp man, teamed up with me for a night session a couple of miles along the canal at Heyford. This was to be an action-packed session for Phil, who had eels of 2lb 6oz, 3lb 1oz and 3lb 7oz. An interesting thing here was that the 3lb 1oz eel had two good-sized crayfish in its stomach. Lobworms (double) appeared to be the best bait, but at times they would be picked clean off the hook, without a bite being registered. On other occasions we had nothing but twitches all night. We had now found out that the crayfish were responsible for this, but it had puzzled us for a while.

My first six attempts at these canal eels drew blanks and I was beginning to wonder whether it was really worth while. It was now early July and my tackle was to taste its first action. The water temperature was 69°F and at 11.30pm my silver paper shot up and a fast run developed. I set the hook in a 4lb 12oz eel, which I landed without too much trouble on 15lb nylon and 2lb test-curve fibreglass rod. I was getting closer to my ambition of catching a five pounder. The area fished was further along from Heyford village in the direction of Bugbrooke.

I had to wait until August for my next run, which was from the Bugbrooke north stretch of canal. Here it was at last; I was hooked into a monster eel. I could feel by its resistance that it was very big. I had gained line to be in control, but suddenly the eel surfaced and thrashed the water to foam. I called for some light, as I wanted to make sure of landing this one. The torch beam settled on the cavorting eel, as I struggled to bring it over the large landing net.

'It's enormous,' I shouted – and with that I felt the sickening feeling of a slack line. The eel had broken, or should I say bitten through, my experimental bonded nylon trace material. I estimated that eel at over 7lb in weight and it had taken a dead gudgeon bait.

I was gutted but now even more determined than ever, as water temperatures were perfect at 66°F. I decided to return to exactly the same swim the following night. Before fishing, and while it was still light, I made up a ground-bait scent attractor; I had great faith in this weird concoction. The mixture naturally had to sink to the bottom and slowly disperse. Raw eggs and pilchard oil was all mixed up with fine soil taken from mole hills. Before it got dark, these mudballs were put out in the area close to where my baits would be. At 10.55pm I had a run on a double lobworm; the eel turned out to be a real beauty of 5lb 8oz. It put up a good fight and took about five minutes to land on straight-through 15lb nylon, risking no trace. The fish was 40in long and had a girth of 9½in. Needless to say I was thrilled and felt a great sense of achievement. It had taken me ten trips to reach my goal.

With the nights beginning to close in and the realization that the first two hours of darkness was the key period for catching these eels, I began to put in some evening-only sessions after work. Yes, specimen hunters used to work in those days!

It was now September and I had moved along further to Bugbrooke south. I remember clearly putting on a small perch dead bait and cutting off its dorsal fin, as I thought it looked more edible that way. This time I used a 15lb breaking-strain fine-wire trace, which was threaded through the fish base.

At 10.45pm the run came, it was a scorcher – 30yd of line disappeared off my reel spool in very quick time, then, as it stopped, I engaged the pick-up, waited for the line to begin to tighten and hit it. Another five-minute fight saw me landing my second consecutive five pounder; this time the scales read 5lb 4oz. I had done it; another big eel was completed, even if I did lose the biggest one. Next season I returned to mixed fishing and my beloved Grafham trouting.

Although I have had the odd eel trip since the success of all those years ago, it wasn't until August 1994 that I tried to turn the clock back almost thirty years. A trout-fishing friend, Kevin Garn, told me of a stretch of canal at Welford, which is a narrow arm leading to a marina. It is full of little roach and he had heard there were good eels to be caught. We tried it, staying after dark until midnight, and two eels of less than 2lb and a little bootlace was our lot. It looks as if more eels enter this system and, as the form book of all those years ago proved, where there are lots of small eels about, seldom is there a big one caught. If I am going to turn the clock back, it seems I must try my old haunts on the Grand Union Canal to succeed – I shall be trying in August if ever I get the time.

For budding big-eel catchers this is what I found out. It was found that water temperature of between 64°F and 68°F was best. Places to favour fishing are where trees and bushes overhang the water on the opposite side to the tow path. Other interesting spots that are obviously good eel hideouts are close to old bridges or lock pounds. I found the first two hours after dark the crucial time for a run, then to a lesser extent around dawn. To be on the safe side, traces of some kind are needed. The modern equivalent of wire is an American braid known as Iron thread; this is a soft abrasion-resistant braid that has a narrow diameter.

Tackle, well, your 11ft pike or carp rods will do – no need to go over 2.25

test though. Nylon of 12lb to 15lb is perfect for canals. A 42-inch landing net is best for a writhing 5lb eel to drop in. Remember that today's thinking is to return any big eels caught, as you would any other fish. I must admit that a five pounder is a whole lot easier to deal with than a two pounder. Big eels are stronger but slower in their movement.

The canal in this area mentioned is governed by the Northampton Nene Angling Club; card and permits are on open sale at all local tackle shops. At the time of writing, the price is £30.00 a season.

Before I leave the subject of eels I must tell you another little story about them. Peter Chillingsworth and I used to fish at Sibson Fishery near to Peterborough. It was great for big net-fulls of tench, bream and rudd. At night though, we both always put a separate eel rod out. At about midnight, Peter had a run on his double lobworm rod on 15lb nylon and, after a brief fight, he was broken up and the eel was lost. Two hours later, I also had a run on similar tackle and this time I landed my eel of 3lb. This I kept for the pot, as stewed eel is quite a delicacy if cooked right. At first light I gutted the eel only to find Pete's hook right down in its stomach. I can not imagine any other fish that would have carried on feeding after having a big hook sticking through its stomach wall.

If you want some good reading on eels, try to get a copy of *Eels*, a biological study by Leon Bertin. Professor Bertin was in charge of the National History Museum in Paris before his death. I have read and studied this book many times; it is very educating on this rare subject.

Tench

Right from the word go, I had a strong passion for catching tench. I think they are one of the best looking of freshwater fishes and pound for pound they fight so hard. You can also make big catches of them if you get it right with your approach work. I have taken 100lb-plus bags of tench from quite a few lakes and reservoirs and usually each mid-June I go back for more.

The build up and preparations for a day's tench fishing at the start of each season is something I look forward to – because I just know that, nine times out of ten, it will mean a big catch. Another thing that has happened over the years is that the average size of tench, on a national basis, has increased quite amazingly. When I first fished for tench, the old record was 8lb 8oz and four pounders were good fish. A possible six pounder was the ambitious dream for me and my friends. It is now known that tench began to gradually get bigger after nitrates started to be used in quantities on the land. Since then global warming and boilie high-nutrition pre-baiting has helped the general size of tench creep up ever higher.

Back to the early and mid-sixties again. Rod Kilsby and I teamed up to have a serious attempt at Sywell and to try and catch our first six pounders there. We selected an area at the end of the left-hand arm. We dragged out lots of soft weed and pre-baited, then we fished the following dawn. We were allowed to fish from 4am, which really was first light in June. Both Rodney and I were pioneering the use of open-end swimfeeders in still water. Don't forget, they were originally designed for use in rivers where the current would wash out the groundbait to attract fish to feed and then take the bait. We found out we could do the same thing in still water by legering with a two rod system.

It was important to cast to the same spot each time. We used a groundbait of brown crumb mixed with blood. This was packed tight to form a stop at one end of the feeder. Then the central part was filled with maggots and finally packed-in tight by repeating the pressed-in groundbait at the other end of the feeder. This now gave a good casting weight and we usually fished about 35 to 40yd out. Our hooks were size 14 or sometimes 16 eyed, tied to 6lb breaking-strain nylon. These were baited with maggot.

The clever bit was to add a bit of fresh bread flake to the hook shank before casting out. Then, after casting, tighten down to the feeder and give a sharp jerk-pull of about a foot or so. This deposits the groundbait and maggots, the feeder then moves forward out of the way and the hookbait also moves forward, right into the groundbait area. Now just sit back and wait for the bite – I tell you it won't be long.

Rodney and I caught the first three six-pound tench from Sywell during this period – at the time this received major news coverage in *Angling Times* and *Anglers Mail*, such was the rarity of a tench that size. But from now on the tench were going to get steadily heavier as the years passed by.

In 1974 I was asked to write a small sixty-four-page book, *Catch More Tench*, published by Wolfe of London. For the contents of the book I took all my tench fishing experiences, but mainly it centred around the Sywell years. I also wrote the foreword for Dr Barrie Rickards' and Ray Webb's book *Fishing for Big Tench*, published in 1976. Finally, I contributed a long chapter in the late Trevor Housby's book *Specimen Hunters Handbook*, published by the Blandford Press in 1987. Of course there were also several articles on tench which I contributed to *Angling Times* and the then-monthly *Fishing* magazine.

Sywell today, 2002, has seen a number of changes since my early fishing there. In 1980, shortly after the local water board stopped using the reservoir for drinking water, there was a scare that it was to be used as a landfill site. However, local opposition brought pressure to bear on politicians and the proposal was eventually quashed. Shortly after that, the council turned Sywell into a country park. It is now popular with walkers, joggers, birdwatchers and the like. They use the top footpath but don't come near the anglers. The circuit right round the 60-acre site is about three miles.

After recent uncertain seasons, which have seen legering banned, we now have a much better situation – which is a credit to tackle company Tekneek, who took the fishing lease over this season. They offer day permits at £8.00 each and a season permit costs £97.00. This seems quite fair for quality tench fishing. If you are interested or want further details you can call Tekneek on 01904 479797. The head bailiff at Sywell is retired policeman George Stevenson, who will also offer advice on the bank.

On 8 July Keith Arthur rang me up saying, 'Bob, Sywell is in the news a lot because of the Tekneek takeover. Can you come and fish it for Sky's *Tight Lines* programme and catch a tench or two?' My memory soon clicked into gear and I remembered that Sywell's tench usually begin spawning on 9 July – in the past you could bet money on it and you would rarely be wrong. Of course, leading up to spawning and during it – for a couple of weeks – one hardly catches a fish. However, never afraid to take up a challenge, I went over the night before we were to fish (which was the 10th) and, exactly as predicted, the tench were spawning big-time in the rushes off the point that separates the two arms.

Gavin Walding, from the Northampton Specimen Group, came with me and we really gave it a good pre-baiting. We took a bucket full of 'tennis balls' comprising mixed broken boilies, sweetcorn, dried blood, maggots and casters, all mixed with brown crumb. I fired mine out with a Whopper Dropper groundbait catapult and easily reached about 40yd. Gavin used his spod, which I have to admit was pretty 'cool', as he termed it. I am now getting into young people's terminology. It consists mainly of two words: 'cool' and 'sorted' – easy really!

We were back at first light, Gavin on boilies and corn, myself on corn and maggot. Nothing had been caught for a few days and I was a little worried because, as I say, 'They don't feed when they are spawning'.

Keith Arthur and the crew arrived quite early and we got on with the basics of the Sywell 'takeover' story, followed by my version of how to catch the fishery's tench. To give the interview a little humour I used the same tactics on one rod as I did all those years ago – maggot and flake 'sandwich' on a size 12 hook. My end rig was 18in long from swivel to hook, and this was baited carefully and precisely. I push the point of the hook into the centre of the rear end of a big maggot and ease it round the hook bend so that it stops at the eye. This hides the hook shank completely. Then I add just two more maggots on the hook (I usually favour red ones) and nick them carefully 'just' through the skin. I put one on by the rear end and the other at the pointed end. This stops the hookbait spinning when casting and retrieving. A tiny pinch of bread flake is then pinched on near the hook eye. At times this can make all the difference between success and failure.

The other necessity is an open-end clear-plastic swimfeeder, which is attached to a quick release, anti-tangle attachment. I have always had a rubber bead as a stop on top of the swivel. This set-up is good for short-, medium- and long-range fishing – in fact, ideal for Sywell.

As the morning progressed I tempted a couple of tench for the camera – an impressive male close to 6lb and a spawned-out female of over 7lb, which Keith landed. With the job done Keith seemed quite happy.

As I write, 26 August 2002, I have just returned from a couple of days' tench fishing at Sywell. Top carp-man Chris Berry joined me, and two friends from the Adams Mill syndicate also came along to fish. We all found the fishing quite difficult, but a few good tench were caught with various methods. Chris and I chose the dam wall, fishing one rod close in, trying to drop the bait in the spot where the wall ends. At this point there is a little drop-off into a silty trough. Fish patrol this line amongst the thick Canadian pondweed, which needs dragging out in order to fish effectively. Chris, being young and fit, cleared a good-sized area and we pre-baited a double swim. The fish were not there immediately, as I thought they might be, but I lost a very good tench in the evening on a small piece of luncheon meat.

I was back the next morning. Half an hour after first light I hooked a big, very old fish, which I reckon had been a ten pounder in its prime. It had a massive tail and head, but was rather thin and empty-bellied. Nevertheless it still went 7lb 8oz, so I was quite pleased.

A few fish began to roll during that first hour, which proved that they were at least there. Chris could not make it until the evening so we baited up heavily again, as he was coming back the following dawn, although I had to work. He started off quite quickly with a nice fish of 6lb 10oz – a young, good-looking fish – which was an excellent sign. Again fish were rolling, but still not feeding as they should be. He lost another tench when it buried its head in the Canadian pondweed and came off. This one took his Dynamite Baits Meaty Bites, which he often uses for carp fishing.

Chris and I will continue to fish this swim whenever possible until the end of September. We hope to hit the jackpot eventually, as I used to in the old days when the fish were much smaller.

Dick Bateman, who I know from the barbel scene, has taken some good catches from Sywell recently. He uses float tactics most of the time, despite the legering ban now being lifted. The following consists of a one-day catch last September.

8am	6lb 14oz Male	3.15pm	7lb 3oz Male
9.30am	7lb 2oz Male	3.30pm	7lb 6oz Female
12.30pm	6lb 8oz Female	4.10pm	7lb 9oz Male
12.45pm	8lb 2oz Female	4.45pm	5lb Male
1.15pm	7lb 2oz Female	6.00pm	6lb 4oz Female
1.45pm	6lb 12oz Female	7.00pm	6lb 8oz Female
3.00pm	6lb 10oz Female		

Another friend of mine from the barbel world is Paul Thompson but, of course, he is also very much involved with tench fishing. Paul is a committee member of the National Tenchfishers' Group and their members have had a soft spot for Sywell dating back to the mid-sixties. Paul was fishing there this month and he told me:

> Sywell is not as easy these days as many anglers think. Of course, on the right day everything goes well and you can expect to catch between four and six fish. But on the wrong day it can be a right bitch, without a single bite.

He added, 'The swim raking chore has usually worked for me.' His final tip was, 'Don't try to cast to the middle of the reservoir unless you are really desperate – then only with one rod. You can catch fish from three rod-lengths out by sitting quietly.'

My Sywell record at the moment is: best female tench 8lb 6oz and 8lb 10oz, and best male fish a colossal 7lb 10oz. I intend to get a ten pounder from Sywell one day soon.

3
Pike

Winter Action in the Fenland:
Getting Serious about Pike

For most keen specimen-hunters the pike is the most natural big fish to go for in the winter months and I was no different. I had caught lots of good doubles locally, namely a lot between 15lb and 19½lb but never a twenty pounder. This all changed with my first visit to Horsey Mere, the then popular venue on the Norfolk Broads, in late October 1967.

My companions from the Northampton Specimen Group were Ray Clay and Rod Kilsby in one boat and myself and Phil Shatford in another. Fred Wagstaffe had been doing so well there that he suggested we all should give it a go. It was indeed frustrating listening to Fred's impressive big-pike stories; we had to try for ourselves. It turned out a great one-and-a-half-days' fishing; we had two 20lb-plus fish, two nineteen pounders and a fish of 18lb, as well as many lesser doubles and smaller pike.

We motored from Martham along the dykes to Horsey. Within minutes of our two motor boats entering the broad, Ray Clay was into the biggest fish of the trip. It put up a good fight on his float-fished roach bait and, as he brought it to the side of their boat, Rod soon netted it aboard. Its weight, 26¼lb, gave us a lot of confidence and I felt this was my best chance yet for my twenty pounder.

It had poured with rain since first light when we picked our boats up at the Martham boatyard but, despite being quite wet, spirits were high. Phil and I were hooking plenty of pike in the 7lb to 10lb class. Then I hooked into a big one after I had put on the largest roach dead bait we had; it must have weighed a pound. Again the pike put up a brave fight in the shallow weedy water. It circled the boat twice before Phil was able to net it for me. I was ecstatic at last, the weight 22lb. Back on the other boat it was the turn of Rodney, who narrowly missed the 20lb mark with fish of 19½lb and 18lb. Phil had to wait until later in the day for his nineteen pounder, but clearly it had been a memorable weekend.

All pike fell to 'bobbed' roach dead baits fished under a float. There was just enough chop on the water to make the dead bait behave enticingly. The float was set at only 2ft deep, allowing the bait to leap-frog over the top of the heavy weed growth where, of course, the pike were hiding in ambush – it worked well.

After putting quite a good effort in for pike locally, I had lots of doubles to 19½lb from Sywell reservoir. A new gravel pit complex near Olney called Emberton Park suddenly came good for the pike as well. Here I was having great sport with as many as eight doubles in a day. The heaviest I managed though was just over 20lb, with Ray Clay getting the best at 24¼lb.

Along with a few NSG members we started to show more interest in fishing various fenland rivers and 'drains' as they are called. It was Jim Shrive and I who motored the one and a half hour journey to fish on the 20ft Drain, but the water there was very murky and we didn't fancy it. So back to the car where we arrived at the 16ft Drain shortly after. The place where we stopped the car was just by luck; we now know it as Jenny Grays Farm. Bear in mind that the 16ft Drain has a road running along the side of it for several miles.

From the moment we both began fishing there was plenty of action, but I seemed to land up in the hotspot catching six pike to 24¼lb in the late-afternoon three-hour session (because of the December dark at 5pm). Jim had a couple of nice fish to 14lb, so it seemed pike had gathered here for whatever reason.

Jim and I were back the following week, which was actually my birthday, Boxing Day 1971. This time we caught a few live baits to try and again, from the word go, we had very lively sport. Jim started with a seventeen pounder, which he netted rather quickly. This pike went wild whilst in the landing net, and actually broke it off at the handle. It was very noticeable on this day how live bait was so superior to the various dead baits that our Fenland friend, Dr Barrie Rickards, was using fishing near by. While he had no runs, Christine Rickards caught a few to 14½lb on live bait. On my right-hand side Jim had seven pike to 17lb, and I had landed seven pike to 17¼lb – all on live bait.

With the light fading in the late afternoon, Barrie and Christine said their goodbyes and drove off to a second Christmas dinner at the mother-in-law's. I had saved one large live bait to use last thing. I cast out over the area vacated by Barrie and my float went instantly. At first I thought this was due to the strong large bait, but no, a giant pike had engulfed it as soon as it was cast out. I was using an instant-strike harness rig, so I made a wind down and powerful strike. Then all hell let loose as the pike sped off down the centre of the drain; scores of roach were leaping out of the water in fright. This all looked more spectacular in the fading light.

I was determined to play this fish out patiently, because we had a high bank and battered landing net to contend with. This I did and when it surfaced and lay there beaten it looked every bit like a crocodile in some jungle swamp. Jim jumped into the shallows and netted the fish minus the pole. It was enormous. The hook hold was with only one point of one hook. I stopped a car to get further witnesses to the weighing and the exact weight of the pike, 31½lb, was a new personal best for me, and remains so to this day. Most 30lb-plus pike that get caught these days are usually from trout reservoirs, so I still regard this catch as one of my best ever. A quick photograph to leave me with a happy memory and back she went.

We had now teamed up with other group members, Mike Prorok, Gordon Labnum, Geoff Smith and also the slightly crazy Coventry Circus Group. My attention was drawn to the River Delph after Cyril Inwood popped in one evening to have a chat. He had just fished in a match on the Delph. 'You've never seen anything like it; the river is lousy with pike,' he said. Apparently pike had proved a menace during the competition. Not only did they attack several keep nets, they struck at rudd and bream as the anglers reeled them in. I didn't need any more convincing; we would go there next to fish for pike.

The place was known as Welches Dam and the River Delph ran side by side with another superb pike water called the Old Bedford River. In four sessions here we all did OK, with lots of doubles up to 18½lb. We got restless and moved further downstream. The others were fishing all over the Fenland – the 20ft, 40ft, Relief Channel, Cut Off Channel – and we were beginning to get a few zander, which was, of course, a new species for us all.

I had heard on the 'Piking' grapevine that, lower down the River Delph at a spot called the Post Office Mile, some good pike were being caught by locals. This Saturday it was Mike Prorok and I who travelled the 70-mile journey together. Our first action came when we were still in the car, for a plump pheasant flew out from a ditch and straight into my car radiator.

On arrival, down an old farm track that stopped at the Old Bedford River, we found the boat that we use as a ferry system had been secured to the opposite side of the drain, leaving me and Mike unable to reach our destination – the River Delph which was only 40yd beyond the Old Bedford. I set up my pike rod, put on an ounce lead weight and my largest treble hook, and cast it across the drain straight into the boat. I then struck the hook into the wooden punt and reeled it back to our side of the water.

We were now soon able to cross the drain with all our kit and fish the river at the spot we had intended. First cast I had a 7¾lb pike, then lost one. Come midday and I put on a fresh bait. Straight away I had a run. I hooked into a big fish, which fought very hard for 10min before it was netted. At 25lb 10oz it was a fine-conditioned specimen. It was 43¼in long, and had a girth of 21¼in. I had to have a photo, as this was my best river pike.

They say that lightning doesn't strike twice in the same place. I don't believe that anymore. Mike Prorok, Gordon Labnum and I returned to exactly the same Delph area the following Saturday. As we drove along Mike said, 'It's my turn for a big one this week.' Actually, we fished about 300yd away from where I had taken my big fish; here the river widened to form a bay that screamed big pike.

Within an hour of fishing the new spot, Mike had a run and landed a fine

25½lb pike, which was a different fish from mine. About an hour later came his second run and he hooked into what he thought was a good double-figure pike – but what a surprise we were all in for.

As the fish fought gamely Mike got a glimpse of it just beneath the surface. 'It's a zander,' he yelled. Now he played it more carefully and it was netted by our regular visitor, river bailiff John McAngus. This was a rare specimen at that time, February 1973. It had taken a 4oz roach live bait, and weighed in at 11¼lb. This set a new species record for the River Delph. It was a great double catch for Mike.

While all this was going on I had landed ten pike, with the best at 13½lb so I was not complaining, and Gordon had two more. Between us it was well over a 100lb catch but, to be honest, the best was yet to come. Before it did I managed another big pike at 21lb and, higher up the river near Welney, we had begun to catch a lot of zander to around 7lb.

The Coventry Circus group, lead by joker Ray Brown (he looked just like Freddie and the Dreamers), was brother Derek Brown, Lol Derricott and David Malin. They really hit the jackpot further downstream from the Post Office Mile. They had ten pike in the day, but amazingly Dave played a 33½lb specimen, while Derek played a 26lb 6oz fish and Ray was playing a 25lb 2oz fish. If only it could have been captured on film. But perhaps not; such occasions will live in their memories forever and probably that's good enough. Sorry Lol, I nearly forgot; your best that day was a tiddler of 14¾lb. I am certain Dave's biggy is still the river record to this day. At this time the Delph was at its best.

A year later, just down from Welney town bridge, I witnessed and weighed a superb pike for Cambridge policeman Dennis Moules. It went 28lb 2oz. Its very noticeable feature was its huge head.

I now moved to the lower Great Ouse and Roswell Pits near Ely for zander, as they were quite new for me and I wanted to catch a big one. I used to fish with Robert Taylor and Mike Leonard and between us we had some fine catches, especially when fishing Roswell from Robert's punt.

Roswell is a fair-sized pit which is connected to the river Great Ouse and I have no doubt both zander and pike could move in and out, according to their needs. As well as zander, where my best two went 10½lb and 10¼lb, Robert's best went 12¾lb, and for a long time Mike held the record for the third-heaviest zander in the country, with a fine specimen of 15lb 2oz.

The big trout reservoirs are producing all the heaviest pike at the moment with Blithfield leading the way. Chew Valley opened for pike in the year 2000 and is very good. I reckon, though, that Bewl Water in Kent could beat the lot when it opens more to the public soon (in 2003); already test fishing produced a forty-two pounder to rod and line.

The other type of trout waters to turn up big pike are the gravel pit fisheries. Barnes Lake in Oxfordshire supposedly produced a monster of

Dave's old Ford 8 1934-model car was used for our first fishing trips in 1954.

Life in the country during World War 2 with Grandma Burgess; I found my first pond in 1942.

Dave Smith, my first regular fishing mate, fishing Fritton Lake for bream in 1955.

ABOVE: Having a fishing weekend with Fred Wagstaffe at Dick Walker and Fred J. Taylor's hut on the upper Great Ouse in 1963.

LEFT: Dick Walker, my specimen-hunting inspiration – with Clarissa, his record-breaking 44lb common carp, in 1952.

Bob with a 25lb 12oz pike from the River Delph in Norfolk in 1973.

Bob's first 6lb tench from Sywell reservoir in 1966.

In the five years before his death the master fly angler Cyril Inwood spent many trout-fishing days with the much younger Bob Church in 1968.

In the early 1960s I fished regularly for chub on the Great Ouse. This five-pounder came from Newton Blossomville.

Bob with his first double-figure barbel from the Royalty stretch of the Hampshire Avon in 1964.

Bob's first eel over 5lb from Bugbrooke north gave a good fight and went 5½lb in 1966.

Bob with his British Record small-eyed ray weighing 12½lb, caught with Peter Wheat out of Poole in 1968.

Bob with Grafham's heaviest limit of 31½lb, six rainbows and two browns of 5lb 7oz and 5lb 2oz, in successive casts in 1973.

Bob and television presenter Terry Thomas after making an Angling Today *film for ATV at Pitsford Reservoir. Bob made twenty-three of these films in the series during 1973.*

Bob's best-ever pike, a 31½-pounder from the 16ft Drain near Chatteris. It was his birthday, Boxing Day in 1972.

Bob's first fly-lure-caught pike over 20lb from Grafham; caught on a tandem Appetiser and sinking line, it went 20¾lb in 1974.

Dave Steuart with a Hampshire spring salmon of 39½lb, from Ringwood in 1977. These fish are sadly in decline.

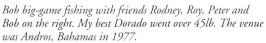

As zander spread through Fenland, Bob caught his share from the Delph, like this 10½-pounder from Roswell Pit in 1976.

Bob big-game fishing with friends Rodney, Roy, Peter and Bob on the right. My best Dorado went over 45lb. The venue was Andros, Bahamas in 1977.

Bob always enjoys grayling fishing, and here he shows a brace of two-pounders from the rivers Dever/Test junction pool. Bob was the guest of Trevor Housby in 1980.

A treasured moment. Bob spent the day fishing with the late Eric Morecambe in 1980. Eric really enjoyed trout fly-fishing and was very good.

Bob was instrumental in helping to form the international youth and ladies, four Home country now annual events. Here he presents his cup to the then youth captain of Wales, Russell Owen, looked on by organizer Moc Morgan.

Bob plays a salmon on the Tweed, the spot just below the weir of Lower Flores at Kelso. It is here he once caught five over 20lb in a morning.

LEFT: *Bob with fresh-in 21-pounder from the Tweed, where very few fish are retained these days. This was 1984.*

ABOVE: *1984 Salamanca, Spain, and the World Fly Fishing Championships. Bob makes his debut and the team finish runners-up with Tony Pawson taking the individual first place. Just look at the trophy.*

LEFT: *Avington, 1984. Bob with the late, much-loved Peter Stone as old Izaak Walton, in celebration of the 300 years since his death.*

Avington fishery in Hampshire, where Sam Holland began to produce some massive rainbow trout and lead the way. Left to right: Alan Pearson, 18lb-plus; Bob, 15½lb; Peter Dobbs, 11¼lb; and the old master of reservoir sinking line style, Dick Shrive, with a 13½-pounder. Quite a day!

By 1990 the tench in Sywell had got much bigger than in those early days, when a 6-pounder was massive. Now fish like this one of Bob's, which went 8lb 6oz, are quite regular.

Avington again. This 3lb 4½oz brook trout was an English record for Bob at the time of its capture in the 1970s.

1991 and Bob was made England Captain for the Home Countries International held at Llyn Brenig, Wales. England won the event and we cleaned up with the trophies.

record proportions. Elinor has given two fish over 30lb to Derek MacDonald and I fish here myself. The trip I remember most was when Des Taylor and I shared a boat for the day, piking at Ringstead Grange Trout fishery. This is a 30-acre gravel pit and it suddenly gave a good number of 20lb-plus pike. The day was special for a laugh a minute; we were both in humorous moods.

A Day's Piking with Des Taylor

I've fished with many of the top anglers and stars of stage, screen and television. For out and out continuous laughs and funny time fishing stories, a day spent fishing with Des Taylor takes some beating. Such was the day we spent together fishing for pike from a boat on Ringstead Lake.

Ringstead is a 35-acre trout fishery, which has the river Nene running only a matter of a few yards from it. Over the winter's heavy rains the river's flooded swollen waters have poured into the lake, bringing in some unwanted pike. As we all know, pike can grow to over 20lb in six years on a good 'stockie trout' diet. This is what happened here.

Harold Foster, the fishery owner, was ready for killing all the pike when he first found out about them. However, he changed his mind and allowed periods of winter pike fishing instead and there were plenty of takers. Good pike fishing thrives on neglect; once good anglers begin to fish a water regularly the general sport deteriorates. This is what happened here, but during the second year it was still pretty good, as our day proved.

We fished small rainbow trout live baits suspended about 10ft beneath cigar-shaped slider floats. Des started the action with a short fat fish of 20¼lb, which he brought to my waiting landing net very quickly. His shock tactics meant the big pike actually started to fight once it was in the net. You should have seen it; somehow the pike bit into the mesh of the net and tangled its teeth, then it did a series of twists (crocodile like) and you've never seen such a mess.

Des looked at the situation and said, in that lovely 'Brummie' accent, 'Bloody hell, its et the f*ing net.' Fortunately, we did manage to untangle it, but it took some time, and the pike swam off safely in the end after having its photograph taken.

The morning ended well, for I caught an almost identical pike, but mine went four ounces heavier at 20½lb. We rowed the boat ashore to see Edward Foster, who had also caught a good pike during mid-morning and kept it in a sack for us to photograph. This was a real beauty of 27¾lb and it proved the water still had quite a lot to offer visiting pike anglers. Good fishing without being too serious is Des Taylor's motto and every time we meet up at a trade show or Game Fair we always have a laugh about the net-eating 20lb pike.

As Des pointed out, both fish had the head size of a much smaller pike – almost like a twelve pounder. Their body thickness and girth, though, were colossal. For this reason don't expect a spectacular fight from trout water 'fatty' pike. It only takes six years for these female fish to reach 20lb and more. Also, they should never be moved to other waters for stocking as they just lose weight very quickly. I go back to the Fens for odd treks most winters and if conditions are anywhere near right I can always catch fish. Zander are now a nationally accepted species, as they have managed to turn up in rivers, canals, lakes, pits, and reservoirs like Grafham, and Rutland, where I now even catch them on deep fly lure tackle. This then brings me to the next subject, which is at last catching on fast.

Jerk Bait Piking

My pike fishing sessions these days are set aside for winter, when it's either too cold for barbel on the Great Ouse or the river is too flooded. My optician, Mike Green, is a very serious and very good pike angler and he offered to show me his successful 'jerk bait' technique a couple of years back. Mike took me to one of his favourite pits where we were to fly fish for pike first and then try the jerk method. The reason for jerk bait fishing second is, 'because it's so effective, it catches most of the pike quickly, leaving the fly method second best'. He was correct. We had hooked a series of smallish pike, about twelve up to about 7lb, and now I urged, 'Show me this deadly jerk method then Mike.' Result: three casts, three pike to around 12lb. 'Here is the outfit. I'll leave it with you while I take the Labradors for a walk round the lake.' After about ten casts I had a nice fish of around 10lb and then we had to go, as we had to meet people for lunch.

Two years have past and, in that time, Mike hasn't stopped coming up with terrific results with the method from a number of waters. First, a morning's catch from the bank at Blithfield reservoir was four pike of 31lb 12oz, 31lb, 28lb 1oz and 18½lb. But, forgetting about the oversized trout-fed pike for a while, how would jerk baits do on non-trout gravel pits?

Mike has been concentrating on the shallow clear-water gravel pits of the Great Ouse and Nene river valleys. His approach in the main is home-made jerk baits; these he makes with precision. As I found out, the commercial ones are OK, but his seem to work that much better.

We had two gravel pit sessions together for pike during the Christmas holiday break 2002. We chose a 30-acre pit, which, despite the very heavy rains, remained gin clear and the temperatures, both air and water, were quite incredibly high. I mean, when did you last fish on Christmas Eve with an air temperature of 55°F? The conditions were perfect for pike to be on the lookout for food. Now, I have never, in over fifty-odd years of pike fishing, found an artificial bait that could catch pike even half as good as natural baits, live or dead. So it was to be my using live bait and Mike using his deadly jerks.

It was the shortest day of the year, but we managed about six hours fishing. Result: Mike nine on jerk bait, which included some lovely specimens of 13lb 12oz, 15lb 4oz, 19lb 4oz and 23lb 12oz, plus six others averaging between 5lb and 8lb. The roach live bait and dead bait tactics produced a measly three seven-pounders.

It continued mild, so Mike and I were back on New Year's Eve and we both fished most of the day just in jumpers. I think this was a first for me. We both fly fished in the morning and we both did very well, Mike taking eight fish on fly to a good size fish of 12¾lb. Any double-figure pike caught on this tackle gives incredible sport. The fight and skill playing it proved what a good angler Mike is. I had landed four good pike on my fly tackle, all about 5lb to 8lb. My disappointment came when a fish of well over 20lb followed my fly right to my feet before turning away. With about an hour and a half of light left I just had to have a serious go at jerk bait fishing.

I had kitted myself up with what appears to be the best reel for the job; it is the Shimano Curado Multiplier. It is so foolproof that even complete beginners cannot get overruns; this was always something that put me off this type of reel with earlier models. To say I was pleased with my next three pike would be an understatement. I had tried a shop-bought jerk for half an hour with only a follow for my efforts. So I said to Mike, 'Can I try one of your silver homemade jerks? From what I have seen, it's the one that does the business!' I put it on and had complete confidence that it would catch. First a fish of 16¼lb, then I had to wait until the light began to fade for two fish in quick succession. One of 15¾lb was followed by a superb fish of 20¼lb, which had engulfed the whole jerk bait. Despite this it was only hooked in mouth tissue, hence the incredible fight.

It seems I had spent quite a lot of the two days' fishing taking photographs of Mike, but now it was my turn to do a bit of posing. I will also say at this point that there is a little bit of extra patting on backs when you catch a twenty pounder from a non-trout water. What do you think? We could run two records for specialist pike anglers; it would help keep a lot more interest going.

Mike obviously loves his pike fishing and he changed to his jerk rods for the last half an hour – yes, you guessed it, he did it again and landed one of 19¼lb. A little heavier and it would have been his eighth pike over 20lb in the last two weeks, with a best of 26½lb. Mike's final quote whilst chatting in the car on the way home was, 'Pike are far more wary and a lot smarter than most give them credit for.' So, to sum up, it just goes to prove you can teach an old dog (me) new tricks. As Mike said, 'You have jerked.' I can tell you, if you have not tried it yet and you like piking, give it a go. Try to choose a clear gravel pit or similar with shallow water up to about 12ft or so.

The following Sunday everywhere was either flooded rivers or frozen lakes. However, I now had the pike urge, such is my all-round attitude to fishing. So when Gareth Hancock my neighbour offered to drive me to the Fens for a few hours' piking, I was up for it. He even took some maggots and caught a few fresh rudd baits.

This day was just too cold for jerking, the big lake of 25 acres had only cat ice in the margins, so we went out in the punt and allowed the boat to drift slowly across the middle on the gentle breeze. Then a very slow row back, trolling the suspended baits at about 30yd behind the boat, then drift back again. We had covered almost three quarters of the lake before my float suddenly shot under. I struck in to a very heavy pike, which fought like crazy in the crystal clear water. We had to drift the boat into the bank before I could net it, a magnificent specimen at 26¼lb. That was my second twenty-pounder on the trot – what a way to begin 2003.

Specimen Pike on Fly Tackle

Of course, I've been catching pike on fly for over thirty years, admittedly most in the early days were by accident. Pike would take my deep sunken-line lure for a small fish swimming along the bottom. This was, of course, a very good method for catching the larger reservoir trout, when at the time most fly fishers were fishing on top.

I recall my article in my *Angling Times* column of 1975, when I was fishing at Grafham in these circumstances. I wrote:

> My white marabou tandem lure fluttered close to the bottom, 18ft down, and then I appeared to hook some obstacle as my fly stopped dead in its tracks. I felt the obstacle shake its head and it swam off slowly but determinedly in an unstoppable movement.

This was a very heavy weight on the end of my fly line and I instantly knew it was no trout. It just had to be a pike and a very large one. My pulse rate quickened as it always does when I hook a big fish at Grafham and my fishing mate, Peter Dobbs, began to lecture. 'Take it easy Bob, this is really some fish.'

After five minutes of continuous pressure – as much as I dared with a 7lb breaking-strain leader – I figured if it was to be broken by the pike's teeth it would have happened by now. This thought gave me confidence, but the fish was dogged and kept deep. It was doing nothing spectacular at this stage and I just had to play it out. After ten minutes I felt the still unseen fish coming up in the water.

'At least let me see the size of its head,' Pete pleaded. The drama of the action had now spread and several boats stopped fishing to watch. Here she comes then, I thought and at that I experienced quite an exciting moment in my fishing life. The pike looked well over 20lb and it opened its mouth then shook its head with gill-flaring rage. I could see my marabou lure clearly right in the scissors of the jaw, with the long shank protecting my line.

The climax of the battle had now passed. I played the fish to a standstill and Peter netted it tail first. The boats gathered for a good look. It was weighed and witnessed by four other anglers, going 20lb 4oz. Although I am a keen pike fisher in autumn and winter and have caught fish to 31½lb on heavier pike tackle, fly tackle is quite a different matter and I was told my catch was something of a record; it was a lucky day for me. I finished with a limit bag of eight trout for 19lb 1oz and Peter had four nice fish too.

After a story like that, which I admit to be glowing over, I can hardly talk about trout fishing, so I want to tell you something of what I know for sure could be a deadly way of catching pike during the warm autumn months.

With the Great Ouse area pike waters now open, pike fishing is becoming a major interest, however, many such productive shallow waters are thickly weeded, making dead baits or live baits unsuitable until after the first frosts. Autumn is the time for wandering about with artificials and I find pike more willing to chase a lure at this time of year.

Since anglers have a wide range of spoons, spinners and American plugs to choose from why should they bother to try something else? Simply because feathered lure fishing with a powerful fly rod can give you some advantages. Two that immediately come to mind are: the weed problem can easily be mastered; also a 4lb to 6lb pike, which would be brought in rather quickly on normal tackle, now becomes a very sporting proposition on a fly rod. I must have caught 500 or more pike on fly tackle over the years; most were by accident when after trout, but a fair number were by intention.

I remember one session clearly. I had spent several early morning trips after tench from Harlestone Lake. I was catching my tench all right, but was continuously having my concentration broken by pike activity as they struck at fry close to weed beds. I decided on taking my powerful reservoir trout rod on the next session. I would fish a fur and feather fry-like lure and see what happened. My choice of fly line could be floater, sink-tip, or slow-sink.

I fished for tench as normal, with my trout – or should I say pike fly tackle – made up ready. As soon as I heard the splash of the first pike striking I was off. I cast a No. 2 keel-hooked black-and-white hair-winged lure on a floating line, next to the bed of lilies. I retrieved in a series of pause and pull, sink and draw movements. That method worked and so too did stripping fast just beneath or across the surface. I had six fish to 8lb and felt quite pleased at such good sport. I repeated similar catches on Great Ouse backwaters and on each occasion the weedy areas were competently fished and, of course, this is where the pike were lying up.

There is just one point to consider before seriously embarking on a fly-tackle pike session and that is traces. I would advise you to use a 12in wire trace, otherwise you will be bitten off too often!

Catching specimen coarse fish by design with fly rod tackle will, in my opinion, be a popular trend for the future in our sport. Most trout fly fishers who fish at the larger reservoirs have encountered accidental catches of coarse fish from time to time. When this is the case, the fish caught are not rated as highly, because really you were after trout. However, please believe me, when you deliberately set out to catch coarse fish on the fly, and they usually are sizable, there is as great a feeling of satisfaction as if you were trout fishing.

I suppose I am so lucky because I have six major trout reservoirs from as little as five minutes to forty minutes from where I live. They all hold a good head of coarse fish as well as the prolific trout. One reservoir, my personal favourite, Grafham, has a new sporting species to try for – the zander – and fishing for them has created a lot of interest. Many years ago, the late David Fleming Jones, who was then Grafham's manager said:

> One day zander will get into Grafham quite naturally through the water pumping-in system from the river Great Ouse. When this happens I will welcome them because they will create bonus sport for fly fishers without damaging the trout. They will also help control excessive shoals of coarse fish which often mature and eat the same food as the trout, namely, aquatic insects of all kinds.

We first heard of the odd zander being caught at Grafham in about 1995. This, of course, was always an accidental catch to fast-sink line and lure fishing. It is interesting to see just how many people have become serious zander fly fishers now that the species has firmly established itself in Grafham Water.

Having heard stories of some good zander and pike catches being made, John Emerson and I decided to forgo the catching of trout and try for these species on our next trip to Grafham, in early September 2000. We also knew we would catch some big perch. From past experience I remembered too that big bream also take 6in tandem lures at this time of year, when their predatory instincts are obviously aroused.

Armed with 10½ft IM 8 Alaskan fly rods and WF8 DI8 fast-sink fly lines, plus a good selection of big feathered and flashabou lures, and link-swivelled wire traces, we set out on our mission. We were soon in Hill Farm bay, near the aeration tower, and kept well out from the shore in 25 to 30ft of water. I had caught plenty of zander, into double figures before from the Fens on bait, but I had caught a few on fly from a lake at Dreux in France. I had also caught lots of pike on fly before, including the twenty-and-a-half pounder from Gaynes Cove at Grafham. We had some idea what to expect.

We dropped anchor and started fishing, and straight away began to catch perch, some good ones to well over 2lb: about 100m away another boat was anchored up and we could see the lone angler on board was using a very specialized shooting head outfit and a massive pike fly, which he was casting some distance. I said to John, 'This guy knows what he is doing.' We saw him quickly catch a couple of pike and also two decent zander to about 6lb: we now know him as Andy Goram from Suffolk, and he and his mate Jim Woolnough have specialized in fly fishing for pike for some years now, mostly on the Norfolk Broads.

John and I moved away from our perch spot because we seemed to have fished it out. I had lost two good fish, which came off during the fight; we think these were zander judging from the way they fought. The new spot was in 30ft of water. John put on his tandem No. 6 hook Appetizer lure and wire trace, and I put on a 7in pearl tube fly. As the eye of the swivel on my wire trace would not go through the thick plastic tube I risked it, pushing my 12lb nylon trace through the tube and tying on a size 4 double salmon hook, the shank of which slid back into the tube leaving just the hooks exposed at the rear.

We both made our first cast together and then left it for 30 seconds to lie on the bottom before retrieving. As soon as we did retrieve we both hooked into very, very heavy fish, which just had to be pike. This was incredible, for after about fifteen minutes of steady pressure both fish came up and showed themselves at the surface. We nearly had kittens as both fish were over 30lb. 'What are we going to do John, there is only one specimen landing net?' My fish dived deep again and was gone, entirely my fault, the fish eventually had bitten through the plastic tube and then easily through the nylon. One problem was solved.

I then set about netting John's pike and got it first time. I am glad we had a 42in-diameter landing net. The fish was really enormous and I unhooked the Appetizer from the scissors of its jaws with my forceps. We left it outside the boat in the net mesh to recover from its fight. Now, being keen and with a fish off this size, naturally John wanted to weigh his fish without harming it and have his photograph taken before we returned it to the deep. We called over to Andy for help and he had the proper equipment: a cushioned mat to lay the pike on in the bottom of the boat so it does not knock itself; also a large hammock-like weighing sling. I did at least have the correct scales for weighing the pike; they went up to a 60lb limit.

John's pike weighed 30lb 8oz exactly and, after the photograph, swam away happily. I would stress here that, if you are thinking of trying for these big pike, you must have the right gear to deal with them once you have netted them. If you don't you will end up with a dead fish on your hands. Big pike do need handling with great care. We both commented on the chances of hooking two pike of 30lb plus at the same time, because we saw mine before it bit through, and guessed at one in several million.

Another move was needed because, after a further hour, nothing else came from this spot. It seems that moving about is a very good policy and, if it is not too windy, we found 'back drifting' to be a good technique for covering a lot of bottom.

My luck changed at the new spot, for I started with a fine 6lb 8oz bream on a tandem Appetizer. These fish are also very good sport on fly tackle and they give one hell of a dogged fight. Without question, big bream fry-feed in the autumn when this food item is found in abundance. They are big enough to make them well worth catching.

After losing another zander in the fight, I decided to give the next one I hooked a couple of extra firm strikes to set the hooks more securely. John gave me one of his large boobies. He had tied them up especially for the zander on this day, but we had not tried them out yet. I put it on the link swivel of my wire trace just in case. Then to my relief a zander at last, not a big one but between 4 to 5lb. I was pleased to net him aboard. David Fleming Jones' words were ringing true; they are a second sporting fish for the reservoir and I am certain they will become popular with the majority of Grafham's visitors in future years.

Just to see if we had fished on one lucky day, because it was quite memorable, we both had a second trip to Grafham the following week. This time Andy was there again with his friend Jim and so too were two more boats, obviously fishing for pike and zander. They all caught several zander and double-figure pike up to 18½lb. John had perch to 2lb 10oz and two 6lb bream, while I had a lovely young pike of 19lb 4oz. This proves our first attempt was no fluke and we look forward to many such days in the future. And do you know, to my absolute amazement, not a single trout was caught.

The way ahead seems to be quite clear if you are seriously taking up this specialized branch of sport fly fishing. For the pike, which really are quite exciting to catch once they get into double figures and more, the tackle needs to be similar to Andy's and Jim's. They used 12 weight shooting heads on specially built 9ft fly rods. Because, at the reservoirs, most of your fishing is deep down with big fly lures, you need this extra power for longer casting and setting those bigger hooks. For the zander, perch and bream our outfits were more than suitable and we just about got away with them for pike.

Once you become good at fly rodding for pike you can take your tackle along to any coarse water, as I did earlier in the year. Mike Green from Northampton has specialized in this for a few years and makes some very good catches. He took me to a shallow lake in Buckinghamshire that has a punt on it; this was ideal to slowly drift along on a drogue. We caught several good pike here and Mike has caught as many as five over-double-figures in a session. His best on fly so far was 18½lb from a more difficult pike water, but he even managed one of exactly 20lb from the River Nene. Fly fishing does often give you the edge over spinning, because you can slow down your retrieve so well without the fear of forever hooking the submerged weed beds.

Finally, Anglian Waters fishery manager John Marshall has had to make new rules at their four waters to cater for the new interest in the coarse fish. As too many fish were being killed, especially at Grafham, the new rules say that only one zander or one pike, not exceeding 12lb, may be taken and retained. This will go someway towards safeguarding stocks for the future. After all, you cannot have anglers willing to pay good money for the catching of pike and zander and yet allow other anglers to kill them.

Before I move on, I do recall a day I was out on Chew Valley Lake near Bristol with Tom Bilson. If I tell you I have caught hundreds of perch between 2lb and 3lb it would be true. But I have to say that, apart from twenty-five or so from the Great Ouse, the rest would have been caught on a fly lure when fishing a sinking fly line after trout. Most of our major reservoirs hold big perch and initially we were after trout, of course, but things changed when I realized what was happening.

It was mid afternoon and a big hatch of damsel flies was taking place in and around the area known as the Roman Shallows. The damsel nymphs were swimming up fast from the bottom and then crawling up protruding weed stems to hatch. Many were being chased and intercepted by good-sized fish. At first we thought these to be trout, but soon I had a follow right to the side of the boat and it was a big perch.

I changed up quickly and fished a size 8 damsel nymph on a slow-sinking fly line. First a plump 2lb-plus perch, then this was soon followed by a lovely fish of 3lb 8½oz. At last I had deliberately caught a big reservoir perch by intention, rather than luck. I can recommend any potential big-perch hunter to try the reservoirs, fishing deep from a boat – usually with a small fish-imitating white lure. This method is very effective indeed. Also the pike-fishing on fly at Chew Valley Lake is excellent, with fish to 35lb being caught by Jeremy Herrman.

4
My Fly Fishing Adventure

Take-Off with Grafham

My tackle dealer, Reg Smith, made a bold statement to me, because he knew how passionate I was about my specimen coarse fishing. Reg said, 'Bob, trouble is, if you take up fly fishing for trout, it will take over from your coarse fishing.' This was around 1960 and I remember answering, 'No, never', but it did.

I purchased a Millwards 10ft split-cane fly rod, a Kingfisher silk-braid fly line and a decent fly reel, and I was off practising my casting. First, it was mainly Ravensthorpe and Eyebrook reservoirs, but then Pitsford opened in 1963, right on my doorstep. This gave me some really good fly fishing, but mainly I was just filling in the close season for coarse fish.

Everything changed in June 1966 when Grafham water (1,500 acres) opened its doors for trout fishing. I had become quite good at catching trout on more difficult still waters, so Grafham's virgin fish were quite easy to tempt and they were 'big' – 3lb, 4lb, 5lb plus – bearing in mind these fish, mostly rainbows, had been stocked eighteen months earlier at only 12oz. Within weeks the big reservoir received national headlines that read 'Glorious Grafham', and it was too.

Since getting into fly fishing I had become a champion of the sunken fly and lure type of fly. I regularly wrote articles in *Anglers Mail*, *Angling Times*, *Anglers World* and *Angling Monthly* magazines. In these, I would have a little 'pop' at the big reservoir fly fishers who would have us all fish floating fly lines and small flies only. To fish this sinking method well you needed to cast long distances, so I was in at the start of using shooting heads. Here I was influenced by local fly fisher Dick Shrive; he was a great ideas man, inventing many deep fishing aids.

I had soon realized that the larger trout fed quite often on small coarse-fish fry, usually roach or perch. This is really why my insistence on pushing modern lures into respectability was a crusade I personally wanted to win and, as time proved, I did. My first lure invention was a perch-fry imitation, which my friend Dick Walker insisted on naming 'Church Fry' after he and I had caught lots of good trout while using it. It has remained a good fish catcher to this day. At this time, or shortly after, Dick came up with the

'Sweeney Todd' lure and the very life-like Polystickle; both were very effective.

This was a good period for fly lure inventions and my pure-white Muddler Minnow was great, as it caught a 5lb 1oz brownie off the bank at Grafham, the first time I tried it. However, it wasn't all lures, as my Claret Hatching Midge fished in close to the surface was also doing very well. At this period Cyril Inwood and Arthur Cove were both fishing at Grafham and in their prime.

Around 1970–71, I started to fish from the boat at Grafham much more and my regular boat partner was Mick Nicholls from Coventry. Mick is a very good angler and, like minded, we formed a good team. Boats were booked for every Saturday and Sunday, and they were rowing boats only. Needless to say, I was as fit as a fiddle. Other boat partners were Brian Furzer, Jim Shrive, John Wilshaw and Dave Allen from Hanningfield. I was now averaging around 500 trout a season, which ran from 1 April to 30 September, extended later to 31 October. In those days, boat bookings needed to be placed one month in advance to ensure you got a boat at all at Grafham, such was its popularity.

I think I was the first person to use chenille, and definitely marabou feather, in this country for tying lures. For example, my Appetizer lure was an incredible breakthrough in fish-imitating lure patterns. It looked so much like a little coarse fish when in the water and, of course, for the first time, we had the life-giving movement of the marabou feather, with its pulsating action.

I introduced the Appetizer in my *Angling Times* column in September 1973, I wrote:

Here's How to Tie a New Fry Lure

Every trout over 3lb my friends and I caught from Grafham, be they brownies or rainbows, all had twelve to twenty perch fry in their stomachs.

We have caught these fish on several different kinds of lures, but I got to thinking, perhaps we would do even better on a more lifelike pattern of a perch fry.

I retired to my fishing room with this in mind; there I sat studying all my fly tying materials. As I tightened a No. 6 long-shanked hook into the vice, I tried to visualize those tiny perch. Here is what I came up with.

Tie with black tying silk. Tail: a spray of mixed fibres from a dark green cock hackle and a silver mallard breast feather. Body: white chenille, spiralled with fine, oval shaped, silver tinsel. A throat or beard hackle only, of evenly mixed orange and dark green cock hackle fibre plus a few fibres from the same silver mallard breast feather. Wing: this was tied in two layers, first a generous spray of white marabou herl, then directly on top of this, a spray of natural grey squirrel tail hair. After building the head to good shape I then completed the lure by adding two green bead eyes, and then varnished it.

Out of the water the white marabou looks positively scruffy, but in the water it certainly gives that lure plenty of life. The general colouration looked very 'perchy' as I pulled it just beneath the surface by the side of the boat.

Now to try it on the fish, in rather poor conditions too. Quickly a brownie of 3lb 11oz was boated followed by a rainbow of 3lb 4oz – not a bad start.

I've named this lure the Appetizer for obvious reasons. I feel confident that in the remaining few weeks of the season I shall catch my biggest trout of the year at Grafham while using it. If you are going to Grafham before the season ends it would be a good idea to tie a few of these up.

Since that day, this lure more than any other has dominated the fry imitation artificials. Over the years it has had a few cosmetic changes with modern synthetic materials and this is OK. The Appetizer gave me, and thousands of others because it was recognized worldwide, some of the best catches. Also, importantly, it accounted for the fishery largest record individual trout. It's still very, very reliable and it was born at Grafham.

Here are a few stories from Grafham shortly after the Appetizer became my main line of attack. Please do remember here that stocking in those days was with maximum size 1lb weight fish. Today the reservoir management are forced to start stocking with larger fish from 2lb up to 3½lb to try and dodge the persistent cormorants.

The dreaded cormorants were not a problem in the seventies, but today they most certainly are doing tremendous damage to the fish stock all over Europe. It makes me laugh at the absurdity of the bird people being in favour of a cull on the ruddy duck, just because it mates with other, rarer, ducks sometimes, while the cormorant, which is eating its way through all freshwater fish stocks in this country and now Europe, remains on the protected list. Why do we, who know the real facts, have to listen to the results of a three-year government report costing several million pounds? They actually found out that cormorants eat our fish stocks, both trout and coarse, but nothing gets done! As I write, I think most people who own fisheries have given up, although others have made it a private war against this very cunning and clever bird.

Back to the Grafham story. As autumn approached in 1973, I was very conscious of the massive perch and roach fry shoals that were present. I now had the Appetizer to attack the fry-feeding trout, so best I recollect the three successive articles I wrote in my *Angling Times* weekly page.

Time for a Giant Trout

Without doubt, these last few weeks of the trout season offer reservoir fly fishers a much better chance for a big trout. This applies to both boat and bank fisherman and you will find the records from previous years support this statement.

When talking of big trout, where reservoirs are concerned, I would say from 3lb upwards are noteworthy fish, 4lb and over is excellent, while the capture of a 5lb-plus specimen remains a real red-letter day for the captor.

Here we must remember that these fish have grown naturally in a wild state since they were stocked, in most cases at less than a pound in weight.

This week I caught a 5¼lb rainbow, but as it came from a small fishery where it was stocked at that size, I must admit I couldn't get all that excited. Now, had it come from a reservoir I would have been over the moon and felt a real sense of achievement.

Six rainbows of 5lb and more have been caught by anglers fishing at Grafham in the last three days. All had been feeding on perch fry, except one of 5lb 15oz and this took a natural dapped daddy-long-legs. As I write, the largest rainbow is 5lb 15½oz, caught by Derek Brown, a winter pike fishing friend of mine. He was trying reservoir trout fishing for the first time and landed three rainbows; all fell to a Black lure. It's a certainty he will be a regular trout fanatic in future.

One of the main reasons why more big trout get caught at this time of year is that they move into the shallower water to feed on the 'small fry' shoals that gather there. At Grafham, for example, just now some areas are heavily populated with good trout of 2½lb upwards, but there are also vast stretches that are virtually barren of any fish.

Consider my last trip to Grafham when Mick Nicholls and I purposely fished our way around the whole reservoir. We scored a double-limit bag, but the fish came in just two small areas only.

With the wind blowing steadily in the direction from the Fishing Lodge to Savages Creek we drifted from the corner right down to the Creek. It wasn't until we actually approached the Creek, where there were ten boats at anchor, that I had a gentle tap take that never materialized.

Then, next cast came a very lively 3lb rainbow. As we drew

close to the other boats we both had two good fish on at the same time, again close to 3lb. In all we had nine good fish from this spot in the next hour. All went over 2lb. Half of the other boats were also catching as well.

After an hour there were fourteen boats in the area and it was too crowded, the fish began to go off through so much activity. The wind had veered slightly, now blowing towards the dam. This presented us with a perfect long drift. Off we set, passing over lots of normally good 'hotspots' at Hill Farm and Church Bay. I estimate that drift is close on 2.5 miles long, yet it wasn't until we came to the end, close to the dam, that Mick had the first take. He lost the fish.

The only other place where we found fish was from the far corner of the dam at Plummer Park to the Valve Tower. We stayed here to complete our limits on floating lines and small flies, but the fish were a lot smaller, averaging around 1¼lb.

As none of the other public reservoirs that I know are producing fish in the class that Grafham is, this is the place to go if you want big fish. You may get a disappointment, yet again you may finish the day like Derek Brown did. Remember that the fry are quite close in, so don't go out too far from the shore if you have a boat. The only exception to this rule is to fish over known shallow submerged islands.

If you are bank fishing, early morning is definitely the best time. Find an area with some weed about, this will harbour plenty of perch fry, the trout will certainly be round at some time to feed on them.

After the first two months of this year's trout season you may recall I made a chart of the popular reservoirs. This followed their progress to date, giving anglers some idea where to visit. With just three weeks to go here again is my chart, so see how it has varied throughout the season.

FOOTNOTE: Can you beat this? Bob Draper was fishing at Pitsford Reservoir when he caught a brownie of 1½lb that had been feeding on fry. Bob did a stomach content examination when he got home. Result – eighty-four small roach fry were found!

The following week came this article.

Catches Turn Back the Clock
The kind of magnificent sport Mick Nicholls and I had at Grafham this week was, for me, like turning the clock back to

1966–67. The sixteen rainbows we caught went over 46lb and averaged nearly 3lb a piece, with the best specimen going 4lb 13oz to Mick's rod.

Yes, these were vintage Grafham results and trout fishing at its very best.

Yet the day had started most miserably for me, after being out in the boat for less than an hour I felt groggy with a violent headache and stomach upset.

I began to get over it by 3pm and, fortunately, this coincided with the big rainbows coming onto feed.

We were drifting our boat along very slowly when suddenly the monotony was broken. Both of us hooked good fish simultaneously. I boated mine, but before I could get the net to Mick, his fish shook the hook.

We rowed back and anchored about 20yd from the spot, reasoning there would be more fish in that area. A steady comfortable cast and our lures covered the spot. Soon we both had another fish a piece, but in netting mine I had tangled my monofilament backing.

In the short period it took me to untangle this, Mick had landed four more big fish, including the best specimen at 4lb 13oz. I managed to get another one before they went off, but the feeding spell had been short and sweet.

Other boats in the vicinity had not fared too well, but the bank anglers were catching a few. After a while the other boats up-anchored to try pastures new, so we decided to try slow drifting again. Fish began to rise for the small fly life on or near the surface, but these were much smaller fish than we had been catching and they proved difficult to tempt.

We had given our hotspot a fair rest so at about 6pm we decided to give it another try. Mick rowed over and I lowered the anchor in the same place.

It was my turn to take the lion's share this time, for they were bang on feed again. I caught five while Mick had three.

There was lots of other action too, with hooking and losing fish, and gentle tap takes. Mick finished with 25lb 9oz and my weight went 20lb 7oz.

We had chopped and changed our tackle about a lot during the day, catching the fish on slow-sink, sink-tip, and floating fly lines. The latter were used when we saw trout chasing fry on the surface. The lures were changed quite a lot too, but my new pattern, the Appetizer, and the Baby Doll were the most killing.

Just like a cat cannot resist an injured mouse or bird, neither at present can Grafham's rainbows resist an ailing or injured perch fry. I say ailing or injured, because a percentage of these 3in fry still have the killer perch disease. When they become distressed and flap about weakly, they become easy prey for the big marauding trout.

There is another reason why you will notice perch fry struggling feebly on the surface. This follows a powerful attack by a big trout. As he bulldozes into the fry he catches some which he eats, but at the same time he stuns a few more.

Naturally, the trout usually picks these injured fish up shortly afterwards. That is if those keen-eyed terns don't beat him to it. If you watch out for activity where terns are concentrated on a spot where they keep dipping down on the water, it's odds on that big trout will be feeding on the fry there.

Mick and I really had a great weekend, for the next day we were at Draycote to fish in the final friendly trout fishing competition of the season. This event certainly proved popular and caught on with Draycote's regular anglers but, as I stressed previously, the event was open to anyone.

David West and Gordon Griffiths won the match with fifteen fish going 17lb 14oz. Mick and I came second with thirteen fish for 14lb 15oz, and Jack Smith and John Hillier were third with 13lb 12½oz.

It was a difficult day, one when fishing on the surface with small flies gave the best results. Notice this last section about friendly competition; this was that period when I began to take an interest in this branch of fishing. The detail of competition has a separate section.

Finally, the third article, which shows you what it was like. I truly believe that because *Angling Times* encouraged me to write up the excitement of the trout fly-fishing scene, between us we created lots of coarse anglers taking up the sport.

This last article also refers to the Baby Doll lure; my friend, Brian Kench, invented this one and, again, it was a very, very successful fry pattern. I wrote:

Two 5lb Brownies in Successive Casts

A violent pull almost jerked my retrieving hand back up to the butt ring and I was into something pretty big. Ten minutes later Mick Nicholls slid the net under a beautiful specimen brownie of 5lb 6oz.

With the light beginning to fade at evening time I quickly despatched the fish, unhooked my 'Appetizer' lure from its mouth and cast out again. I waited for a few seconds for my slow-sink fly line to go down (it was only 10ft deep), then with my first retrieving pull, 'Bang'. I was in business again. This fish fought every bit as hard, and it turned out to be yet another specimen brownie of 5lb 2oz. Of course this sort of thing could only be happening at Grafham Water, the reservoir I have been advising you all to fish this back end.

These two fish had crowned another successful day's trout fishing at Grafham for Mick and me giving us a 50lb total for fourteen fish. My limit bag went 31lb 7oz and broke the record for the season's best catch, and Mick's six rainbows went over 18lb.

Naturally we feel we understand the feeding behaviour of these larger trout more than ever before, so this is how we set about catching them.

As I mentioned last week, location has been no problem at all. But the trout only feed in short spasms when they are on the fry, and if you are not careful this can put the angler off his stride. For example, it was obvious that Mick and I would return to the area where we had caught the 46lb double-limit bag the week before. We knew there were stacks of fry there and we hoped the trout would still be there too.

Fishing at anchor has paid better dividends than drifting when the trout are on the fry. However, earlier this summer when these same fish were feeding almost exclusively on daphnia, drifting the boat was then easily the best method.

In the first half-hour at anchor on this latest trip I caught three big rainbows of 4lb 3oz, 4lb 1oz and 3lb 7oz. All these fish fell to lures tied on extra-long-shanked hooks. This gave the finished job an overall length of 2½in.

Now to Mick and me this was a most important factor towards our success. The big trout were feeding on perch fry of 2½in long, and our normal No. 6 ordinary long-shanked hook size, was nowhere near the correct length. Also on the previous week Mick had pointed out that these perch fry were a rather anaemic, almost white looking species. So this was the reason for concentrating on lures with mostly white in their dressing.

This combination of the correct length and colouration of the lures, made our Appetizers and chenille-bodied 'Baby Dolls' almost irresistible.

It was midday before Mick had a take, then he had two 3½lb rainbows quickly. The next feeding spell came in mid-afternoon when we caught a rainbow each, again both over

3lb. At this time we also hooked and lost a fish.

During this particular brief feeding period we witnessed an incredible sight. A perch fry was being hounded by a big rainbow, the small fish leapt three times from the water in absolute terror as the rainbow closed in on him. A quick shake of the head and the perch was swallowed alive; we saw this all happen at only 3yd range.

Now came a very long wait right up to the final hour of the day's fishing, but it was worth waiting for. It was all-action stuff from then to the close; I had four fish, including the two 5lb-plus brownies, while Mick had three more good rainbows. Had we become restless when the fish went off, we could easily have moved and missed out on that tremendous last hour.

We figured it out like this – when the trout came on feed it was a chain reaction, they all came on together. However, it didn't take them too long before they had had their fill of these large food items, and sure enough they all went off the feed together.

A resting-up period would follow, I suppose for the trout to digest their food, and during this time there would be no takes. I noticed twice when I had hooked big rainbows, during the lively fight that followed, that other big rainbows were swimming around with them.

I reckon they thought my hooked fish was having a feeding frenzy and they came up to look for their share. Grafham has now produced over 20,000 fish so I wasn't far off with my earlier assessment. 'A new arrival will give sport for the future.'

Zander on the Fly at Grafham

Around 1995, following the news that Grafham had fished well for the Midlands Eliminator Final, Frank Cutler went to fish at the big reservoir with Malcolm Eade. A big wind had discoloured the water and this seems to be the situation there these days. Because his thoughts of a big catch disappeared, Frank put on a sinking-line outfit and a fry-imitating lure. He caught a trout then a perch, but what followed turned out to be a bit of a shock, as he found himself playing a decent-sized 4lb zander.

Many of us regulars had heard stories of zander in Grafham for some time and it was obvious they would get in with all that water pumped in from the Great Ouse. I had never come across anyone who had caught one there on a fly lure before Frank's catch. It seems like these could provide bonus sport for the future and create an additional sporting species. Certainly they will do no harm to the trout and their dorsal fin, which is very spiky, might choke the cormorants!!!

Seriously though, I have caught zander on the fly before at a lake in France where they also fish for trout and pike on the fly. I once caught five zander in an hour there on a White Tinhead lure. Now, to date, I have caught a few by Grafham's north aeration tower up to 7lb. I like them.

I have also fished for zander for many years while using bait in the Fenland Rivers and drains. I find them fascinating and a very good species to try for. The late David Fleming Jones, who managed Grafham in the 70s, said this would happen one day and that he would welcome the extra sport zander would give. Now they have been caught there to 12¼lb and I do think that, in a few more seasons, the UK record for zander will be broken at Grafham with a fish over 20lb.

The Other Trout Reservoirs

I make no bones about it, Grafham has been my favourite trout fishery since its opening in 1966. I suppose I know it so well I could almost tell you the position of every pebble on the bottom. I don't need a depth sounder. I could fill this book with Grafham stories alone, but I must move on. That does not mean to say, though, that I ignore all the other top-class reservoir trout fisheries. Looking back at the early days, I spent many weekends at Chew Valley and Blagdon; it was always good sport and a lovely place to be.

Closer to home I had Pitsford on my doorstep and also Ravensthorpe, with the lovely Eyebrook just up the road about half an hour. When Draycote reservoir opened, this too offered superb fishing. Then finally the largest of all, Rutland Water. I have spent countless days from both boats and banks fishing; at all of them my fishing life has been kind to me. Obviously I can not go into detail about every good catch or all techniques, so I will retrace my memory just to whet your appetite.

Prior to the opening of Grafham, Eyebrook reservoir took some beating for quality and size of trout. Brown trout of around 2lb to 2½lb were caught on most visits. In particular there was always an early rise in the mornings, something I have never really seen anywhere else. I still go to fish Eyebrook a couple of times each season and it's as good as ever. I even caught a 3½lb blue rainbow on my last visit.

Draycote reservoir, near Dunchurch in Warwickshire, is so easy and quick to get to. It is also very good at producing top catches. When it first opened in 1970 it was only half filled and gave short fast sport with lots of browns and rainbows to around 3lb best. During the second year, 1971, there was quite a controversy over the fishing at Draycote. Some season ticket holders had made strong complaints, for many of them had poor results, especially from the bank. I agreed that some of the stock fish were very small, but I never fished for them. I and my close friends who fished there, and went for the three-year-old 'brownies', going from 3lb to 4½lb. We fished very deep and exclusively for the browns that were feeding on the bottom.

We fished mostly from drifting boats with similar tactics, which we had used with success at Grafham. The only difference was that we used a new idea in sinking line, deep fishing, namely the 'lead core' shooting-head line. This was an improvised home-made effort, being a 10yd length of Gladding multi-coloured trolling line. This in turn was attached to 100m of my flat Black Streak Shooting Head backing, which was known for its no-tangling qualities. The outfit was completed by using the first improvised wide-arbour trout fly reel, namely an Allcock's Aerial 4in coarse-fishing reel. The fly rod to cast this heavy head was a fibreglass light carp-rod blank, which we made up as a powerful fly rod.

In the main we kept around 100yd from the bank, mostly along the natural shoreline rather than the stony dams. Depth was usually 18 to 20ft deep. To complete the new deadly tactics was a new lure invention of mine called the Black Chenille; this was tied on a No. 6 long-shank hook.

Don't forget that these big browns – lots of three pounders, some 4lb – were stocked at less than 1lb. So they were good fish, but were definitely feeding much differently from the norm. They were, in fact, taking advantage of the freak natural food explosion. This was brought about by the second year of the reservoirs filling up and flooding more natural bank. Stomach content checks found they were full of large food items, like frogs, newts, sticklebacks, minnows, big snails and so on.

Of course, the way these brown trout were feeding at Draycote didn't suit the normal style of fly fishing used by the majority. This caused a lot of irritation and frustration. Nevertheless, this was a time for change on the big deep reservoirs and we had hit on the key to extreme deep fishing. Namely, putting the lure quickly right along the bottom where the trout were. Today this crude early find of ours has been made into proper fly lines such as the DI8 and the Bob Church Competitor Fast Sink Line with Tungsten Impregnation. From those Draycote lessons, other fly fishers soon cottoned on that floating lines with three wet flies or nymphs was not the only way to catch trout.

Rutland Water

We had all waited with great anticipation for Rutland Water to open its doors for the first time. Everything was right in 1978 – big attendances at all other waters and the coarse-fishing closed season was still on. It was the peak time for all anglers to want to catch themselves a few trout. At 3,300 acres, Rutland was the biggest man-made trout water in Europe. The high numbers of fly fishers who turned out to fish will never be equalled again.

Naturally, at the beginning, it was quite easy to catch a lot of trout from bank or boat. The fishing lodge in those days was at Whitwell Creek. It was in the second season that things began to get interesting as the boat fishing began to produce lots of 3lb to 4lb brownies.

The deadly rudder method, which I had promoted somewhat at Grafham, years earlier, was now banned there. But here at Rutland the large, very good boats had inboard motors. This meant they had a very good built-in rudder and all one had to do to set the boat drifting straight, bow-first downwind, was to wedge a piece of cushion foam-rubber beneath the tiller arm. Many soon got into this method, using sinking lines and good-size lures, and soon we were to see the 'waggy' lure in action. It was time of 'limititus', as most average fly fishers were catching their eight fish. I, of course, was in there with them. I cringe sometimes when I see photos of the past, with piles of dead trout and the rest. But it was all the done thing through that period, and still is on many waters.

Fact is, once you have paid for a ticket for fishing and a boat for the day, you tend to keep the eight fish you are entitled to (if you catch them). A catch and release day ticket is only a couple of pounds less – this is not enough to encourage anglers to return their catches. A much lower-price ticket and the use of a barbless hook fly are really needed for returning all fish.

I suppose Rutland has been kind to me. I have fished there in the World and Commonwealth Championships for England, both times getting a team gold medal. I have qualified to fish for England in the National Championships there on two occasions. Also our team, Bob Church Tackle, has finished third, fourth and a couple of fifths in the National Benson and Hedges Championships. There are a number of other memorable trout competitions I have been involved in at Rutland, but there is a separate chapter covering competitions later.

One of the major things that happened at Rutland was when the Anglian Water Authority put up Rutland for privatization. Our good friend Roger Thom took it on with a nine-year lease and the option of a second nine-year lease. However, he made such a good job of it that Anglian Water paid good money to get it back, after Roger's five successful years, in which time Roger had shown them how to make a good profit with, for example, breakfast, restaurant and bar, and also a very good tackle shop.

Rutland has produced both browns and rainbows into double figures, but I have to say I have never caught one. I would love to. Trout of this size grown on naturally are a very rare fish. For the specimen fisher they are the ultimate prize.

One of the major lures I invented to catch the fish deep down at Rutland, was the No. 6 hooked tandem Goldie. It proved so good for Peter Gathercole and me, when used from the boat. Peter even created a 'waggy' version of it that worked quite excellently.

My favourite area at Rutland is way down the south arm in Manton, or over on the Bunds. By contrast the north arm is usually more difficult, unless a good hatch of buzzers appears. Then a lot of big fish will rise for them, producing some of the water's best ever fishing.

With the fishing lodge back at Normanton and the whole fishery under the watchful eye of the likeable John Marshall, things look good for the future. I have to admit though, as good as the Wembley of fly fishing really is, I still love Grafham the best.

Pitsford – My Home Water

Five minutes' drive from my house is Pitsford Reservoir. At 800 acres it is a good size and it is a great summer trout fishery. From mid-May onwards Pitsford becomes the best real fly-fishing reservoir I know. The hatches of fly life here are far more numerous than at the other major large reservoirs. This makes fishing here a very interesting proposition. It is then perfect for the fly fisher who likes to 'deceive' rather than 'attract' the trout.

I always start my serious fishing at Pitsford about the time mentioned, for it coincides with the first few hatches of pond olives. These delicate little flies with their upright wings sail across the surface for quite some way before taking flight. This, of course, is guaranteed to make trout rise and I have always found at Pitsford this includes good rainbows and browns.

Following the small black chironomid of late April, we have another olive fly hatching quite often throughout May and that is an olive chironomid (buzzer) of slightly larger size. With all these natural olive-coloured flies about obviously it pays to use a similar shade in our artificials. Greenwells Glory, Olive Quill, Golden Olive and Sooty Olive are all well worth a try, but I have easily had most success with a wet fly of my own development called June Fly. When fishing the nymph version I use a pattern with a dubbed-on marabou body called Spring Favourite. For some unknown reason a 'bob fly' with orange in its body, like a Grenadier, makes the most effective top dropper when the olives are coming off.

As well as these flies, daphnia is common; so too are sedges and the phantom midge, and caenis can be very thick. Damsel vary with each season; snails, corixa, leeches, coarse fry and shrimps all help to complete this very good natural trout larder. The trout naturally thrive well here and fish are always in tip-top condition once they have been in a short time. A systematic stocking policy is operated and, like Rutland, John Marshall is in charge of this.

Bank fishing is quite good, but a boat does give a lot more scope at this time of year. I personally favour traditional short-line drifting best of all, not only for the extra pleasure that this method gives me at this time of year but also because it catches more fish. There is nothing as thrilling as watching a trout rise two or three times to a natural, then you cast to it and observe your artificial being taken.

Some of the best drifts at Pitsford, in order of my preference, are close to the bird sanctuary limit in the small half of the reservoir. The whole area has thick Pond Olive hatches and trout rise well in the fairly shallow depths. Another good drift is from the far side of the Walgrave Arm, to drift into the spot where the old road can be seen to run into the reservoir. Finally, a drift to take you down to the centre of the Holcot Arm is also well worth a try. These spots mentioned are all in the shallower part of the reservoir, which is the fishing lodge side, separated by a main road causeway dam.

To get through into the main deep part of the reservoir there is a tunnel through the causeway. At each entrance there is a deep hole and when a good wind is blowing a strong current is forced through the tunnel. This situation often attracts good numbers of trout to the spot, so anchoring the boat out from the upwind side and then casting back to the tunnel is a good tactic.

The Stone Barn Bay area has always been a lucky spot for me for big fish. It is a good spot from both boat and bank. Continuing along the gravel bank to the holly bush, this is all very good bank fishing. Because it is the furthest spot from any access, you will have great stretches to yourself if you are prepared to walk. Under these conditions fish come in very close and you are able to stalk them with nymph tactics. By the way, John Goddard's pattern and floating Suspender Buzzer is quite excellent here in this situation. One final tip, if you try this don't wade.

There is a little creek, known as the Pitsford Arm, as you approach the main dam. This creek is probably the best area to concentrate on at the back end, as we know many of the large elusive browns home in on this spot for their pre-spawning gathering. At this time it will be best to go back over to fish-imitating lures, and try to make an early morning start.

Two other very good spots are Sailing Club Bay and Brixworth Bay with the drift from the left-hand corner of the main dam and back to the creek mouth, or in reverse if the wind is the other way. A team of skinny buzzers on the 'bung' method is deadly here.

Blagdon Reservoir

Now we go back to our 'roots' as regards reservoir trout fishing, for it was way back in 1904 that Blagdon opened. Centenaries are well worth celebrating and as I write I am preparing for a trip to Blagdon in mid-April. Standing the test of time is a great achievement and, for continuing consistent sport in completely unspoiled surroundings, Blagdon has the edge on all other reservoirs. Blagdon was the first still water in Britain to be stocked with rainbows and even 100 years ago it soon became obvious that this American immigrant was going to provide more exciting sport than our native brown trout could offer.

Set in the picture-postcard Mendip Hills, Blagdon has its own special charm. The lodge has the atmosphere of bygone days as large, cased trout stare down from its walls. The one-time record rainbow of 8½lb, caught here in the 1920s, is there – a fine wild fish grown on naturally in Blagdon from stock size.

All the boats were rowing only until recent years. The stock fish are always of the highest quality; both Blagdon and Chew Valley have this reputation that goes back many years. Bright silver fish of 2lb to 3lb are commonplace.

For well-read anglers the name that instantly springs to mind when Blagdon is mentioned is Dr Bell, the father figure of our nymph fishing as we know him today. His Amber Nymph and Blagdon Green Midge were the forerunners of our Sedge Pupa and Buzzer Nymph patterns, of which there are now so many. It is an interesting fact that, even with all the modern developments that have followed, Dr Bell's original patterns are almost as effective at catching trout as the new ones.

My favourite bank fishing spots at Blagdon are down in the shallows at Dr Bell's Bush, off the point of Holt Bay. This is a good spot for intercepting cruising rainbows. The shallows of the north shore also offer good bank fishing, for when the aquatic plants begin to grow they become a haven for all sorts of creepy crawlies. Common insects at Blagdon are chironomids (buzzers), corixa, damsel fly nymph, sedges, shrimp and snail.

After the initial opening week has passed, when a medium sinking or home-made sink-tip line would be of use even in the shallows, all you need from the bank is a floater. I would advise anyone who is likely to fish Blagdon from the bank to nymph fish using patterns such as Buzzer Nymph (various), skinny and bung method. Pheasant Tail, Corixa, Damsel Fly Nymph, Stickfly, Footballer and Olive Nymph are a good set.

Before we leave bank fishing and after advising you to nymph fish, on second thoughts I should also mention that Blagdon rainbows go for a single small No. 10 Dog Nobbler type lure fished on a floating line. They work so efficiently everywhere. Keep this choice of method as an alternative to nymphing.

Most times when I make the journey to the west country I travel with a fishing mate and we book a boat, stay overnight in the village inn and fish again the next day. This makes a good weekend break, which I recommend. I always look on a boat as a sort of insurance policy, for it is most rare, no matter what kind of day it is, not to find feeding fish somewhere. You may get a few resting fish later in the day, so you know most trout will be on the bottom.

For early-season cold water conditions the easiest way I know to find trout is to use a drogue. You need to take your own, by the way. Don't put it out from the normal broadside position, put it out from the central stern and attach the rope with a G-clamp. Now you will drift steadily along allowing both anglers to cast out from different sides of the boat with sinking lines and a single small lure. The slow drift will mean you search over a lot of bottom until you find a shoal of trout, which early in the year may be fairly stationary. Carry on drifting but remember the spot, so when you motor back you start the next drift to begin just upwind of it. If you have drifted half a mile or so with no takes then both get a fish on at the same time, this is a sure sign of quite a large shoal in the area. Now a little tip; if you stand up and start waving the net about so all the other boat anglers see you, they will probably move in and spoil the drift. So use a little cunning; keep the rod low while playing the fish and don't touch the landing net until he is beaten and ready to lift out.

Lures I have had the most success with at Blagdon are, in the early days, Missionary and Black Chenille. Other good patterns are Muddler Minnow, Ginola, Green Pea, Appetizer and Black Tadpole. A size 10 Black and Peacock Spider normally used as a wet fly near the top is also quite good here when fished deep on a sinking-line dropper.

It can well be a good idea to anchor at this shallower end of the lake, as it is an ideal spot to try nymph fishing from the boat. Once again, it is a good idea to take your own anchor with you. Actually, if you are to be a serious boat fisher, having all your own boat equipment is essential. In this way you can handle any weather conditions without it spoiling your fishing.

Let us move on to those lovely summer days and evenings when at last you can fish the top with confidence. Traditional drifting with a team of three small flies then comes good and, to be honest, there are not many better places in this country you could be. Old traditional favourites like Greenwells Glory, Claret and Mallard, Invicta, Wickhams Fancy, Olive and Ginger Quills still catch as many fish as any modern pattern. Use these in conjunction with a Grenadier or Soldier Palmer as a 'bob' fly and I guarantee you some fine fishing like I have had.

Chew Valley Lake

Just three miles from Blagdon, along the Mendip, lies Chew Valley, the largest and best known of the west-country trout reservoirs, Chew Valley Lake. At over 1,000 acres and very well managed, Chew encourages a lot of visitors each year. As well as the experienced Bristol locals, many Welshmen and Midlanders can always be found fishing here and every so often it is used for an international event.

Similarly to Blagdon, stock fish are of the highest quality. One point perhaps needs clarifying; the large double-figure rainbow that have come out of Blagdon and Chew of late are, of course, stocked at that size. But it must be added that, from the pictures I have seen, these were all well-proportioned silver trout and not clapped-out dark brood fish. If you catch a large brown from either reservoir you can be sure that this will be completely wild and grown on in the water from 1½lb or so. A set-up 10½lb fish bears witness to this in the fishing lodge.

Chew Lake has a number of interesting features, many of which are good trout holding spots. The comparatively shallow bank areas on the east shore at Wick Green are always a good early season spot – this applies to both bank and boat fishers. In complete contrast is the deep-water bank fishing to be had just out from the fishing lodge at Woodford Bank. This area always holds a lot of roach and perch fry and from August onwards this is a very good early morning spot. At this time use fish-imitating lures and it is important to get there early to fish this section of the bank hard before other anglers get a boat. The deepish water continues as you move in the direction of the dam to a spot known as Walley Bank.

Chew's buzzer (chironomid) hatches are very good and often a large species of brownish shade and around 1in long can be seen coming off. When these are hatching it is guaranteed that fish will be up very close to the surface sipping in the nymphs trapped momentarily in the surface film. Two very good bank spots for evening nymph fishing are Nunnery Point and Moreton Point to Stratford Bay. Another good bank spot is on the north shore by the picnic area.

These days at Chew I tend to fish the boats most of the time and I can always catch fish at the back of Denny Island. When it has been very hot in mid-summer and the water green with algae, conditions have looked impossible. Yet at these times you will usually notice three underwater oxygen-giving aerators are switched on in the area of deep water out from the dam. This area really does get stuffed with trout at these times and the late Frank Cutler and I had two heavyweight double limits here when, if we had fished elsewhere, we would have drawn a blank – remember this one.

Without doubt, for me the most consistent boat drifting area of all at Chew is over the Roman Shallows. This quite large area lies roughly halfway across the reservoir between Nunnery Point and Wick Green. The depths vary, of course, according to water levels and usually these are down in summer. Depths from 10ft to 2ft, averaging around 5ft, mean excellent fishing in warm weather. The shallows get very weedy and harbour a lot of the trout's natural food, so fish are always frequenting the area.

Because of the shallow nature of the spot it is all too easy to completely ruin your chances before even casting a fly. Always make sure you cut off your motor long before you get to the Roman Shallows, then drift quietly on to them. When the drift is finished always motor back in a big semi-circle keeping well away from your actual fishing spot. If you religiously stick to this and there is a reasonable wave action of 6in or more you will catch well. Remember that, even if there are no fish rising at all, the water is shallow enough for trout on the bottom to see your surface-fished fly. If they do see it and you have done as I said and not frightened them there will be no hesitation and they will rise to take your fly.

I have been on Chew when masses of buzzer, sedge and caenis have all been hatching at once and the fly I hold greatest faith with is the Olive Quill. Other flies and lures that have given my friends and me our best results are Ginger Quill, Dunkeld, Invicta, Grenadier, Red Dry Emerger, Peach Doll and Appetizer, and a White Muddler was the best of the fry patterns.

After saying that, a recent trip to Chew was in bitter cold weather and strong winds. I had anchored my boat 60yd from the bank on the east shore at Wick Green. The season was now two weeks old and the fishing difficult. I kept saying to my boat partner, who was fishing Chew for the first time, 'Never known it as hard as this.'

At such times persevere; keep trying different lures and different spots is the tactic I employ when I know I am struggling. I was rewarded with a 2lb rainbow after my first cast to a Yellow Dog Nobbler when six other different patterns had failed. As the day crept on we had not seen any other boats. I moved to a new spot 80yd along the bank but still only 60yd from the bank. Finally I changed yet again, this time to a White Frog Nobbler. In quick succession I had a 2¼lb brown followed by an over-wintered brown of over 3lb. This fish fought quite magnificently and jumped three times before coming to net. Another fish on and off, then a couple more takes and 'I am in again'. I knew this fish was heavy, but no trout. What a specimen it was, a very fine perch going 3lb ½oz; just imagine catching such a fish on your local river or canal. It would make headlines.

Of course this was not Chew at its best. I reflect back, though, on that day as how it can be for early season fishing. These days, of course, I sometimes fish for pike on the fly at Chew, as there are some very big specimens to be caught – up to 35lb.

Bewl Water

Bewl Water in Kent is a big reservoir favoured by many and used for national and international events. I like fishing here very much, as it has been kind to me. I suppose my best memories of Bewl would be coming third in the European Grand Slam, which was a half boat, half bank competition.

I was also fishing there on the day they allowed boats to go in close to the stockie cages. I fished with Jeanette and we decided to approach the day with fast-sinking lines and lures. Anchoring close to the cages and fishing beside them was rather exciting because we knew there would be some big resident trout lurking about. These would be looking for free food bits that come through the mesh of the stockie cages. We caught some good-sized fish, Jeanette boasting the largest, a 5¼lb rainbow. Then I had a few minutes of high drama. I was casting my fast-sink line equipped with a tandem No. 6 Goldie lure to land really close to the cages. It was quite deep here, some

24ft. During the late afternoon I hooked a very solid, slow-moving fish and it took hard right at the bottom.

I played the fish on my adequate tackle for a few minutes before it eventually came up on top and we saw this magnificent brownie, which looked to be at least 11lb to 12lb. With that a boat motored past and he turned to come close in to me, chatting away. 'Hello Bob, have you had a good day?' The almost beaten monster was scared by the engine and took off once more, right under the boat, which you will remember was anchored. I could do nothing about it but try to haul it back and in doing so it touched the coarse plastic rope. Just my luck, the fish was hooked by one of the single tandem hooks. The other was hanging just out of the trout's mouth and this caught fast in the rope and the trout de-hooked itself and swam off, leaving the lure firmly stuck in the rope. The trout was none the worse for his experience and I would have put him back alive and well, but it would have been nice to take a photo.

Needless to say I had a few words with the oblivious over-friendly stranger. I couldn't get too mad, even though he definitely cost me the prize of a very rare double-figure brownie.

Tittesworth Reservoir

I sometimes visit this lovely lake. This is my best memory of some years ago.

Nestling beneath the Pennine Range in a completely unspoiled part of England lies Tittesworth Reservoir. It is the closest one can get to an Irish lough or Scottish loch this side of the border. The surroundings alone are worth quite a lot even before you catch any trout, but that is no problem either as I found on my couple of trips to this most attractive 200-acre water.

Although Tittesworth is a very good bank-fishing reservoir, after driving a fair distance I like to treat myself to a boat. There are several good reasons for using a boat here. I soon found three very important ones.

First, because the bottom feed is not as rich as at some low-lying reservoirs, the trout become free risers and lend themselves perfectly to traditional loch-style short-line fishing from a broadside drifting boat. Second, many interesting areas close into the bank are steep sloping and very deep. This is virgin fishing territory, as thick woodland and undergrowth make any bank casting impossible. The boat, therefore, is the perfect platform to fish these holding spots at anchor or on the drift. Third, Tittesworth is full of browns, both stocked and also a high percentage of wild fish that breed mostly in the Churnet feeder stream. This rises as a spring at Middle Hills, Ramshaw, on the edge of the Pennines. The big browns that sulk away in the deeps of Tittesworth, in my opinion, have never been touched. If ever a water was waiting to receive some attention by big brown trout enthusiasts, this is the one.

Just to whet your appetite, they have been caught to 9lb 5oz and bailiff, Ken Scragg, took one out from the margins that had choked to death on two stock fish. This was a double-figure fish. Then there is the resident, approximately sixteen-pounder who regularly shows himself near the boat moorings. He has a patrol beat that takes him from the lodge area around into Churnet Bay and back; he lives on stockies and coarse fish. Need I say more?

The late Selwyn Hughes, the Welsh ex-international fly fisher, was a classic participant of the delicate art of short lining. Viewing him fishing from some distance I could not help but be most impressed by his control of rod, line and flies, and he used a white line too!

It is the done thing for expert fly fishers these days to catch a lot but also return most of them unharmed. I met Selwyn back in the lodge and he called me over to show me a fish. It was a perfect rainbow of about 6in. Every fin was intact, it was very silver and solid fleshed and we both agreed this could not possibly be a stock fish. The reason Selwyn had killed this fish was to get a second opinion. Certainly that was the first wild rainbow I have ever seen in a still water in this country. That Churnet stream must be very pure and ideal for successful breeding, as are many of the Pennine rivers.

Talking to regular Raymond Inney from nearby Stoke, I learned much of the reservoir's background. Ray has fished Tittesworth since it opened in the mid-sixties. He loves the place and admits that the water's popularity has had its ups and downs, mainly through varied stocking policies.

The very first trout I caught from Tittesworth came from Churnet Bay; a superb brownie of 2½lb, as wild as any I have ever caught. It had twice as many red spots as black and I am sure it had grown from wild stock in the stream. Because it was early season and cold with gin-clear water my boat partner, Keith Robinson, and I decided on fast-sinking shooting heads. My fish came to a size 6 pure-white Muddler, while Keith caught on a Black Chenille lure.

As newcomers, we wanted to explore the reservoir. We rowed across to Badger Bay, pulled the boat ashore and fished from the bank. The wind was awkward, which gave us plenty of elbow room. After about my sixth cast with a size 8 Jack Frost I had a solid take. A silver hen rainbow of over 3lb cleared the water with a succession of spectacular leaps before eventually being beached. Keith and I finished with a limit apiece split between browns and rainbows. We went home most impressed. This was in the mid-1970s and it is only recently I have found time in my trouting calendar to return to the water.

This time I took Geoff Smith with me, who is known more for his specimen coarse fish captures but who also loves his fly fishing. It was late April and just a few days after a horrible weekend of snow, wind and rain that caused havoc country-wide. We were not expecting a great day, for we knew the feeder stream would be filling the reservoir with murky brown cold water. This, in fact, is what we found on our arrival and we felt rather disheartened as we tackled up with sinking lines for slow and deep tactics. The bailiff told us not to worry. 'Go down to the bottom end of the reservoir to Scar Hole. The coloured water hasn't reached there yet,' he guided.

We made our way to this area, slowly moving the boat at about 60yd from the bank. Side casting and steadily moving a small black lure was as good as anything I could think of, but neither of us had a take. Suddenly, as we approached the point top side of Scar Hole Bay, we saw a rise and the water changed to normal clarity, almost as though some unseen barrier was holding it back.

Scar Hole has a high wooded bank behind it and this was giving shelter from the strong cold wind. It was like another world, for here conditions were incredibly perfect; a good hatch of small black chironomids was coming off and fish were moving upwind and rising avidly.

According to how far we drifted from the shelter of the wood we had a ripple that steadily increased to about 9in high – conditions were perfect for bringing confident takes from rising fish. The sinking-line outfits were soon forgotten as we set up with full floating lines and leaders carrying two droppers. Geoff immediately put on size 14 flies, consisting of Black Pennell on the point, March Brown on the centre dropper and Black and Peacock Spider on the top dropper or bob position. I had set up also with Black Pennell, whilst a Claret and Mallard and a Blae and Black completed my leader. Geoff could do no wrong, taking four browns in fifteen minutes but retaining only a brace. The wild browns of around the pound mark are so perfect it's a real conscience-pricker to kill one.

While Geoff had been hooking his fish I had been rising plenty but they were coming short. I got him to row back for another drift while I changed my size 10 and 12 flies, replacing them with all size 14s. This was all it needed for instant success and we both continued to catch very well. I hit the first rainbow, a fish of some 1½lb. On this light gear and small hooks it was all proving to be a fine day's sport. The rise continued through to 6pm when we packed up. Geoff caught twenty while I had eighteen. We kept only the fish that were hooked well in the mouth for our six-fish limit apiece.

This then was a most enjoyable day and every time I see Geoff he says, 'When are we going back to Tittesworth?' From this you can judge how good it was, for he lives close to all the big Midland reservoirs.

Blithfield Reservoir

Although Blithfield Reservoir in Staffordshire is a season permit water, it caters quite adequately for the fly fishers of the area. Guest permits are quite generous – so when Alan Barker from Bloxwich invited me to spend a day boat fishing the 700-acre water with him, I readily accepted.

The day was perfect – grey skies with a fair ripple and the threat of a thunderstorm brewing. Of course, in these ideal conditions there was a tremendous hatch of buzzers on when we started fishing at 10.30am. These buzzers varied tremendously, from tiny right up to ¾in-long giants. Colours varied too, but mainly they were green, brown, grey and black.

The trout were seen to be rising only occasionally as we motored to our fishing position, but obviously they had to be up in the water to take these nymphs. I set up with a floating line and team of traditional wets, putting a size 12 Butcher on the point, a Mallard and Claret on the second dropper and an Invicta on the top dropper. I rubbed my home-made 6lb nylon leader with some heavy mud to take the grease and shine off it. I always use the six-turn water knot for attaching my droppers. As well as being very strong it allows the flies to fish better on the retrieve.

My second cast saw me into a good rainbow, which I rose to the Mallard and Claret with my traditional style short-line technique. Alan decided to use a contrasting method, that of a very slow sink line and size 10 all-black Muddler. Both methods worked well throughout the day, though the old traditional tactics just had the edge.

By the time I had taken my fourth fish, a rainbow of 1½lb, I decided to spoon it, knowing full well what I would find – lots of buzzers. Not for the first time I was able to shock my boat partner. I could see a sizeable red tail of some recently eaten fish in the trout's throat. I needed to use Alan's artery forceps to remove it, and even this was difficult for it was a 6in perch, more than a third the length of the trout. Quite incredibly, after eating this stomach-bulging meal, the trout was busily knocking off buzzer nymphs, for a number of these were sticking to the body of the removed perch. On top of all this, the trout had risen to the sub-surface to take my small wet fly with real confidence.

As I have said several times in the past, where reservoirs hold a good head of coarse fish, even small rainbow trout will feed on them. Once the summer gets underway, reservoir rainbows become quite fit and vicious predators. Obviously they thrive better in the warm weather conditions, when they appear to be continually eating. Their diet changes according to availability, and I find that buzzers (chironomids) are perhaps the most common item on the menu.

By mid-afternoon at Blithfield, the storm that had threatened all day broke quite violently but we were able to take the boat under the arches of a road bridge. The rain stopped and we went out again to fish, but the storm began to double back. I made some joke to Alan about carbon fibre rods acting as lightning conductors, but there we were, standing up and swishing them around. In between the storms fish were still rising to the fly. We had almost reached our double limit, retaining fifteen fish, when a sharp flash of lightning struck down on the water making all my hair stand up like a hedgehog's prickles, and I tingled all over. I can tell you, it scared me half to death.

We quickly caught the last fish and packed up, before more heavy rain spoiled the late evening fishing. Blithfield is certainly a trout reservoir to be compared with the best, and if you live in the Staffordshire area it is well worth joining this season permit club. It is run by the South Staffs Water Board.

The next trip to Blithfield came as an invitation for Frank Cutler and I to fish as the guests of local fly fishing instructor Bill Birnie. This was in the scorching hot summer of 1976. On arrival, Alstair McKenzie, the fisheries officer, apologized for the heat wave. 'Sorry Bob, they haven't been biting for three days now. This will put your fishing to the test, for it's even hotter today,' he said.

We paid for our boat, and even though it was a late start there was only one other boat out. However, I was pleased to note the water was a perfect colour for fishing. Today was going to be a reverse of the first trip, and once again I needed to use my experience to reflect on similar heat-wave conditions when fish were seemingly not feeding. At Grafham they go very deep – even the rainbows – and they will be prepared to take a lure at such times if you get the depth right.

The water was absolutely teeming with coarse-fish fry, which could be seen showing on the surface. Our choice of single lure was naturally a fish-like pattern rather than a gaudy one. As these coarse fish were roach and perch my Appetizer was a good fry imitation. Lines were fast-sinking shooting heads with long leaders – around 5yd of 7lb breaking-strain nylon.

Incredibly the very first drift produced six offers of which we landed four, all rainbows. I had a good brownie next drift and, to be honest, we could do no wrong. It really was hot, so we slowed the situation down by taking a two-hour break for some pub grub and iced lager in the local village.

On resuming we kept on catching at this pleasing rate, in the end breaking the barbs off our hooks to release fish more easily. We retained our limit of ten fish apiece, but it must have been more like forty that were actually brought to the side of the boat. They were quite pleasing results for a period when the fish were not supposed to be feeding. As I said many times, versatility in approach is a must to combat varying situations.

Hanningfield Reservoir

Hanningfield is a big reservoir and one that I have fished a few times each year since the early seventies. Then I used to meet up with Essex policeman, Dave Allen, and we would usually have great catches of brown trout up to close on 5lb, mostly to the deep-sunk lure tactics.

In more recent times Hanningfield has produced terrific rainbow trout fishing, the size of the fish being very impressive due to the very large rearing-cage system operated on the reservoir. Many wild trout would spend a lot of their time milling about beneath the rearing cages, taking in the free sinking pellets at feeding times. The size of these rainbows reached up to just over 20lb, easily the highest of any reservoir. We must remember, though, that the fish were just perfect specimens but their unusually high weights were only because of the free feed beneath the cages.

Eventually the massive rearing programme operated at Hanningfield, as they provided stock fish for many other waters, including Rutland, back-fired. Pollution began to accumulate because of the massive amount of waste product shed by the thousands of stock fish. Shortly after 2001 the whole rearing project had to be abandoned. However, the fishing, albeit false, was good while it lasted.

The two concrete-bowl type of reservoirs that I have fished quite a few times are Queen Mother Reservoir at Datchet and Farmoor II near Oxford. In particular, the Datchet reservoir was opened by the late Queen Mother in 1976 when I was an invited guest, sharing a boat with Fred French from Thames Water Consultants. The reservoir soon became known for its specimen trout, both rainbows and browns, and it produced browns up to double figures. These were naturally-grown fish and very pleasing to catch. My best was a 6lb 10oz rainbow and a near 6lb brown, both on my Appetizer lure. This water is now closed, but was excellent.

Oxfordshire's Farmoor II was built some years after I had fished Farmoor I and it was here that I met the late Syd Bruck, that larger than life character and a really excellent fly fisherman. Syd's casting ability was one of the best I have ever seen. He could reach the fish at greater distance than most others and this is one reason why he was regularly top man.

I first used the 'bung' method here long before it ever became popular with skinny buzzers. When I practised it I used ordinary Pheasant Tails and Fraser Nymphs, and it worked very well.

Another reservoir is Ladybower near Sheffield, where I shared a record barbless hook catch-and-release opening day catch from the bank with my good friend Brian Furzer. Our combined catch of 197 trout included browns and brook trout to 3lb and I had a beautiful over-wintered rainbow of 5¾lb.

Carsington Reservoir

Carsington is another beautiful picturesque trout fishery and, again, it is mostly brown trout that you will catch. A visit to this Derbyshire water is something I try at least once a year and it never fails to produce at least a brace of 3lb-plus browns. If you go, book a boat first.

Roadford Reservoir, Devon

Another lovely reservoir full of brown trout and one where, in fact, I was told by officials that *only* browns were stocked. Fishing with my wife, Jeanette, from the bank I landed a perfect 4lb rainbow. After we had just got over the shock of this, Jeanette also hooked a rainbow, again a perfect fish of around 3lb. Both fish were slipped back. For a water with supposedly no rainbows these were cracking fin-perfect fish.

Foremark Reservoir

Foremark is a sort of forgotten trout reservoir as far as the travelling fly fisher is concerned. Yet only a few years ago I enjoyed some great fishing days there. Again, the brown trout, especially in April, were quite good size! If you like looking up new places check this one out.

Others

I have enjoyed my fishing in Wales, mostly at Llyn Brenig but also at Tal-y-Llyn, a 222-acre lake tucked away in the Snowdonia National Park. Standing towering over Tal-y-Llyn is the impressive Cader Idris mountain at 2,927ft, making the lake a lovely place to catch fine brown trout from a traditional drifting boat. The other superb reservoir I love to spend a weekend at in Wales is Lake Vyrnwy. I highly recommend a visit here. I've fished lots more, such as Malham Tarn in Yorkshire, Ardleigh near Colchester, Ogston, Thornton, Ardingly and more.

When it comes to Scotland I visit there mostly for salmon in its mighty rivers, but Loch Leven and Lyntrathen Loch near Dundee are superb waters to fish – Lyntrathen for its browns. This is the home water of my good friend and Scottish International stalwart, Sandy Forgan.

Then right up in the north of Scotland is the lovely Loch Watten at Thurso. Here I spent many happy hours with local tackle dealer Sandy Harper. We would make long drifts right across the shallow loch to catch some lovely brown trout. I remember a Wingless Wickhams was a superb top-dropper fly.

5
Trout

The Merits of Catching a Big Trout

To me the merits of catching a big trout seem fairly obvious. You either catch one that has just been put in from a small water or you go to a big reservoir and try to catch a few trout of 4lb plus. There is another equation of hunting large wild browns from the big Scottish lochs and Irish loughs. This I covered at the beginning of the book, a very exciting experience. So I will stick to normal fly fishing, that is with fly rod and castable fly line. First, let me say I enjoy fishing at the small fisheries very much; it is just that when I catch a very big fish from one of them I don't get the same thrill as I do at the big waters. Thoughts immediately creep into my mind when looking at, say, a nice 15lb rainbow – perhaps it was only stocked this morning, I imagine, and that spoils my moment.

On the other hand, as you will be aware, it is in September when the bigger fish begin to show at the reservoirs. Most water authorities stock with fish up to around 2½lb with the odd bigger ones put in occasionally. For this reason I rate trout of 4lb plus from a reservoir as specimens. For if a fish has doubled its weight after being stocked, feeding on natural food, and then has the chance of getting lost in the freedom of 1,000-acres plus, if caught it is well earned and I get enormous pleasure out of catching such a fish.

Before leaving the subject, there is a third type of water. That is the larger gravel pit fishery, up to around 50 acres. These usually fish well in early season then suffer with lush heavy weed growth in the heat of summer, which makes them difficult.

The Gravel Pit Trout Waters

The Massive Trout of Earith

The late Dave Hughes kept nagging me. 'You ought to get over to the Earith trout fishery, it's been fishing so well with big fish I've lost count of the doubles I've caught! You really are missing out.' Then a friend, John Emerson of the Mid-Northants Trout Fishers, told me he had been to Earith and said, 'Bob, I've never had such sport, had three doubles with the best a 14½lb golden rainbow.'

I can take the hint and I asked veteran Frank Cutler if he fancied a change from our local trout waters. He jumped at the offer. The fishery was owned by Ken McLennan and I was well impressed by his set-up. A 12-acre lake allows for a six-fish limit and a 25-acre adjoining lake offers catch-and-release fishing only. The ticket cost for each water is a moderate £20 and the catch-and-release water is stocked with fish of minimum size 3½lb up to 25lb. Ken had spent eight years developing this old gravel pit site, and his fine house and ticket office is the central point.

Frank and I were late as usual and so we took out a punt on the catch-and-release water. The idea was to go to the tree-lined bank area into which the wind was blowing, anchor up and then cast into the submerged branch area. It looked a perfect set-up to us, for the down-wind shore always fishes best during early season.

Frank set the ball rolling with a perfect rainbow of over 6lb. 'I am not used to putting fish back of that size!' he joked. Frank had taken his first trout on a Green Pea – this is a lure, black in colour with marabou tail and fluorescent green head. We were both using Wet-Cell II lines as, typical of this type of lake, there were various areas of 3–4ft shallows and deeps up to 12ft. This line is just right for such a situation and is best described as a medium-speed sinker. I broke my duck with a four pounder, then we missed a couple as the fish wriggled free from our barbless hooks.

A couple of hours passed by and we spotted two or three double-figure goldie trout. They were so easily spotted in the clear water as they cruised about 2ft down. We both managed only follows from these quite wary fish, which had probably been caught and released before.

While all of this was going on, one angler, Darrell Wanson from Mildenhall, was having a tremendous time. He was in the corner and casting into a bay towards the tree-lined bank and we could see he was using a large-sized white lure, which turned out to be a pure White Zonker. This was weighted beneath its dressing and fished singly on a very slow-sinking fly line. Darrell finished with fifteen trout, five of which were doubles including two goldies. Darrell said, 'This is nothing, last week I had twenty-four fish, which included four doubles.' Now this kind of sport – fish, catch and release – is the best I have heard of yet in this country and, being a large water, the fish toughen up and handle well.

The climax of Frank's and my day came when I copied Darrell and tied on a white lure. This was a variation of a Cat's Whisker, one of my patterns which I call the Bee's Knees. Its only difference is short-fibred lime fritz for a body and the chain-bead eyes are painted red but, boy, did it do the trick. Third cast with it I was into something very, very big. I kept my cool by thinking it to be a big double. I took about ten minutes to beat it and Frank netted it expertly the first time – at 23½lb it was my best ever rainbow. It was bright silver, very deep and firm and was incredibly thick across the back. We handled it very carefully and that was one massive trout to swim away – time 1.30pm.

The session produced six fish for Frank and four for me. I couldn't concentrate properly after that. Ken later said there is one larger rainbow in, a 25½-pounder, four 20lb-plus fish having been stocked three months before.

After a couple of years Ken sold up to Ray and Tally Bermesister and I wondered if Ray would continue with the big fish policy on the catch-and-release lake. I am pleased to pass on to you that he did and the fishing is still spot-on – I really love the place. I have spent many pleasant days fishing there, but I must tell you of my special red-letter day. This was spent fishing with John Emerson, who also enjoyed his fishing here.

I have had a few red-letter days in my fishing career, but this trip to Earith trout fishery will stand out amongst the best. Catching six trout for 62lb 10oz is mind-boggling and you need to be lucky enough to select the correct tactics right from the start. Also, a huge slice of luck is needed to be in the right place at the right time on such a big lake.

John Emerson and I were fishing Earith for the first time that season, it was Spring Bank Holiday and we were interested to see how the new owners were getting on. We arrived late morning on what was a lovely fishing day. Two anglers from Ipswich had already caught fine rainbows of 7lb and 8lb – a great start, but they said it had now gone off despite a massive hatch of the large lake olives and some ginger buzzers.

I soon observed that only the smaller trout and some lovely rudd of about a pound were occasionally rising to these. So the choice of fly line, I felt, would be very important. It had to be a very slow sinker as the lake is not that deep, so I put on my Bob Church slime line, which is a milky clear colour, blends well as it goes down and does not 'spook' the fish. Why some companies manufacture bright coloured sinking lines I shall never know – 'trout scarers' I call these, especially in clear water.

A long 5m leader of 6lb breaking-strain green Maxima and with my weighted newly invented 'Ginola' fly on I was ready to go. John had set up with a floater but also a long leader and weighted Olive Tinhead as the single fly.

Why, you might now ask, were we not using a dropper or two as we would at the reservoirs? Well, we were fishing Earith's sporting lake, which is catch and release and the fish can get quite big to hook two at once, which is always possible with droppers on, and you would be asking for trouble. Also there is always the risk after hooking a big fish on the point fly that it could run you around and get the trailing dropper fly caught up in a snag and you would still lose the trout. So, better safe than sorry.

There was one of the new boats going spare but we decided to bank fish to begin with, starting in the deep corner by the island. After fifteen minutes John had a take on the drop, which turned out to be a perfect 7lb rainbow. He soon let it swim off, none the worse for its brief encounter.

As I worked along the bank to the corner I spotted a decent goldie, which this water is known for. It was slowly cruising about 2ft down on a regular route. I patiently waited for it to return and then I cast accurately about 2m in front of it, paused for my weighted fly to sink into the fish's vision then retrieved quickly away from it. My tactic was correct as the goldie accelerated to full speed taking the Ginola fly confidently. At just over 6lb I was well pleased. We then had a quiet spell as the sun came out and John said, 'Let's use the boat.'

Now it is here that I believe luck played a part because as John slowly rowed out I said, 'Where do you look for a really big fish on a lake of this size?' To which John casually replied, 'This looks a good spot, we will try here.' Bear in mind, a 20-acre lake is very big for a so-called small fishery.

I knew the goldies liked a quickly pulled fly, but with the rainbows taking on the drop I decided to concentrate on this method. After half an hour at John's chosen anchoring spot nothing had happened, except he had got restless, changed to a suspender buzzer and missed a small fish on this. 'I'll make one more cast then we can move,' I said. I cast long, the fly plopped as it turned over and I paused for about ten seconds waiting for the fly to sink. Before I even took up the slack I had a fish take on the drop. I bent well into it as John said, 'Come on, get that in and put it back and I will pull the anchor in.'

'Hang on a minute, I think this could be a decent fish, perhaps a ten pounder the way it is fighting.' Then suddenly it came up on top and wallowed. John's comment – 'Shit, there is no way that will go in the net.' It was enormous. Ten minutes later it did go in the net; I left it there still in the water as John up-anchored and slowly rowed us ashore. I kept it in the water while a nearby angler fetched the fishery manager, Oren. He brought the Avon dial scales. We quickly weighed and photographed this huge fish and then watched it swim off – the weight of the rainbow, 27lb 2oz. It beat my previous best by nearly 4lb and was a new fishery record, and I believe the biggest fish caught in the country that year.

Everyone had come to see the weighing and the size of it, and as they dispersed from the bank spot where all this commotion was I cast out once more, again on a very long line. The pause, waiting for the fly to sink, 6, 7, 8, 'bosh'. I was in again and what a spectacular fight this was. Where the big fish was more heavy and dogged, this was speedy long runs of the full fly line and lots of backing. At one stage it ploughed straight through a rush bed but came out on the other side. Eventually, after a fast and furious ten minutes, I netted an over-wintered spot-on 11lb rainbow, an immaculate fish that quickly went back. All this action and no one else was catching – it was to be my lucky day. By 4.00pm my scorecard read: rainbows of 27lb 2oz, 11lb, 6lb and 5½lb; also goldies of 7lb and 6lb. A total of 62lb 10oz for six fish, over a 10lb average weight. I doubt if I can ever beat that again.

Eventually, after much persuasion, John took my rod with the deadly set-up of line and Ginola fly. Within ten minutes he had caught a 6lb goldie. We fell about laughing.

Points to note: there are days when fish will take on the drop far better than any actually moved fly or nymph. Sometimes you will find this out by accident but, if so, really concentrate on it. The last time it happened in a big way for me I won the Midlands Final at Grafham, so it works on all waters. After saying this, when we visibly spotted a goldie we knew they wanted a fast fly and we changed accordingly.

Ginola Fly

Just leading up to the beginning of this year's trout season, I watched Tottenham Hotspur in a couple of games and Frenchman Ginola was absolutely brilliant. So as I always try a new fly pattern out at the off, why not a Ginola fly? I would use the colour white for a tail, and a black hackle and shell-back head, long-fibred pearl fritz for the body. This was white for Tottenham's shirt, black for their shorts and the pearl for Ginola's greying long hair.

This same fly caught four trout to 4lb at Hanningfield, six at Grafham, five at Elinor and seven at Earith – the catch at Earith being a record breaker when other good fishermen there on that day found their flies not working too well.

This fly is very versatile because it was Hi-Di sinkers at Grafham and Hanningfield, a floater at Elinor and one of my own slime lines at Earith. Noticeably, takes on the drop of this weighted fly are regular. One for the future. Why not tie one up?

Ginola Tying
HOOK: Size 10 Kamasan, lead-wired beneath dressing
TYING SILK: Black
TAIL: White marabou three times the body length
BODY: Pearl fritz long-fibred
HEAD: Yellow fluorescent chenille
HACKLE: Black
SHELL BACK: Black feather fibre
HEAD: Clear varnish

Lechlade

Lechlade, a mature gravel pits' fishery, is another of my favourite waters and I have had many super days' fishing here. Tim Small prides himself on the size and quality of his stock and they fight so well. Lechlade, like many other Cotswold waters, has quite a prolific mayfly hatch. Although you would expect the best hatches to be in May, in fact it is during the first two weeks in June that this takes place and frenzied trout feeding is regular.

Hundreds of mayfly patterns have been devised over the years, but so far as the nymph is concerned in still waters only one is necessary – Dick Walker's leaded Mayfly Nymph. Here trout feed naturally on the nymphs that live on the bottom in little burrows. Try Dick's nymph out – to this day it still works just as well and there doesn't have to be a hatch on.

Lechlade is very clear in summer and it is possible to stalk trout using this single nymph on a long leader and floating-line outfit. For this type of fishing you don't want too many anglers on the lake, for the tactic is to walk the bank very slowly equipped with a good pair of Polaroids. When I see a trout, perhaps slowly cruising or even resting stationary, I take great care not to spook it. Now cast ahead of the fish's vision and steadily retrieve closer and closer to its mouth. Usually you will see a quick flash of the head and he's on. To be honest, though, mayfly time should be reserved for dry-fly fishing only. The sheer pleasure of seeing a trout rise and take your artificial off the top cannot be bettered. Remember Lechlade next early June and spend a pleasant day in the Cotswolds. It will be worth it!

Milestone Trout

A day out in the lovely Cotswolds is always something to look forward to. So when fishing pal John Sheppard said he had found some excellent trout fishing there and he didn't think I had been there yet, I soon started asking questions.

Milestone Fishery at Fairford was created by the land owners, Bob and Sue Fletcher, five years ago. The 11-acre lake was originally dug out for gravel in the 1940s and now forms part of the Coltswold Water Park. When the project was first started it was so overgrown you couldn't get near to the lake. Being country people, Bob and Sue were very sympathetic when clearing the banks, leaving some wooded areas that can only be fished by boat or float tube. The finished lake is now stocked with rainbows, browns and the very popular golden and blue rainbows. As the photographs around the fishing lodge walls indicate, there is a very good chance of a double-figure trout on any day.

Fellow Northamptonian Con Wilson (new Dever Springs' owner) and I took the scenic drive and in less than two hours we were tackling up. I started on the bank while Con and John Sheppard went out in the boat. I soon noticed their rods bending as they fished catch-and-release, which this fishery allows. Orange or brown fritz-bodied tadpoles were doing the business for them; nothing fancy, just a 4m leader of 6lb nylon on the now very popular slime lines.

I hooked a couple of fish from the bank and they both fell off before I could release them. Then I saw a good-sized carp swim in close. As it grubbed about on the bottom I twitched my now deadly Ginola lure in front of its nose. In a split second I saw the carp's mouth and it ejected the lure. I am glad I witnessed this because I feel more carp could be caught on fly tackle than is realized. Already a twenty pounder has been caught at Eyebrook and one of 24lb at Rutland.

Local angler Dr Wayne Jones said he would share a boat with me, so we set out and anchored close to the overgrown shoreline. Wayne preferred a faster-sinking line; as he pointed out, the water was quite deep here and weed free. He knew his water alright for he caught twice as many as me and one was a fine 12lb rainbow. His size 8 orange fritz tadpole was proving quite deadly. I had to copy his tactics to get my best fish of the morning, a bright silver six-pounder, which I soon slipped back.

In such idyllic surroundings there was no need to flog the water hard all day so we adjourned to the fifteenth-century Bull Hotel in Fairfield for a pub lunch. Refreshed and relaxed, this was a far different trout fishing day from my more recent competition days.

Back at the water Wayne and I took the boat again, but it was soon obvious that the fish had become very wary of taking the lure. Wayne said he would change up and try what is usually a good afternoon method here. This was so simple; a floating line and about a 9ft nylon leader. A plastazote 'bung' (floating sight bob) was set around 6ft from the single fly, which in this case was a size 10 black buzzer. Casting across the wind from the anchored boat, then allowing the light wind to drift the nymph naturally round at the 6ft depth was again quite deadly. Wayne hooked and released four quick fish while I only had one to the original technique that we had used in the morning.

Not being the shy type, I asked Wayne to loan me his rod and set-up. Now casting out my side of the boat I too was into three fish in three casts. It was a bit like float fishing with bait, but I can assure you it was utterly devastating on the day. I praised Wayne for his fishing performance, choosing the right tactics at the right time. He was spot-on. Just as we were about to pack up I noticed a bank angler creeping about in the far corner of the lake close to where we had ended up. I realized I knew him. It was Len Colclough, the big-fish stalking expert from Hampshire.

To end the day in classic style Len hooked into a big rainbow, which was giving him a hell of a fight. He eventually got it in the net, another double-figure rainbow of just over 12lb. Len said he often travels to quality waters that give good chances of catching the magic double-figure fish. His tactic was floating line and leaded bug, the standard stalker's approach. Of course, the clear water of Milestone allows you to use this skilful method from the bank. Also, because the water is trickle stocked on a daily basis after the day's catch is checked, you get a true consistent stock level.

As we called it a day, there had been six double-figure fish landed and also some superb goldies to 8lb. From what I saw on this casual day out, without hesitation I would place Milestone up with the best of the small fisheries that cater for bigger trout of quality than normal.

My local gravel pit trout waters are Ringstead, 36 acres, run by farmer Harold Foster, and the 50-acre Elinor, run by his son Edward, who is himself an excellent trout fisher. He has fished for England in the four country internationals and also my Benson and Hedges team. As you can imagine, he runs a great catch-and-release fishery. My best fish from here went 8¼lb.

Small Trout Fisheries

How this classification came about I don't know, but it usually means purpose-built small lakes from a little over 1 acre up to perhaps 6 to 10 acres. I've fished lots of them. In the earliest days it was Two Lakes in Hampshire where Alex Behrendt started it all. I did fish here a few times to begin with as the guest of Barrie Welham.

However, it was Tony Chattaway at Packington Estate who really got the big rainbow situation started. He stocked the newly opened Burnt Iron pool with a few over 8lb. Soon Brian Jones broke the old long-running British record of 8½lb (grown on) from Blagdon with a fish of over 9lb. From then on the record rainbow steadily increased with fish reared and fed especially to do just that.

Major players were, first, Sam Holland at Avington, then Nigel Jackson at his own created lakes, Dever Springs. Sam was a great mischievous character and had a regular angler visiting Avington, Alan Pearson, now my long-time friend. We began our friendship with a verbal argument that raged for a few weeks on the letter pages of the press, both *Angling Times* and *Anglers Mail*, until Alan invited me to fish at Avington in 1976 and try these easy, tame, stock fish, as I had called them, for myself. The day went like this.

Alan and I had clashed several times in print on the subject of the oversized rainbows. Would I have to eat my words? This trip to Avington would reveal all. A look round the stock ponds at Avington showed fish from this year's hatchings. They were almost twice as big as normal yearlings and all through the graded age groups these rainbows were quite frighteningly advanced.

There was a choice of three lakes to fish, as there is today. They were all very clear and as I walked slowly down the first one I spotted a good-sized rainbow. I watched this cruise back and forth close to the bottom about 7ft down. But the trout wanted none of my offerings! Neither did a pair of rainbows I located later. As nothing was doing, I walked to the next lake where I found an excited Peter Dobbs fishing a shaded area beneath a large tree. He had landed three fish of around 4lb and been smashed on 8lb leader line.

Apparently Peter had hooked one of the really big rainbows, on a size 10 yellow thorax Pheasant Tail Nymph. Alan eventually caught a fish of 8lb on a Mayfly Nymph and I returned to the first lake. There I caught the fish I had been after all day. It went 8¾lb. I must have changed flies twenty times before the fish made a mistake. Although my successful fly was black and silver, I feel it was the presentation that eventually did the trick. Certainly I found that, to get any interest at all, my fly had to be at the exact depth of the cruising fish.

Although catching these big artificially fattened rainbows gives a lot of people a great thrill, I felt the real worth of Sam Holland's work was yet to be seen. I felt these trout needed the space of the big reservoirs to really show their colours. If they were stocked into food-rich Grafham at 12in (the normal stock size in those days), I believed we could have average size fish of 4lb to 5lb with doubles to 15lb a top weight. This was my summing up in my weekly *Angling Times* column the following week. One thing came of the day: Alan and I cemented a firm friendship and we still keep in touch.

Interest was now being shown in Avington and its jumbo trout from all over the country. So a day was set up to bring an *Angling Times* team of experts down to Avington to really see what could be caught. Features reporter John Wilshaw was there to cover the story, in April 1977.

To fish in the party were some pretty good anglers: Dick Walker, Dick Shrive, Peter Dobbs, Alan Pearson and me. 'Dobbie' started the ball rolling with a beauty of 11¼lb. By mid-morning I was into my first-ever double, hooked in the middle lake on a size 10 Ace of Spades. I remember watching my whole 30m of white floating fly line being stripped from the reel. However, I steadily brought back to net a lovely proportioned 15¼lb specimen and, obviously, personal best rainbow for both Peter and me.

Dick Walker caught six fish wandering here and there, with the best two 12lb and 11lb 4oz. Dick Shrive had a thirteen-and-a-half pounder, but it was Alan who showed his knowledge of the water to find a massive 18lb 7oz rainbow, which was a new British and World record at the time. The party looked on the day as a good fishing and social day. We all learned a little bit about dealing with such huge fish on fly tackle. The day was well covered in the press and we all came in for a bit of criticism – someone compared it to 'shooting tigers in a cage'. I clearly knew what he meant.

That was the start of many trips to Hampshire, not only to fish at Avington, but to visit Leo Jarmals and Leominstead; this also gave me some lovely days of sport. Then there was Peter Atkinson's Rooksbury Mill at Andover with, again, quality fish and Dave Riley's Nythe Lake; they were all good and really they were following Sam's early ideas. Anglers clearly liked fishing for big rainbows in small pools – stockies or not, it made no difference.

It was local fly fisher and good friend Con Wilson who first alerted me to the big fish of Dever Springs at Barton Stacey. At first I couldn't understand why Con made the two-hour journey to Hampshire each week, sometimes twice, when his own town of Northampton was literally surrounded by top trout waters.

It was May of 1987 that Con took me with him and I met Nigel Jackson, the very hard-working creator of Dever. For whatever reason, in those days if you caught your limit early on, namely four fish, it was a normal thing to buy a second day ticket. This we did that first day and well remember that Con's Jag boot had sixteen rainbows in it from 4½lb to near 8lb.

With time, I began to enjoy Dever more for a combined fishing and social day out. No longer do I approach it with the idea of catching every fish in the lake; I pace myself, go up to the village pub for a lunch and so on. I wasn't at all surprised when Con decided to purchase Dever, after all he is a very successful businessman and it was a rare present to himself, but of course also a sound investment.

Right from the beginning Nigel had some lovely stock fish. He obtained these by his 'ranching' style of rearing fish on. This is done by allowing the stock fish to grow on in a large, shallow, nearby lake. Naturally they are pellet-fed twice a day but, when he removes them by netting to on-site stock pools, they are perfect with no tatty tails and so forth.

I've caught lots of doubles from Dever and one mid-May day I had a rare situation develop at around 11am. Suddenly lots of hawthorn flies began to get blown on the surface of the small lake and a rise began to them. Quickly putting up a trailing leg hawthorn dry artificial I was able to take advantage of the situation to land a brace of 8lb rainbows. As soon as the hawthorns disappeared I walked on to the big lake, going back to a leaded Mayfly Nymph; I then hooked a beauty of 16¼lb. Then a rise began right out in the middle of the lake and out of casting distance. The stiff summer breeze was blowing some mayflies well out. I searched through my tackle bag and, sure enough, in it was my floating shooting head, which I used for very long casting and 'muddler' stripping on Grafham. My idea for using it to get the extra long-range on this day was about to be tested. So, on went a single dry Mayfly, on a 6lb breaking-strain nylon leader of 12ft.

First I hooked and lost a couple of fish at 40yd-plus range. Then a superb rise and this time a proper hook up and I was into another good double – this time it went 12lb 9oz. I enjoyed that day because, as I say, it's rare to catch on dry fly at Dever.

Chris Ogborne and I made a fairly good video, 'A Day At Dever Springs', and it's still on sale today. We did catch a lot of trout that day and it made good viewing. Why? Because I think Chris and I passed on lots of tips on how to catch fish easier. I do get a kick out of helping genuine keen anglers, no matter what species they are trying for.

6
Competition

Competition Fly Fishing

This became a massive part of my trout fly-fishing life. I suppose I had proved to myself that I could catch plenty of trout at all waters with various techniques, but I was best known as a sinking-line lure fly fisher.

I first became aware of the four country home internationals when Cyril Inwood told me about them. Cyril was a member of the then English International Fly Fishing Association and it was this private invitation-only club that chose the England Team for the four home country internationals from their members. Cyril fished for England a few times through this route.

In 1969 I received a letter from Captain Michael Moylett from Ireland. It just said, 'Tie me fifty flies that catch the fish at Grafham.' Cyril had told me of the international that would be held at Grafham in May, so I put two and two together and guessed right. The flies were for the Irish team – so I provided them with the deadly fly-lure of that period, the bright orange Whisky Fly. Although Ireland did not win, they did have the heaviest basket, a catch of eleven trout caught by their first reserve on the Whisky Fly. The Irish, how I love them, invited me to my first international dinner held at the White Lion Hotel in Buckden. It was an atmosphere I enjoyed very much.

In 1972, Scotland, Wales and Ireland accused the English International Association of being undemocratic. The England Team was not open for all fly fishers to enter and a bitter dispute arose. I went to the open meeting that followed, when the English Association resigned and removed the word 'international' from their title. This left the way open for the formation of the Confederation of English Fly Fishers. It immediately caught my interest as I felt I would love to have a go at this. Straight away I could sense things were not all they should be and the new English Secretary, Don Fulcher, preached 'democracy' but practised something completely different.

I entered the qualifying rounds and got through at club level and then came third in the Midland Final. I then received a letter from the democratic Fulcher saying I was 'deemed to be a professional angler as I wrote a weekly column in the *Angling Times*', the fee for which in those days was £10.00 – some professional fee; more like expenses. Somehow he convinced his committee to make it stick, even though democratic Don picked himself for the England Team as captain just because he was Confederation Secretary. This situation kept me in the wilderness for twelve of my best prime fly-fishing years. I really got to hate that man. However, in the end he was forced to resign. Thanks to Moc Morgan and Tom Bilson, the professional situation was dropped. I had to take my chance and soon got into the team through elimination for my first International, held at Llyn Brenig in North Wales.

Going back to those wilderness years, I was invited to fish in the Gladding Masters Competition fished from the bank at Draycote. I managed to win that, beating Dick Shrive into second place by ounces. Then I had a great idea; because the new English Fly Fishing Association had no big international events any more, perhaps they would compete against me and my friends in a Pro-Am event. Bill Radley Searle made a positive reply and the annual event, usually held at Grafham, has been running for almost thirty years. Just a note here: the Ams won the first competition, but the Pros have won every other match since. It is always a great day.

So came my first home country international to be held at Brenig, North Wales in autumn. I was told by the officials to keep my head down, so to speak, as the professional subject was still going on behind the scenes. Anyhow, I fished and England were runners up, but I had finished well, coming second in the England Team performance, and so kept my place for the following Spring international. Brenig was the place I found to be a lucky omen for the rest of my international career as an England team member: as captain of England I won gold, as a member of the world team I finished runner up in the still water heat, I was individual winner of the first ever catch-and-release unofficial Brown Bowl, as manager of England I won gold. I had a full set.

So I had qualified for England's 1984 World Team of five fly fishers plus a manager, David Swatland, Chairman of the Salmon and Trout Association. England's team was Tony Pawson, Dennis Buck, Bob Church, Mike Childs and Mike Smith. To fish for your country on the world stage is a proud moment and the pinnacle of achievement for any angler.

Spain was the host, staging this event on the River Tormes, which runs from Salamanca, a central city, and travels west into Portugal where it enters the sea. The river's wild brown trout had been augmented by some freshly stocked browns and we realized that these stocks were only in certain sections of the water.

Our team suffered a serious setback when Mike Childs broke his arm and ankle at a bullfight. Bulls were running the ring and members of the crowd volunteered to be charged at. Some young men, who had visions of being matadors one day, were in the ring, so too were members of the Luxembourg and French world fly fishing teams. One lone British spirit,

Mike Childs, said, 'There is no Englishman in the ring, I'm going to have a go.' Jumping from the high wall into the ring he landed badly on his ankle and fell back, hitting his arm on the wall. David Swatland had to stand in and fish, as Mike was in hospital for the rest of the week.

The draw favoured the Italians. Tony Pawson and Dennis Buck had favoured spots in the first four-hour sessions and made it pay, by taking twelve and thirteen fish respectively. David Swatland had five from a reasonable peg, but Mike Smith and I drew badly, Mike not catching while I took one good wild fish that put me first in the poor 'A' section. Oh yes, and I caught three 8lb barbel on a March Brown fly, lovely fish, but unfortunately they did not count in the competition.

We were lying second after this round. In the next session Tony and I had five each from moderate pegs, while David took one good wild fish from a poor peg. Dennis and again, poor Mike, had no-hoper swims.

At the start of the final round we were clinging to second place. I was happy with my draw near a bridge where I had practised and caught a few. Tony was now very confident, even though his last spot had produced two blanks to previous competitors. He had checked the scores and found the Italians had taken sixteen from the peg downstream in the first round. Tony did very well, getting another seven fish, while I caught ten but unfortunately had to return four as they were just undersize.

Dennis was a hero, taking four wild fish from a 'no-hope' area and with two more blanks this gave us a team place of runners-up with the Italians clear winners. France were third, Poland fourth and Spain fifth, followed by Belgium, Luxembourg and Holland. At sixty-two-years of age, Tony Pawson was the oldest of all the competitors, but a very popular winner of the individual event. Certainly this is the best performance yet by an English team.

The placings were: Tony, World Champion; Dennis seventh; I came, luckily in this case, thirteenth; David our reserve was twentieth; but, alas, poor Mike, who was a still water fisher, only drew three blanks. Even so, England had got the individual crown and were runners up in the team event. I would point out that, in this year 2003, this is still the highest position England have ever achieved in a river world championship. So I received a silver medal at world level.

Tony's trophy was the largest cup I have ever seen for any sporting event. It had to be strapped-in to its own seat on the plane journey home. The Spanish were excellent hosts and for the duration it was one whole festival party. If you ever wander away from the sands and sun of southern Spain, try a visit to Salamanca; it's a beautiful historic university city.

I did make a good friend in our translator, Count Raphael De Madrigado. He was also our fishing guide to instruct us in practice. He told us upstream dry was the best method for the Tormes but there had been heavy rain for two days coupled with snow melt off the mountains and the river was running high and coloured for our first practice.

Our tactics were obvious to me. 'Forget the dry fly,' I confidently advised. 'This is a medium-sinking mini black lure job if ever I saw one. Cast out, swing with the current and then slowly figure-of-eight retrieve up the side of the bank.' Black and Peacocks and Bibios worked well, and we did enough to give us a high in confidence as match day approached.

Although by competition day the river had begun to clear, because the majority of fish being caught were stocked browns our method of slow and deep with something black remained the best tactic. If ever any of you budding competition fly fishers reading this ever face this set of conditions remember this simple solution, because it always works.

My next international appearance was the Spring four country event to be held at Chew Valley reservoir. But trouble was brewing again for me, as the professionalism thing had reared up quite nastily again and the national angling press was full of it. Of course I was the test case, but they also brought in Brian Peterson of Scotland, who sold tackle. I was no longer termed a professional for writing fishing articles, but now I had started the Bob Church Tackle business, so they tried to ban me again.

Read some of the press cuttings from that time. It was pretty pathetic really, when looked at in today's light. Many top anglers and teams receive full sponsorship these days. Perhaps they need to thank me a little for that. What really happened was, they didn't want me to get publicity from my England team place to help my business. However, in trying to stop me I got thousands of pounds' worth of publicity. As I say, read for yourselves.

My uncertain situation as the Chew International approached dramatically changed with a statement from the international body that the word 'professional' be dropped completely. So that was it. On paper England had one of their strongest ever teams and Chris Ogborne tempted fate by saying as much in a *Trout Fisherman* magazine article.

Came the day of the Chew competition – the wind was cold, gusty, gale-force, the water was clear as gin and it was very bright and sunny. The England stars all struggled and had a very bad result, winning only the wooden spoon for coming last. I didn't like it much, and of course you must be a good sport and take some of the stick, but this was the first and last time it was to happen in my competition fishing career. One of Wales' best ever internationals, Tony Bevan, won the individual Brown Bowl that day with a very creditable seven browns.

I was pleased to qualify again for England in the national held on Rutland. This was for Spring again on Ireland's Lough Conn. I knew Conn reasonably well and was so looking forward to it. Two days before the event the team were allowed a free and easy fishing day. So Tom Bilson and I went to fish the Owen Duff for salmon. That was the day when, still fit as a

MIKE GUNNELL'S

TROUT GUIDE

ENGLAND'S FLY-FISHERS BACK BOB

THE CONFEDERATION of English Fly-Fishers have confirmed that Northampton tackle dealer Bob Church WILL be fishing for England in the home international on Chew Valley Lake in May.

They gave Bob unanimous backing at their annual meeting in Droitwich recently by stating that the original selection of the England team made in November last year still stood.

But the dispute over his selection could linger on until two days before the match when the International Association meet to consider, among other matters, objections by other countries to teams put forward.

"We could be left with a split vote because England have been backed by Wales and Ireland have sided with Scotland. The casting vote could rest with the chairman of the International Association who this year happens to be England team manager Tom Bilson," explained England secretary John Hedges.

Both England and Wales have called for the deletion of international rules 16-18 which govern professionalism in fly fishing and urged the substitution of new rules to define "commercialism" in the sport instead.

"We have been given verbal and written backing by the Welsh team and will be bringing the matter up at the international meeting before the Chew match," said John Hedges. "It's time we put these differences behind us and returned to the friendly competitive fishing that internationals are supposed to be about," he added.

CHURCH IN THE COLD?

NORTHAMPTON tackle manufacturer Bob Church cannot fish for England in this year's troutfishing internationals without breaking the rules on amateur status.

Alastair Nicholl, secretary of the International Fly Fishing Association issued this clarification in a letter to Angler's Mail last week – see full text in page 47.

According to Mr Nicholl, a ruling protecting amateur status was reinstated on the International Fly Fishing Association statute book last year and became operative as from January 1, 1985.

"Without breaking the reinstated rules, there is no way in which Bob Church can be included in the English team for the Spring match at Chew valley next May," says Mr Nicholl.

Bob Church said he had been instructed by the English Confederation of Fly Fishers to make himself available for the Home International at Chew rather than travel to Poland for the World Championships.

"I have been selected, paid my membership fee and will be at Chew," said Bob.

ANGLER'S MAIL Week-ending March 2, 1985

Church in England fly team

NORTHAMPTON tackle manufacturer Bob Church has had his place confirmed in the England team for the next international competition.

"I have received a letter from the Confederation of English Fly Fishers asking me to fish in the Chew Valley international in May," said Bob.

Scottish international Brian Peterson hit the headlines recently when he announced his intention to fight a ban imposed by the Scottish National Angling Clubs' Association.

All four British Isles' countries have strict rules regarding the amateur status of competitors.

It was once thought that Bob, who qualified for the England team in last year's eliminators, might fall foul of the amateur rule.

But Bob added: "I'm most definitely in the team for Chew Valley. I've tied up my flies, prepared my tackle and I'm raring to go."

fiddle, I jumped off a 4ft-high wall. In landing I trapped the sciatic nerve in my back, causing me quite dramatic problems on and off ever since.

I had a pain-killing injection from the local doctor in Ballina so I could get through the competition on Conn OK. England were to finish runners up. We fished the competition in difficult big wave conditions. Gradually now I was beginning to get to know many of the leading anglers from the other three home countries on a friendly basis. Men like Moc Morgan and Gwynfor Jones from Wales are good friends today. So too is Sandy Forgan, the gentleman tough guy from Scotland, and my old pro sparring partner Brian Peterson. From Ireland, Frank Reilly, Murt Folan, Toby Bradshaw and Basil Shields have all become good pals. We bump into each other when I go on my regular visits to the west of Ireland.

As well as the home internationals and other big competitions that I became involved with there was the first European Grand Slam event. I remember the first one quite well because it took place at Dreux, a quiet little town some 50 miles south of Paris. In our team was John Wilshaw who was editor of *Trout Fisherman* and he did so well winning the individual event with twenty-two trout on a fly we had both invented, the white-and-silver-bodied lure on a small 10 hook. Yes, we christened it the 'Frog' Nobbler.

The European event became a big thing for leading fly fishers. It became officially recognized and was fished over three legs in England, Belgium and France, and teams were of three anglers. This type of fishing suited me well and for a few years of fishing I managed some good results.

Our team of Dennis Buck, Chris Ogborne and I won the first event. Coincidentally we were all driving Audi cars at the time, mine being a pearlescent uniquely coloured Quatro. Thinking about it, I've had some great motors over the years but that was probably my favourite, followed by the extremely quick first Ford Cosworth in Northampton. A lot of water had flowed under the bridge since that 1934 Ford 8.

In this European Gold team performance of 1990 Chris had come first and I had come third over the three legs, with Dennis not too far behind. Apart from this performance I scored three more bronze medals and finished third in the individuals. Jeanette was at the height of her competition career and she put in a great performance to finish individual sixth. Don't forget there were over 100 of Europe's best fly fishers taking part over the three legs, so I was very proud of her as, along with Peter Cockwill and Micky Bewick, she won the Belgian heat.

Better was to come though; she was automatically teamed up with Dave Grove and Chris Ogborne who had finished fourth and fifth overrall. So this was England's Team 2 for the following year, 1993. The first leg was fished on Grafham; Jeanette won that session and she put in good performances in France and Belgium. The outcome was that her team won the European

Grand Slam that year.

In all, Jeanette fished eight times for England Ladies in internationals, she was outright individual champion twice on Rutland and once at her favourite Grafham. Jeanette had a terrific ten years of competition fly fishing. She became Club Champion of the powerful Mid-Northants Fly Fishers. She became Leeda Individual Champion from 110 nationwide entries – this was from the boat on Rutland. Then the ladies team entered the Benson and Hedges in her zone final held on Grafham in a force-8 gale; she again won the individual and the team also came first on a difficult low weigh-in day. Several other events went her way, like an England versus Wales small-fishery international event. Jeanette won this with nine big rainbows for an over 50lb weigh in. Finally she was selected for the England team to fish in the Commonwealth Championships in New Zealand. On this occasion England were a close runner up, but she again fished consistently.

It was Jeanette, Tom Bilson, Graham Smith, Moc Morgan and I who started the Ladies Home Country Internationals. First with a challenge to Wales, then Scotland joined the next year, finally followed by Ireland. The foundation of the Youth International system was similar; again it was the same people who got it off the ground, Tom, Moc and I. Then Graham managed the England Youth Team, as he did for a while the Ladies. Moc Morgan, 'Mr Wales' of fly fishing, has been a close trout-fishing friend now for twenty-five years. A superb speaker, organizer and very good fisher.

Looking at the rest of my family's performances at competition fly fishing, my daughter Nicola has also excelled. Nicola fished for England eight times, winning the four country top rod on Lough Melvin in Ireland and coming second on Scotland's Loch Fitty. Nicola also won a Benson and Hedges Midland Final on Pitsford Reservoir. She put in a particularly fine performance by entering the open (normally men's) Confederation of English Fly Fishers eliminators. In the first two club-level rounds she easily won through, then again qualified well in the Midlands Final. When it came to the National Final she finished with ten trout on Grafham, but you needed eleven or twelve to qualify for the England Team – a good effort Nicola.

Stephen Church fished for a few years; his efforts winning a couple of club eliminators and coming second in the Midlands Final. He missed out by 1½oz one year to get in the England team and after that he packed up to turn more seriously to his beloved golf, where he plays off five at Woburn Golf Club.

At my fourth time qualified for England's Home Country Team I was voted to be captain, a job you can only have for one international at this level. The water was once again Llyn Brenig in North Wales, my lucky place of the past. I was full of confidence as soon as I knew the venue. Confidence is a great thing to have, when you are brimming with it you can almost talk the fish into taking your fly. The opposite, low confidence, nearly always means a defeat. Some anglers would look on high confidence as big-headed, but I would sooner my teams be like that than quiet wimps. Always be kind to your opponents when you are doing well, be sporting and enjoy the competition. You must also be a good loser as well as a proud winner.

My team were determined to win gold for me on Brenig; we knew it well, we practised well and we comfortably won the match. It was a proud moment making the winning captain's speech and receiving all the trophies. I was again in the team, qualifying through the elimination, to fish at Lough Melvin in Ireland. For this event I had been asked by the committee of the English Confederation to take on the manager's job. It was a good start as manager and I went on to manage for ten internationals, in which England won gold six times and never the wooden spoon.

In the run-up eliminations trying for a place in this England team, you have to get through the Midlands Federation Final of over 100 of the best at Grafham. Most agree that it is more difficult to get in the top twenty here than in the next and final round, the National. I had some great results in this; during a ten-year period winning it twice, coming second twice and third once. The two best opponents I came up against in my competition days were Brian Leadbetter and Chris Ogborne. In one of the Midland finals I won with twenty-one trout, Brian coming second with nineteen. Fished in a flat calm on Grafham, it stands out in my memory.

As I got older and past my peak in competitions, I still occasionally could turn it on. But fast coming up through the ranks from success in the juniors was a young fellow so full of confidence it was unbelievable. I took up a friendship with Jeremy Herrmann and, I hope, helped to guide him in the right direction. He was very, very good and motivated completely to winning. But I would add he kept no secrets; he would tell his boat partner or anyone else around exactly how he was winning competition after competition. In the space of four years he won everything. He won two Brown Bowls, that is to say four countries individual champion, in two successive internationals. He won the Benson and Hedges final, European Grand Slam champion and, finally, individual World Fly Fishing Champion when the event was fished on Lough's Mask and Corrib in Ireland. Then he promptly retired from competition fly fishing and he was still not thirty years old!

The Benson and Hedges six-man team annual contests have always been good competitions for my team and me. In seventeen Midlands Finals we qualified in fifteen of them through to the English National. I won two of these individual spots. When it came to the English finals I had one terrific day on Rutland with fellow boat-partner George 'Geordie' Davidson. We were motoring our way down Rutland's south arm in a light wind that was blowing warm but easterly. Right in the deepest water in the centre of the arm our engine was frightening trout after trout. So instead of going to our intended Manton Bay at the bottom of the arm, I just cut the engine to start a drift there in the middle of nowhere. There were no other boats in sight. We finished the match with me sixteen trout for 24lb 2½oz and Geordie twelve trout for 15lb 15½oz.

The top three teams qualified for the sixteen-team International Final and we were third. I had finished second for my efforts, beaten by a few ounces by Terry Oliver. I just pipped my old rival Chris Ogborne that day as he weighed in fifteen fish for 22lb 4½oz. The fish were beautifully on top and it was floating-line loch-style wet fly fishing at its very best. I caught mostly on size 14 and 12 Grenadiers. At least Geordie and I had the heaviest boat combined weight, which was a match record at the time.

When it comes to the Benson's final sixteen, our team have never won it but had some near misses; three fifths, two fourths and a third showed consistency. The event was passed on to Hardys after the tobacco advertising was stopped. Now Anglian Water have just taken it on. I like this competition and will support it as long as it runs.

I had been entering the World Open Wet Fly Championships, held as a week-long festival on Ireland's massive Lough Mask, for quite a few years. The hand of fate plays many different roles but this experience takes some beating. Here I was, having a fabulous day's fishing on Lough Mask in County Mayo on the western side of Ireland. My genial boatman and ghillie for the day was Michael Arness from Ballinrobe. Mike had lived and worked in England for fifteen years during the late fifties and sixties. One of the very last contracts that he worked on was digging out the 600-acre Draycote Reservoir. This nearby trout water of mine is a mere puddle when you consider Mask is over seven times as big as Rutland at 22,000 acres.

In my opinion Mask is the most wild and challenging trout water in the whole of Europe. It is scattered with many islands, and has great depths and equally large areas of limestone rocky shallows. It is while drifting over the rocky shallows that the cream of the traditional wet fly fishing is found. For this reason it is best to hire a boat with a ghillie, for these experienced locals know all the productive spots and are more aware of the safety factors.

During April and May the small black chironomids (the Irish call these duckflies) and the olives form most of the hatching fly life. From the last week in May one of the best mayfly hatches to be seen anywhere in the world begins. I suppose this peaks during the first two weeks of June, but it continues in some form or another right to the end of September.

Why did I choose August to fish on Mask this year, 1985, for as everyone knows it is the dourest month of the season for catching many trout? The reason was to take part in the World Wet Fly Fishing Championships held annually on Mask and organized by the very efficient Ballinrobe Angling Association. Some six hundred-plus expert trout fishers travel from all over

Ireland, the UK and the rest of Europe, America and Canada to take part in this event of eliminating rounds and a grand final of qualifiers. To qualify to fish in the final is an achievement in itself and this is what I hoped to do.

In our party was Peter Thomas, the English International, and top photographer, Peter Gathercole, in one car and Brian Bromley from Wolverhampton and myself in another. For those of you contemplating a fishing trip to Southern Ireland, it really is straightforward. Book your car on the Stenna Fast Ferry from Holyhead to Dublin, taking approximately one and a half hours. Then there is a 150-mile drive across Ireland to the West, staying at Ballinrobe in County Mayo.

We had a few hours practice fishing on Mask and each caught trout, which cheered us. There were still plenty of mayfly coming off and also sedges were very plentiful. There were two main varieties, a medium-sized brown and a very dark, almost black, smaller sedge. The larger great red sedge, which the Irish imitate with their Murrough artificials, and the green sedge, known as the Green Peter, were few and far between. We caught trout on floating lines, using Mayflies size 8, small Brown Sedge size 10, Invicta size 10, Goats Toe size 10, Green Peter size 8, Claret Murrough size 8, Claret and Mallard size 10 and I did best of all on a yellow and green palmer hackled pattern given to me by Ted Frost, a Ringstead Grange regular. He calls it his 'Punk Rocker'. I tried it simply because it had the same colouration as the mayflies hatching and it fooled the trout.

I noticed many top Irish anglers were using fast-sinking fly lines, yet they were only making short casts of 10yd or less. They were, in fact, using these sinkers the same as they would a floater, for very good reason (this is not an Irish story). In the strong wind and high wave, light floating lines get blown about too much. When it comes to the important part of the retrieve, hanging the top dropper 'bobfly' quite static on top of the wave, the short section of heavy sinking line acts as a controller and makes presentation much better. This is a very good tip we picked up on this trip. I was sure there would be times at Rutland and Grafham when the idea would pay off.

During the eliminators the two Peters caught fish but just failed to get through, while Brian Bromley and I did manage this first hurdle.

We spent our rest day fishing the adjacent Lough Carra, which is about 4,000 acres and very alkaline. On this lake, damsel flies were mating and dropping on the water where trout were rising and taking them. Our confidence was given a further boost by taking ten fish in a couple of hours. This lough is a superb place to fish and adds to the attraction of this area.

So, to the final. I was drawn to fish with Irish International Mike Gilmartin from Sligo, our ghillie was the very experienced Noel May. Noel has a favourite area towards the canal outflow of Mask where he knows every rock and he skilfully manoeuvred our boat to go in and out of the dangerous, but fish holding, shallows. With my very first cast of the day I hooked a good brown of around 1½lb on the Goats Toe but, unfortunately, after playing it for a while it came off. Little did I realize at the time what an important fish that was to lose. Mike took a 1½lb fish on a Claret and Mallard as we drifted onto some rocks. Shortly after this I repeated the action with my yellow and green Ringstead Fly.

It is a tradition in Ireland to go on to the nearest island for lunch and this we did. We found only a few fish had been caught and it was definitely going to be the most difficult session of the lot. We had risen a few more fish but had failed to make contact with them.

After lunch Noel suggested we go and drift an area known as the Black Rocks. I changed up, now fishing with four flies, which is normal on Irish loughs. On my second dropper I had a very nice Olive Mayfly and as we rounded a large rock I dropped my cast in the lee of it. A much better trout took it. I had a heart-stopping fight as the fish dived down amongst the rocks with my droppers trailing. I applied as much pressure as I dared to stop the droppers tangling in the sharp rocks. Eventually Noel netted the fish at the second attempt. Naturally I was very pleased. Then I had a fish of about a pound which was an eighth of an inch too small on the size measure. We rose a few more, but they were not interested in the least after five days of being hard fished for.

At the weigh-in there were lots of blanks, several ones, just two had a brace and one a catch of three. A German angler, Kurt Menrad, had a brace and it looked to be between the two of us. In the end just 1¼oz separated our fish. He won and I took second place. In a field of that class I came home very pleased. However, I can tell you, in such a big high-quality competition, the difference between winning and finishing runner up is massive. You always say to yourself, 'If only!'

World Champions

The year, 1987. The big one. England was to host the World Championships for the first time. I was very excited as I had been chosen for the England team. A team, I might add, which was to prove the best ever to represent England. The team championships were to be held on Rutland and Grafham, our showpiece large reservoirs, with excellent facilities for the competing twenty-one countries that entered. The top thirty-two in the individuals would then go on to the River Test and Avington to complete the event for the final placings.

During my prime competition years my two toughest rivals, in my opinion, were always Brian Leadbetter from Bedford and Chris Ogborne from Bristol. Not to be confused by those who followed later, like Chris Howitt and Jeremy Herrmann.

On the run up to this championship our manager, Geoff Clarkson, said he had never been part of any team, be it military, business or sport that oozed such incredible confidence. The practice sessions on Rutland went exceptionally well and we found an area in the north arm where a big shoal of rainbows were congregated. They were in reasonably shallow water up to 15ft, but mostly they were staying deep. Brian Leadbetter and I practised together the day before the event. We had both caught fish from the same spot a couple of days earlier. They were quite straightforward to catch, but would they stay there? So Brian and I went to see one more time the day before, and they were still there in big numbers. No one else seemed to know about them, despite everyone practising. Of course, we only lightly fished for them in practice, and only for about half an hour at a time, when no one else was about.

So that night at the hotel the draw was made. Brian and John Pawson were on Rutland, while Chris, Dennis and I were on Grafham. I must admit I was hoping to draw Rutland first because of what we had found and, boy, did Brian and John do well there. Brian had thirty-six fish and John thirty-one, taking first and second place.

Over at Grafham on day one, I had been drawn to fish with Dick Willis of Ireland and as we sat in the boat at the jetty waiting for the off I noticed Dick had a floating fly line on. With Grafham all stirred up with a milky tinge, due to some good winds, all our team knew it would be sinking fly lure HiDi tactics and mini lures. I couldn't help myself. I said, 'Dick, haven't you got a fast-sinking line? Because you won't catch anything on a floater.' Of course I should not be helping the opposition, but I couldn't let him suffer on what was a strange water to him. After all, it was my local water that I knew so much about. Dick had one of my Canadian leaded impregnated fast-sink lines in his bag and he quickly put it on.

With a wave of good luck from Chris and Dennis, who were competing in other boats, we were off. I took the engine and we went into Church Bay. On the first couple of short drifts adjacent to the bank and off the point, Dick boated three stock rainbows, while I hooked four, but only lightly, and landed just one. Losing fish in such an important competition is very worrying, but if anything it spurred me on. After about two hours, with Dick leading five to two, we moved to the Sludge Lagoon area, into which the wind was blowing. Dick had another rainbow just as we neared the bank. I hooked a lively fit brown trout of around 4lb, which scurried across the shallow, jumped twice and was off. I said, 'Damn' – or words to that effect.

We realized there were a few decent fish close into this bank and on the next short drift I at last boated one. With my next cast, and we were now right in the shallows, I hooked another decent rainbow on my middle dropper. It dived into some old submerged hedgerow twigs and stuck the hook of the point fly into them. I could see the fish, a decent rainbow, hanging there. It was then that my luck changed. I automatically tweaked the rod top two or three times to try and release the fly and fish. In doing this I of course bobbed the top dropper up and down enticingly. You guessed! Another rainbow rushed in and took the top dropper, and in doing so hooked itself, but broke the other fish off. At least I boated this one and I had broken the spell of losing fish.

For the rest of the match we continued on short 300yd drifts in towards the Sludge Bank. In and out, moving along its whole length so as not to go over the same water. The good thing was there were no other boats near us. It wasn't all serious, as Dick and I had a good laugh all day. I now began to put on the pressure, ending the session at 5pm with twelve trout. Dick hooked his last fish of eight right near the end of the competition. It was a big one and I told him to take his time. Says Dick, 'Bob, you never told me that grilse run into this lough.' Says I, 'Dick, it's a big, fit, over-wintered rainbow and this is a reservoir.' 'Jesus, some anglers in Ireland don't like the rainbows. I'll never listen to them again.' Dick's magnificent fish came aboard. It weighed 4½lb and it was time to go in.

Chris had won the heat with sixteen fish and I was second with twelve and Dick third with eight. Our other man, Dennis Buck, had six fish and held eighth placing. So after day one England was miles in front, well over double the points of Australia who were lying a creditable second at the halfway stage.

Day two; a change of waters for all competitors. Those who were on Rutland now fished Grafham and vice versa. There was, of course, a new draw for boat partners and I drew Jackie Lemmer, a Belgian team member. Naturally, everyone who was now fishing at Rutland knew where the fish were in the North arm – roughly from the Finches, down and past the transformer. With the wind steadily blowing along it, we and the rest of the boats began our drifts with the aid of a drogue to slow us down. We kept to about 80 to 100yd from the bank.

It was standard HiDi sunk-line tactics, which I had perfected from my sunken-line big-lure fishing days – the principle was exactly the same. Cast a long line and have on various mini lures, with orange, black and white-based designs as the main colours. During these two days our team had success with Peach Doll, Church Fry, Stickfly, Zulu and Appetizer. For some reason fish like to be in around 15ft of water and this is what we kept to. Cast, allow to sink, vary the retrieve, some fast, some slow, some jerky, finally lift the flies up from the bottom with a lift of the rod – then hold for several seconds. This is the secret of the method 'lift and hold', as any following trout, which was never going to take the fly but just follow, now often takes the static presentation. Watch out carefully for takes as you will not, or rarely, feel them by hand. Visually watch the top of your fly line and it dips down or moves sideways a few inches. Strike then and you have hooked a trout you would never know was there.

Our man Dennis Buck came good and won this Rutland heat; he had twelve fish and I was fourth with ten fish and Chris fifth with nine fish. At the weigh-in we were ecstatic, for the three of us knew Brian and John could have blanked on Grafham and we still would be world team champions. As it happens, Brian was again in first place with John dropping back to a respectable fifteenth. Remember, there were 100 fly fishers taking part. It was a massive victory; England had 85,330 points, to Australia in second spot with 41,350 points and New Zealand third with 27,815 points. The southern hemisphere teams had done well, but in reality it was a one-horse race. The celebrations that night at the Saxon Hotel were a little wild as we all got rather tipsy on champagne.

We noticed that the Rumanian team looked rather sad after dinner and were not drinking at all. Of course, this was still the time of the Iron Curtain for eastern European communist countries. However, we invited them into our celebration party and it was a night to remember as somehow I acquired top Aussie angler Terry Piggott's hat and still have it. Terry had fished well to end up in seventh individual place.

After this team event the whole party moved down south to Hampshire for the final placing in the individuals. Our hotel was the Royal at Winchester. It was an historic and traditional setting for angling. The thirty-two top individuals were now poised to take on the River Test and Avington's three lakes.

Two sessions on two beats of the Test saw an element of luck emerging as competitors drew for pegged positions. Avington was also pegged, but positional moves every half an hour meant you moved from lake to lake. On the Test the mayfly were up and Brian continued his incredible form and took first place again with eleven fish on a variety of mayfly patterns. Dennis was second and John also did very well to finish in third spot.

While they fished the Test, Chris and I were at Avington and I was the only one who knew it well. I confidently told Chris in the car park, 'Whoever draws the far end peg in the first lake will catch enough trout in the first half hour to win it'. Chris, bless him, drew it, and did exactly what I predicted. Chris finished first and I was second. I did manage the heaviest fish of the whole competition, an 8½lb rainbow that put up one hell of a fight just as the television cameras arrived.

The Test sessions, where Chris and I now were, was three hours in one spot in the morning, followed by a super lunch at the Humbert's Kimbridge lawn, where a big marquee had been put up. I clearly remember eating the most excellent gravad lax and tiger king prawn salad. But my fishing during the halfway stage had been a nightmare. I had over thirty fish and not one of them reached the size limit measure of 36cm. I had drawn a nursery area of the river along a water meadow.

Chris had caught four fish from his beat close to the house and, guess what, I drew his same peg for the afternoon. I didn't fancy following Chris, he is too good an angler, but follow him I had to. I set up with a big Grey Wulff dry mayfly and slowly began to work my way upstream. First a 3lb rainbow, then a 3lb brownie, and these were followed by three more big grayling, one over 2lb. It was a very satisfying catch for me indeed. Chris had caught another couple, putting him sixth on the day and I had rallied round to seventh.

The scoring was done with the lowest points counting from all four sessions, that is Grafham, Rutland, Avington and the Test, so it would be very fair. Brian came a little unstuck at Avington, but still managed fourth place, while John completely excelled, winning his session comfortably.

At the end of the day not only did we have the team event but in the individuals we also had Brian Leadbetter World Champion, (seven points) Chris Ogborne runner up (twelve points), Bob Church a bronze medal for third (fifteen points), with Dennis Buck fourth (twenty points) and John Pawson, who had pulled right back by winning his last session on the Test, sixth (twenty-one points). Dave McLellan of New Zealand came fifth (twenty points), just stopping our England team short of a complete set. It was an incredible performance. There was never anything like it before and I cannot see such a thing happening again.

Tasmania

And so to Tasmania. The following World Championship, in 1988, was to be held in Tasmania on the central plateau, which is a completely wild and untouched wilderness. Brown and rainbow trout were introduced there 100 years ago and they thrived in this perfect, for them, environment. The team was chosen of the same people but, as Chris couldn't make it, our reserve, Brian Thomas, took his place.

The cynics were saying that it was easy for England fishing at home for stocked fish, they would not do so well with Tassy wild trout. We knew this, so it made us all the more determined. The Australian organizers gave us their top guide, Noel Jetson, and his wife Lois; we all got on fine and they have since visited us a couple of times. We were all staying at Bronte Park, Highland Village in the scenic Highlands.

For the first two days of practice, Noel, bless him, tried hard to get us on to his favourite pattern, the Red Tag. He had all kinds of versions of it, dry, wet, nymph, bug and so on, but try as we did with it, we got nowhere. On the other hand, every time we used English-style wet-fly tactics we caught well in practice. After two of the five days practice Noel declared, 'You boys do your own thing and you will walk the championship'.

We were using Wickhams Fancy, Fiery Brown, Bibio and Orange Palmer and putting on a floating or intermediate fly line. We totalled over one hundred wild browns to 4lb and rainbows to 3½lb practising with these. So this would be our approach. These lakes are hardly fished, so with so many anglers in action every day the trout soon retreated from the margin to deeper water. Of course this suited us, but each day it was getting harder and towards the end it was almost impossible to tempt the fish from some more accessible stretches.

The three testing venues to be fished in the World Championship were Bronte Lagoon 2,000 acres, Little Pine Lagoon 1,000 acres, and London Lakes, two lakes of similar size. Each angler was to get a generous 400m bank section to himself plus his controller.

We discovered the best plan was to cast and retrieve, then walk two or three paces so you didn't frighten too many fish. You may get away with staying in one place at a reservoir back home where stockies behave differently. These were wild, spooky fish – make a wrong move and they had gone. Our tactics were spot-on and no one in the England team blanked, but it was very tough fishing on competition days. The extra bonus points gave us another massive victory, again doubling the tally of our nearest rivals, France, who were runners-up. It was a great team effort once more.

I won the first session on Bronte with four fish and then Brian did brilliantly on the very difficult Little Pine, winning his heat, and finally John Pawson caught eight in the last heat to win that one as the weather improved. For the most part it had been windy and wet, typical English conditions you might say, and that's one reason why it suited us.

So England first with thirty-seven fish for 1,393cm, second France sixteen fish for 625cm and third were our hosts, Australia, with fifteen fish for 673.5cm. When the rank scoring was added, namely low wins, the result was: England 32, France 136, Australia 150. It was as big a margin as in England the previous year. The proudest couple at the presentation dinner were Noel and Lois.

Individuals were: John Pawson New World Champion, Brian Thomas second, Terry Piggott of Australia third and I was very content with fourth overall. Brian wasn't too far behind in twelfth position and Dennis a lucky thirteenth. A few drinks were downed that night I can tell you, and our general manager Geoff was, to put it mildly, ecstatic. We received a letter from the Minister of Sport, Colin Moynihan, congratulating us on our efforts when we returned home. I now had two golds, a silver, a bronze and a fourth at World Level, and I felt I had achieved my ambition.

Lapland, Finland

Geoff gave the very successful team the chance of doing the hat-trick of wins at world level when he announced the same squad for Lapland. Finland itself seemed a strange place, as everyone always looked miserable and fed up. However, we were here to fish but what a nightmare for us – we were staying at Kuusamo. Without wishing to whinge too much, the draw was so unkind to the England team we had no hope of coming in the top six. This is the first time in a fly fishing contest I have noticed the draw for beats upsetting the form book so dramatically. Now we understand what coarse match anglers have to put up with every week.

The two rivers fished in the competition were the Kitka and river Kuusinki; both, I would add, were excellent. Plenty of grayling in the Kitka and some lovely big wild browns in the Kuusinki. These were only few and far between but we did catch them to 8½lb in practice. The organizers made a terrible mistake in stocking several pools in the Kuusinki river with lots of browns. This just caused a lottery situation, whoever drew the pegs, no matter what angler from what country, scored maximum points.

In my first heat on the Kitka I caught fifty-one grayling and four small browns, but only three grayling were over the minimum size for measuring by my controller. Still I finished third in the section, which Brian Thomas won. Brian was our best rod overrall, finishing eighth. Did I enjoy it? It is difficult to say but it was certainly very different from anywhere else in the world I've been. From now on those reindeers on the Christmas cards will never look the same again and with a pint of lager costing around £4 life was quite tough. However, we did beat the Aussies, even if our cricketers cannot. Congratulations to the Scots for finishing sixth and to Brian Stuart who also managed sixth in the individual stakes.

To sum up, it seemed wrong to have to rely on a lucky draw for a beat that held stocked browns to give you a high weight. The organizers also raised the size limit of grayling from 25cm to 28cm, and this proved difficult.

My Last World Championship

My fifth and last appearance in the World Championships was when it was held in Wales. This was fished on my favourite Llyn Brenig and the delightful river Dee. The first session was the still-water event fished from drifting boats on Brenig reservoir. I could hardly wait to get going. I was drawn to fish with Jerry from the Czechoslovakian team. I beat him five to one on the morning session, finishing runner-up, and Chris won the heat with six fish. After the first day, England were back in pole position again. It is noticeable we have the beating of everyone on still water but other countries were far better on rivers, as we were about to find out.

In short, our river results were only average and we finished fifth. The Czechoslovakians were easy winners, followed by Poland in second place, Belgium third and France fourth. Chris did the best for us, coming ninth in the individual. Our team also had two newcomers in Chris Howitt and John Horsey. That was my last appearance on the world stage, but I was able to compete further in several European and Commonwealth England teams with a good measure of success.

Commonwealth Events

We now go back to 1987, when Arthur and Anne Humbert hosted the World Event for the river Test finals at Kimbridge. Both enjoyed the socializing and friendship between the fisherman and they had the idea to begin a Commonwealth Country Championship, which would follow the World Event. I had fished in a few of the early ones in Tasmania. We were all celebrating our world win from the day before so we were non-starters, but we started to take things more seriously when Tony Pawson began to run the event.

We finished second to the Aussies in Wales, then second to New Zealand, and after that event Tony Pawson retired as organizer. He said to me, 'Bob, you are next in line in age and experience. I am handing the England Commonwealth organizing to you, I am sure you will do well.'

Briefly, the criteria was to pick a team of ex-England world team members, or up and coming anglers, or indeed anyone who had missed out for whatever reason. Remember, these competitions, although now seriously contested, are based around Arthur and Anne's ideas of close friendship. I can certainly say this has been achieved in this event more than any other I've fished in. So I picked a team to compete in Canada of Brian Thomas, Dave Grove, Charles Jardine, Chris Howitt and myself. It was a great holiday in British Columbia and we won the event held on Lake Nimpo in the north.

The next Commonwealth event was in Scotland, to be fished on Loch Leven and Lintrathen from boats. Of course Leven is Scotland's number one loch for size (3,300 acres) with wild browns and now superb rainbows as well. The addition of rainbows to this water has been very successful and has eased the pressure on the browns. England won the event with the same team that won in Canada. We all had our moments; Charles and Chris winning their heats on Leven. I went one better on Lintrathen, taking fourteen brown trout to 2¼lb fishing barbless catch and release. All fish were measured by our controller. My fish fell to a size 14 black Heather Fly with red legs, tied for me at the breakfast table by my wife Jeanette. This catch was a new Commonwealth record at that time.

Following the World Event held in England at Chew Valley and Blagdon reservoirs, which I might add turned out a complete disaster for England as they finished a lowly twelfth on their home ground, I was organizing the Commonwealth event that followed on Grafham and Rutland Water. I had added newcomers to the team in local expert Dave Shipman, Tony Curtis, also local and top of his form, Geoff Clarkson, our old manager, with Dave Grove and myself, the follow-over from the Scotland match. Could we manage a hat-trick of Commonwealth wins? I told all the team what had happened eleven years earlier in Finland, using this as motivation. Of course, Geoff didn't need reminding as he was our very frustrated manager at the time.

The newcomers all fished very well, especially Dave and Tony, and we won the event with Scotland just behind in second place. As Tony Pawson, long retired, said in his after dinner speech, 'The system of having a manager with experience, and who knows his team well, can get the very best out of them. If you are successful as a manager you keep the job, if you're not you are soon kicked out.' Committees and statistics and the like will never pick a winning team. Geoff, by the way, was awarded the OBE a couple of years back for his efforts in managing the World Team. Since he has retired from that position nothing has gone right for England's World Team.

Competition Sunken Line Tips

If you are a budding competition fly fisherman and you feel you can be successful without a fast-sinking fly line in your armoury, I must tell you most definitely, you cannot. During April (not many competitions held) and May (lots held) a fast-sinking fly is the correct choice 99 times out of 100. The fact that things usually alter dramatically around the end of the first week in June is another story. We are speaking about the period up to that time.

When I started competition fly fishing seriously some years ago, I suppose I did so purely as a challenge, to see whether or not I was good enough to make it. I *did* make it and I *did* like it. Now, I am pleased to say, everyone wants to have a go. Looking back, I had a great advantage over many others at that time because I had just completed a twenty-year study of bottom-feeding trout, and how to catch them. It merely meant a few easy adjustments, like fly size, and having to fish the unfavourable in-front-of-the-boat situation. To be honest, my early season competition results were amazingly one-sided. I was beating my boat partners by 16–1, 12–0, 12–1 and 13–2. I tried to help my partners where I could, like advising them to use the right fly lines and flies. Even though this helped, there was obviously far more to my success than that.

I suppose it's having the 'feel' for the sinking-line method that is most important. Couple this with complete confidence that you are going to catch anyway, and you're halfway there; never think doom and gloom – negative even in the worst possible conditions. Locations of certain fish-holding spots and the in pattern fly of the moment are next on your priority list and, finally, if the wind's blowing half a gale, the winning post is already in sight.

Let's now go through these points in as much detail as I can, for I know it will help you to do well in any reservoir competition held early in the season.

Feel: You must be mentally alert as to where your flies are and how they are behaving at any given time. Naturally, as long a cast as is possible should be made, then the pause, for the fast-sinking fly line to take your flies to the bottom.

While you are waiting for this, the inevitable is happening. The boat is drifting forward quite quickly despite the slowing-down action of the broadside drogue. You are left with exactly what you don't want, a lot of slack line between your retrieving hand and your flies. I counteract this from happening, keeping in touch, by carefully and slowly retrieving the slack as the boat moves forward *without* moving the fly line.

In reality a 25 to 30m cast finishes up only half that distance as the boat closes down on your flies, but not to worry.

Flat Retrieve: By doing this, I get around 15m of retrieve along the bottom where the fish are lying. The retrieve is slow, long, even pulls. Good taking times are on the first or second pull. Another time to anticipate a take is when the flies leave the 'running along the bottom' motion to rise up in a vertical lift. Often, following fish are induced to take at this point. By the way, you should accentuate and lengthen this action by lifting the rod slowly and continuously in one sweep.

Now comes the most important moment of all, and it is that that has given me my success in many of the early competitions. As you bring the flies to the surface in the 'one sweep of the rod' action, watch carefully for the top dropper to appear. Very often you will have a trout following this fly or a lower fly, about 6in to 1ft behind. Nearly always they don't take; remember, the water is still cold so they are not really in a chasing mood as they are in summer. It can help to steer these potential followers out to one side of the boat by making your retrieve, and rod lift, end there.

The technique to ensure takes is this. Bring the fly to the surface with a fish following, pause very briefly and then lower the rod top quite sharply so the fly sinks naturally. I keep a sharp eye on my nylon leader because, nine times out of ten, as the fly disappears from sight my leader takes on a new unnatural angle as it moves left or right, or even plunges downwards sharply. Watch the dropper too. A well-timed lift is absolutely essential and practice makes perfect, believe me. Practise the technique before the actual competition day.

A common mistake is an over-hurried retrieve and lift-off to recast, where the angler never sees a follow anyway. This type of angler seems intent on a casting competition, and will have very few fish to show for it at the end of the day. Being impatient and taking your fly from the water too quickly must be avoided at all costs.

Having complete confidence stems from many motivations. I feel experience is a key factor in the success chain. Fly fishing, unlike many other sports, actually allows you to get better as you get older. Having a good memory, as to how you approached the tricky conditions on a day some years earlier, is a huge advantage.

Bob's daughter Nicola, at four years old, sees her first salmon, an 8-pounder caught on fly by Dad from the Aberdeenshire Dee.

Bob with son Stephen and a combined catch of six perfect silver rainbows between 7–11lb.

Nicola Church with a 7lb 10oz 'wild' rainbow she caught at Grafham. Later she won the Ladies four country Internationals match at Ireland's Lough Melvin.

Bob's grandson Jordan Church, eleven years old, now goes fishing with him, this time for carp; he's learning fast.

Bob's wife Jeanette with a fine wild 5lb New Zealand rainbow – this one came from Lake Tarrawera.

Bob's best 'wild' rainbow (overwintered) to date, an immaculate 11-pounder which he returned after a quick photograph.

Bob's best-ever wild brown of 7lb 6oz caught on a GRHE on the Kuusinki river in Lapland.

Bob's heaviest rainbow is this 27lb 2oz fish from Earith Lake, which was returned. It was a massive fish.

Bob fished in Sweden's river of giants, the Morrum – this 52lb early summer fish, was caught on fly and shows the potential of this river.

Bob's heaviest UK salmon is this 28lb 2oz cock fish taken from the deep hole in Bridge Pool from the Tweed at Kelso in 1993.

This 11¼lb sea trout from the River Test remains Bob's personal best; it was a fine fish.

If you need further evidence, here is Bob's Morrum guide Isaac with an 18lb sea trout.

Left to right, Bob, Dennis Buck and Chris Ogborne, at the European Grand Slam team championships for the year 1991.

The victorius England team after winning the World Championship in Tasmania. Here we are at Government House, Hobart. Back row: John Pawson, Geoff Clarkson (manager), Brian Leadbetter; front row Dennis Buck, Bob Church and Brian Thomas.

The winning team, England, made it a hat trick in the Commonwealth fly fishing Championships. Previously they had wins in Canada and Scotland; now in England in 2000. The team was Tony Curtis, Dave Shipman, Dave Grove, Bob Church and Geoff Clarkson.

Rutland rainbows are of top quality when they have been in the reservoir for a while, like this over-wintered 4½-pounder.

Jeremy Herrmann qualified on Grafham to fish for England for the first time and this 6lb-plus fish was part of his catch.

Bob with a lovely Chalk Spring golden rainbow of 8lb 6oz. It took on the tenth fly change in gin-clear water.

The Newport River in Ireland is usually good for its salmon and sea trout, and produced a shock for Bob with a catch of sea-run rainbows that behaved like steelheads.

Chalk Springs fishery is known for its clear-water stalking style of catching selected trout. Bob was pleased to say this is how he caught this striking 7lb 2oz blue rainbow there.

Bob fishing at Lac de la Landie in France catches the best fish of the day, a 7lb steelhead rainbow.

Bob's barbel-fishing friend Steve Curtin from Bedford with his British Record barbel of 19lb 6½oz caught from the Great Ouse at Adams Mill, October 2001.

Bob likes his pike fishing in winter; this is his recent 26¼-pounder, caught in 2003, a fine specimen.

Bob's personal best barbel to date is the perfect 15lb 2oz specimen, again from the Great Ouse and the Mill.

Bob often goes for trout in the morning and the rudd in the afternoon in an adjoining lake. The rudd are a handsome fish and are becoming quite rare.

At long last Bob started trying for big carp and was over the moon with this 31lb common; in the same daytime catch he had a 28½-pounder and a 13lb wildie.

TOP LEFT: *Bream are another species gaining in popularity and Bob intends to try for one of double this size next season.*

TOP RIGHT: *The early summer tench fishing always holds that attraction. Bob re-visited Sywell in 2002 and caught some nice fish topped by this 7½-pounder off the dam.*

LEFT: *Chub have always been a favourite of Bob's; here is one of many 5lb-plus fish he has caught from the River Great Ouse. This went 5½lb from Harrold.*

Bob's pal John Emerson boated this 30½lb pike while fishing with Bob on Grafham. They fly-fished properly for these pike and helped start a trend. This took a tandem Appetiser.

Competition Dry Fly Tips

My local large reservoir, Pitsford, had run into marvellous form during the summer. All sorts of things had been happening there to entice the trout up from the bottom to feed on the top. First, thousands of snails left the reservoir bed to float on top, as they do on their annual migration. These easy pickings for trout meant surface feeding for both rainbows and browns, and fish could be seen rising everywhere. The actual catching of fish became quite difficult for a while, as trout became preoccupied in the snail exclusively.

With that phase passing, I had a boat trip with Kevin Garn and some friends from Staffordshire. The trout were still in the mood to take off the top, but those who caught the most found that chironomid emergers fished in the surface film, that is to say just under, was best. This method was better than a proud dry fly, sitting high on the top of the water. Jeremy Herrmann is so good at dry fly fishing that I was going to take good note of exactly how he does it one summer's day on Pitsford. We started fishing in bright sunlight and the lightest breeze. There was just an odd fish about. When the first trout rose within casting range it was a fifty-fifty fish, about in the centre of our boat. Being the gentleman I am I said, 'Jeremy, you go for it.' He did and of course he hooked and boated it. That was the beginning of some hectic sport, because we witnessed the largest fall of flying ants, both red and black, that I have seen in over forty years of trout fishing. I would say, by mid-afternoon, every fish in the reservoir was up feeding on top – the dry fly fisher's dream situation.

As Jeremy pointed out, there are no secrets to his phenomenal success using dry flies. He fishes three well spaced-out emerging chironomid patterns on a 4lb breaking-strain Maxima green nylon. In flat calms he may reduce this to a single dry fly. He is forever de-greasing his leader with a fuller's earth and washing up liquid mix. It is most important that your fly floats and your nylon just sinks a little.

When Jeremy casts, he swishes the rod quickly with a couple of fast false casts, to dry the fly or flies out well. On the shoot of line he deliberately casts a slack wavy line so as to ensure the dry fly does not move or drag along at all – he feels this is the kiss of death. If an interested trout sees this it just will not touch the fly. If Jeremy spots a rise form by way of a sip or a splash anywhere near where his flies are he strikes, he certainly does not believe in this pause nonsense when a lucky fish gets self-hooked. If on the strike no contact is made he quickly drops on the fish again. He may rise the fish and miss it again, as he did with me, but then he got it on the third attempt. Presentation and concentration are Jeremy's secrets of success, nothing more, nothing less.

Catch and Release

It was fifteen years ago that I first started to mention the benefits of catch-and-release trout fishing. This was after I had fished to these rules in the World Championships in Tasmania. It worked very well there and these were hardy wild fish. Barbless fly hooks and a controller, who rapidly measured your fish in a special tray before quickly releasing it, made for the success of the championship and safety of the trout.

Some fisheries in this country do practise catch and release and say it works – last year's Ravensthorpe experiment is a prime example of success. However, the whole subject is as emotive as ever, and this includes both anglers and fishery owners. Many anglers think that, if they pay a high price for their day ticket, they are entitled to their pound of flesh. Therefore, limit bags are always on their minds. I know this is so because I have been down that road myself, but times change. Now there are certainly many fly fishers who are supporting the catch-and-release policies of the ever-growing numbers of fisheries. But I would stress that catch and release is not being forced on any angler; I just think it is a step forward to have the option of choice.

Some river and loch fly fishers must be thinking, 'What is he on about, there is nothing new in catch and release because we have been doing it for years with all the little wild browns? We think nothing of slipping these back all day and we know the trout are none the worse for it.' But they still reserve the right to occasionally keep a brace of better fish for the table.

Reservoir fly fishers showed signs of being conservation minded when they began to put all the early season easily caught browns back. This has been a voluntary policy for quite a few seasons now.

On the popular competition fly-fisher's scene all the reservoir's boats are booked up regularly. Legally you are allowed two tickets, equalling sixteen trout, but times are changing here as well. The method used by some clubs, of fishing to a limit of eight and then having a time bonus, is very unpopular because you can get a false result. Much better is the idea we have adopted for the Bob Church Classic. We are fishing to catch and kill a limit of six fish; from then on you fish a de-barbed fly, fishing catch and release with your boat partner acting as witness to your extra fish score card. These will be allocated at 1½lb; each average weight to add to your retained limit catch.

At the pre-match briefing we issue score cards, to be used by those fortunate enough to take a limit. They must hook any bonus fish on a barbless hook and net it, leaving the fish in the net mesh in the water *outside* the boat. Once the boat partner agrees the fish is caught, you just lean over the side, slip the hook out and let the fish swim off. Finally, mark your scorecard with a returned average of 1½lb per fish. At the end of the session your partner will check your card and sign it.

Some fisheries in this country do practise catch and release and say it works; although in years gone by other experienced owners of the smaller fisheries would claim that the practice would mean a lake full of fish that nobody could catch. In my experience it does not seem to work at places like Dever, where the fish are stocked big and daily into quite small pools. But it does work at the larger gravel pit fisheries such as Elinor and Earith. At the latter I have caught a number of double-figure rainbows up to 23½lb and 27lb 2oz, and the larger fish was caught again after I had returned it, a month later. This situation is certain to progress further.

7
Salmon and Sea Trout

The Atlantic Salmon

The Atlantic salmon is quite rightly rated the finest freshwater fish there is and few who know them would argue with this. One of my good friends in the angling world, both as an angler and a business confidant, is Barrie Welham from Southampton. He has been a very successful tackle-trade businessman and also an excellent salmon angler with the fly. Thirty years ago I briefly mentioned to Barrie that I would shortly be on a family holiday in the Bournemouth area and straight away he was putting ideas into my head.

'Now listen Barrie, I've only just finished making promises like – Yes, I will sit on the beach all day – Yes, I will build sand castles and eat gritty ice creams.' You all know the promises we make under duress.

'When and where are we going then Barrie?' I asked, risking the consequences from the family. 'The River Itchen, to try and get you a salmon on fly tackle,' said Barrie. 'Sounds good, I've never fished the Itchen, but I thought it was mainly a trout river?'

Barrie explained. 'It is, of course, better known as a superb chalk stream producing dry fly trout fishing of the highest quality, next to the Test which is England's finest. However, downstream of Winchester, during the latter part of July and into August, we usually get a short summer run of salmon and grilse. It's a fly-only beat so bring your 10ft reservoir trout rod and a No. 8 floating fly line; you just could be in with a chance,' he told me.

About ten days later I met Barrie as instructed at his Southampton home. Twenty minutes' drive and we were at the Itchen and, on the way, I heard how Barrie had caught two salmon earlier in the week. The news gave me a bit of confidence until I remembered that Barrie is an expert at this type of fishing and catches salmon on a fly at a rate that most people catch trout. I reminded him I had never seen this river before and had never caught a salmon on a fly. (This was the early 1970s.)

What a lovely sparkling flow the Itchen has; it made a change for me to be fishing a decent river again.

'It will take us no more than two hours to fish the whole beat, so get tackled up and put on this No. 8 Blue Charm,' he recommended.

I did as Barrie advised, then we walked across the meadow until we reached a part of the river which had a fast run along the far bank. Fifty yards downstream the river turned sharply to the right disappearing from view. 'This is the best stretch on the beat,' said Barrie. 'Fish it carefully down to the bend; the crucial taking spot is about 5yd before you reach the corner.'

I needed to drop my fly consistently accurately about 1ft from the far bank, casting slightly downstream. This then gave my fly the deadly swing across the current – a similar tactic to my reservoir rainbow style. Here the river was only about 5 or 6yd wide and, following each cast, I took a step downstream. Barrie had been off upstream and fished out a shorter stretch without a take. As he passed me he said, 'That's good, keep it up, but you have only got about six casts left to that piece, then you've had it.' Three casts later and at the spot where Barrie said was crucial came a great swirl and I had a 'Grafham-type take'. A salmon had hit my fly very hard and took off downstream.

I called to Barrie and he walked back to watch me play my fish and show me the best landing spot. The reservoir trout rod performed well and it was very exciting to watch the hooked salmon's every fighting move in the clear shallow water. The power of this salmon was very similar to a big reservoir rainbow. Soon he was out and the priest administered, a fine conditioned cock fish of 7lb, which is about average size for these Itchen summer salmon. As we admired the salmon it was congratulations from Barrie.

'Only one "first" fly-caught salmon you know Bob,' he said. I thanked him for unselfishly putting me in the right spot and I believe he was more pleased than I was. Then I thought of the fish's last few days. Just a short time before he must have swum through the Solent and up Southampton Water before entering the Itchen.

As we walked back to the car, out came Barrie's characteristic saying. 'Well, Mr Bob, life isn't so bad after all.' How true it was at that particular moment, but for me it was back to the beach where I suffered, scorched with red blistered skin and a bout of sun stroke – can't win 'em all!

Although I had caught a few salmon before, including one over 20lb, they were on Toby spoons. They came from that lovely River Findhorn, but it was the magic of a fly-caught fish that now captured my interest. I started to go to the River Dee in Aberdeenshire, as it was known as the classic fly water, especially in May and June. Not only that, but you could catch them on a floating fly line and very small flies, as I was about to find out.

I was joined on this trip by my fishing pals, Peter Dobbs and Frank Cutler. We paid a good price for the beat, which came with a big house, and we were looked after by a resident super-ghillie, Rod Grant. Rod could only be described as the man who knew as much about salmon – and fishing for them – as anyone on Deeside. Things could not have been better, for our arrival saw the river rise about 1½ft after a prolonged period of low water. However, instead of dropping back to normal for our following morning's fishing, it had risen to 5ft above normal and was the colour of brown ale. Only spinning would give us any chance, so this is what we reluctantly did.

During the early afternoon, Frank hooked a salmon on a Mepps. This took him the length of a 200yd pool before it was ready for netting. Pete sunk the landing net into the water and Frank guided the beaten fish towards it. Then, suddenly, the spinner pulled out and it was lost. Frank's second salmon, a smaller one, came adrift after only a few seconds, but he redeemed himself later with a fine sea trout of nearly 3lb.

The river dropped considerably for the second day, but the unusual brown peaty colour remained. Rod Grant advised us to continue on the long deep holding pools, called upper and lower Roe Pot. We fished the spinner to start with, then tried a sunken fly line and, by evening, a floating fly line. But all we could catch were small brown trout and some nice sea trout.

Rod Grant showed his expertise that evening when he fished a difficult lie between two large boulders on another pool, which looked barely fishable. His deadly method for these middle reaches of the Dee is a very short-bodied and lightly dressed Stoat's Tail tube fly and a No. 12 treble hook hidden away beneath the hair. This is fished on a floating line and a double-handed 14ft rod. There was one salmon resting in this spot and he caught it. It was the first fish to be landed all week from beats upstream, downstream and opposite.

I can now begin to understand the frustrations of a salmon angler, for, following heavy rain, the river once again rose to a brown flood for our third day. With the river up and down like a yo-yo, salmon just would not take and all our enthusiastic efforts were in vain, except for more sea trout.

Frank's fishing week ended on Thursday when, after catching a brace of sea trout to 2½lb on his first two casts, he fell down the bank and broke his ankle. On Friday the river was beginning to fine down nicely and the sea trout obliged once more. Pete had the best of the week at more than 3lb. I had a take from a salmon and made the fatal mistake of holding on to the line too soon. The fish came off.

Our final session was Saturday morning and, with the river now coming back to normal, Pete and I made an early start. We were blank at breakfast time, but Pete spurred me on as I began to lose heart. He reminded me of his last trip when he had been fishless all week until the final two hours, when he caught fish of 20lb, 17½lb and 13½lb.

At midday I hooked my fish after raising three others. This came as I was ready to throw in the towel after a difficult but enjoyable week. I had a classic take and let the reel run on check, as Rod Grant had told me. When landed, I found my tiny hook in the back of the salmon's throat. The fish, a fresh 7½lb grilse, was far more rewarding than if it had come easy. Also, it proved persistence pays when salmon fishing. I had also learned the lesson in those early days of my salmon fishing. Very small flies in summer are better than big ones. Also, allow the taking fish to pull a yard of line freely off the reel ratchet before striking.

From now on it was once or twice a year either up to Scotland or Ireland's West Coast, even to Wales on the River Conway or the south of England on the River Test. I caught some good salmon from all over, but I was beginning to get a love affair with the Tweed.

The Tweed has the big salmon that come into the river at the back end of October and into the season's end in mid-November. Known by the regulars who seek to catch them as the 'Grey backs' they are all 20lb plus and up to 35lb, usually cock fish.

I had twelve years' fishing on this prime week on the junction beat at Kelso, where our party and other friends fishing other beats would all stay at the Ednam House Hotel, which catered for salmon anglers' needs very well. I have some happy memories of these trips, sometimes with remarkable results. In the early days most fish would be kept but as time went by nearly all were returned, which is good.

The junction beat caters for six anglers who fish in pairs on three stretches: the Junction Pool, where the River Teviot runs in and up to the little weir at the end of lower Floor's Castle beat; then there is the Bridge Pool; and, lower down, Hemsford. You get one boat and a ghillie at each pool, while the second angler wades the bank. I have always enjoyed deep wading and fly fishing for salmon, having never been afraid of the water. My best catch in the twelve years was five over 20lb in a day, four of which came while wading from the weir and down past the Ednam House Bank, after having a lift across the river in the boat. I fished a special sink tip No. 10 fly line that I have had for years and have treasured because it's been my most successful salmon catcher.

On this day I fished a Comet tube fly, just trundling it along close to the bottom. I had four salmon, keeping one of 21½lb but releasing three others, which were between 20lb and 23lb. That morning, much to Jeanette's horror, I also fell in while playing the last fish. I was deep wading and had the fish under control; I began to move backwards towards the bank when I encountered a large round stone. Next thing I know I had fallen backwards and was drifting along with the current with rod held high and fish still on! I recovered, landed the fish and put it back. Jeanette said, 'You had better go back to the Hotel and change your clothes,' to which I replied, 'At the money we are paying, there is half an hour to go before lunch, that's nearly £100 worth. I'll empty my chest waders and fish on!' No wonder I have all these aches and pains in my joints these days.

I have a serious problem, I know, and that is I still think I am young. In fact I've been around a very long time really. Fishing so much has given me time to try seriously for most species as the years have rolled by.

When I hear some anglers go on about the fight of certain fish, I always stand in judgement and say none can fight like the true king of fish, the Atlantic salmon. My best Tweed salmon to date is a 28lb 2oz fish, which proved this the way it battled. I have notched up around twenty-five over 20lb, mostly from the River Tweed, and the best method is to fly fish using a 15ft double-handed rod and a weighted brass tube fished on a medium-sinking fly line.

I was fishing with ghillie Billy from a boat in the deep hole at Bridge Pool at Kelso and I had returned two hen fish of good size earlier in the day. The afternoon was pressing on and it was very cold, with the bank-side frost not thawed all day (mid-November). I put on a yellow and black hairwing with a gold mylar body and cast out once more, well across the current. The line swung round deep and I had an almighty take, hooking a monster cock fish. The fight lasted for twenty minutes and I was giving the fish all I had got with my 15lb breaking-strain leader. It gave one spectacular leap towards the end of the fight then soon he was in the net. At 28lb 2oz, he was a big brute of a cock fish, my best to date, and also a record for the best of that season. Take it from me, specimen hunters, salmon are worth a try.

Going back to the late 1970s, I had an invite to fish on the River Avon, which is a tributary of the mighty Spey. One of the party was Reg Righyni, a well respected salmon angler who specialized on the River Lune – nowadays poor by comparison. Reg wrote regular articles in *Trout & Salmon* and was well known as a top stillwater trout fisher during the boom years of the 70s. I caught two salmon on day one and three on day two, nice fresh fish from 8lb to 12½lb. At breakfast on day three Reg said, 'You will be fishing with me today Bob,' more of a command really, but I was very pleased because I knew I would learn something.

We fished the shallow low-water Factors Pool and Reg said, 'Go down the pool Bob and I will tell you at the end what you did wrong.' His way of teaching I suppose, and a good idea. So I got in the water with my light floating-line outfit on a new 17½ft Bruce and Walker carbon rod, one of the first made. I had caught the other five fish by going small coupled with a finer leader than normal, because I found that was the way to get offers. The bigger flies, Waddington's and others, and heavy nylon leaders produced nothing in the gin-clear low conditions, although the fish were there and we could see them in the shade of the bushes of the far bank.

About my tenth cast and the line straightened and I was in. Reg got the landing net and was ready for netting, but after ten minutes I was still playing it. Eventually, after around twenty minutes, I was able to guide the salmon, a fresh 12½lb, over Reg's waiting net. Up the bank, a tap on the head with the priest and I waited for Reg's verdict.

'Well Bob, you entered the pool correctly, wading was good, casting and presentation excellent, but playing the bloody fish was atrocious. He did what he liked with you.'

I said, 'But Reg, I am only using a 7lb breaking strain leader so I had to be careful as I would be broken.' 'Why go that light?' Reg replied. 'Because it's the only way I can get these takes.' And it was too! Reg admitted later that I had been fortunate to realize so early in the week about the light line. When I went on in the evening to catch three more salmon on a size 10 small black dry fly, I had really arrived as a good salmon fly fisher.

River Ness in Massive Flood

While writing this book, retired Northampton optician Mike Green gave me an invite to join his party of six rods on the Castle Ness beat of the River Ness. Mike is a keen all-round fisherman and he has fished the Ness annually since his father first took him as a young man, so he knows it well. I took up his offer and asked if my wife Jeanette could share the rod with me, and this was OK.

The team consisted of Mike and his son James, Rod Barley from Wellingborough, Ken Dawes from Worcester and, the joker in the pack, Ken Heath from Stoke on Trent – and, of course, us. We arrived at Inverness on Sunday 8 September to find one third of the town flooded, which was covered on national television news. There had also been a landslip somewhere upstream on the flooded River Ness, which turned the water to the colour of very strong coffee. I took one look and thought that we ought to turn around and drive the 525 miles back down to Northampton. I am glad we did not.

The main ghillie, Davie Stewart, badly sprained his ankle the day we arrived and we were looked after by Ian 'Fluckie' Mclellan, a very experienced Ness man. He had not encountered a brown-water flood in over thirty years. Floods yes, but the river always remained gin clear. So, on Monday, Jeanette and I fly fished all day and as they say, 'It was like peeing in the wind', no chance.

The rest of the team failed with their attempts at fly fishing too, but soon changed to spinning also with no results. It wasn't until Rodney put on a large gold toby, that things began to happen. I suppose it showed up best in the murk. They took twenty-one salmon to this method, but all hooks were de-barbed and most were returned. Meanwhile Jeanette and I blanked, as we thought we would fly fishing.

The following day the water rose higher and was still the same colour, so it was spinning again. I was now glad I put a spinning rod in just in case and I did have two gold tobies. It was a great day's sport for all of us. We finished the day with a total of forty-one fish. I kept a brace of cock, quite silver fish of 12½lb and 10½lb, but returned others to over 14lb. These were all we needed for smoking.

That night over dinner at the Lodge everyone was bubbling, we were now going into day three with the knowledge that we had caught sixty-two salmon and that the beat (and whole river) record for a week was seventy-five fish. To cut a long story short, at 3pm on day three Jeanette had the honour of landing and returning salmon number seventy-six, which broke the record. With the river beginning to drop, but not right for the fly, we still all fly fished.

Most of the fish ran through and, as the water dropped and became clear again, the fishing was more difficult than normal. Total for the week ended at eighty-six, clearly a new record. Mike put in a captain's performance that came to a climax at 10am Friday morning. Fly fishing the 'Lady Pool' he landed a fresh-run sea-liced fish of 18lb and with that he stopped fishing and ghillied for the rest of us – the fish took a size 10 black and silver shrimp.

There were in fact three records broken: eighty-six salmon, a record for a week on the Ness; forty-one salmon caught in a day, a record for the Ness; and fifty-six salmon returned, a record for the most ever returned in a week on the Ness.

We decided to report the catch to *Trout & Salmon*, not to boast how clever we were but to give the salmon fisher (long suffering) some good news for a change. It was also good for all of our group to be in the right place at the right time for a change. I asked everyone for a brief comment on the week's sport.

Rodney said:

> I have been salmon fishing for thirty-five years and this is the best I have ever known . . . I've caught twenty-one fish in a week, it's unbelievable.

Stoke's Ken Heath modestly commented:

> Conditions were so favourable and our team fished hard and well . . . Most of the fish returned on the barbless hooks never came out of the water and were completely unharmed.

Ken Dawes from Worcester:

> This is my fifth salmon fishing holiday and I normally fish for pike or nile perch in Lake Nasser . . . Fishing for these Atlantic salmon is by far the most exciting sport I have ever experienced . . . I will never forget this week.

James Green, now twenty-six years old, has been fishing the Ness since early on:

> I caught my first salmon here at the age of nine . . . We arrived to find the river Ness, which has never coloured in living

memory, completely chocolate brown . . . Most people would have never have fished in these conditions, but we soon found different after giving it a few casts.

Jeanette Church:

> After being apprehensive about the holiday, I soon changed my mind when I realized how good the fishing was . . . I was very pleased to catch salmon number seventy-six, which actually broke the record.

Bob Church:

> Certainly made the right choice on an accumulation of dates . . . Before driving to Inverness I had a problem of clashing dates. No.1, Con Wilson had invited us both to Dever Springs' new fishing lodge opening day. No. 2, Bob Church tackle team, had got to the international final of the 'Hardy' at Rutland Water. I had fished in the other heats when we won through and I love the buzz of the final. No. 3, Mike Green's early invite to the Ness. I am really glad I was part of the latter . . . I was very impressed by the river Ness, the fish were mostly from 7lb to 18lb, we put quite a lot back between 10lb and 14lb. When the river eventually cleared I noticed the shallows were full of small brown-trout and salmon parr. It seems a very prolific game river . . . The whole system is in very good shape.

Mike Green sums up:

> The pleasure of a salmon fishing holiday revolves around the companionship and camaraderie of your fellow fishers and in this respect the team gelled perfectly . . . The bonus was that by a total fluke we encountered a unique situation, which provided the opportunity for this record-breaking catch . . . The conditions were hopeless for fly fishing but we thought spinning might give us a chance for a fish, or two . . . In fact the salmon were there in great numbers and only too willing to take our lures . . . As the water cleared we reverted to fly fishing . . . On the first day, in view of the size of the catch we instantly de-barbed the hooks for easy release.

The Castle Ness beat and lodge lets are handled by Bob Robertson of the Estate Office at Greenwood. There are some lets available for spring bookings when a few salmon are caught but the brown trout fishing in river and loch is outstanding. By the way, we caught sixteen brown trout to 4lb during our week, Marks out of ten? Ten!

A Big Sea Trout

The poor old River Test in Hampshire is only a shadow of its former glory days of years gone by. Now most of the fishing is put-and-take rainbow or brown trout, which in fairness offers good sport to those able to afford it.

I have fished for grayling and sea trout on many of the well-known beats throughout this famous river's length, but one day stands out in mind. I was the guest of David Train and I had been invited to fish Testwood Pool, which is the tidal limit ending at the weir pool. The idea was to fish bait for salmon during the day, then rest the pool and restart after dark using the fly for sea trout. David had caught a couple of salmon as usual on shrimp bait, but I was trying a large lobworm. I fished this on a very light lead that slowly rolled bottom, out of, then away from the fast water. Often the lead would stop on a minor snag and I would free it again with a flick of my rod tip.

After four hours of fishing the lead stopped again, but this time the line began to move off as a fish had obviously taken the bait. A firm strike saw me doing battle with a hefty double-figure fish that at first I assumed to be a salmon. Then it leapt a good 3ft out of the water and I heard David shout from the far bank, 'Bob, that's a sea trout! Slacken off!' I didn't need telling twice. The fish's next run was as spectacular as it tried to run up the face of the rushing water of the high weir. It made over halfway up and fell back. From then on I was in control and soon brought it to the net. The perfect fish was indeed a sea trout of 11lb 4oz – the heaviest from the River Test that year.

I finished the day with a 12lb salmon carrying sea lice. Then, after dark, some good sea trout on fly. I fished this pool with David a number of times for twenty-five years, and now, of course, everything goes back.

Sea Trout after Dark

Many fly-fishing experts would agree that the ultimate thrill of this wonderful sport is night fishing for sea trout. Gavin Brown, a ghillie whom I know from my Tweed salmon trips, offered me an invite. 'Next time you are in Scotland during summer I'll take you night fishing for sea trout.' So I surprised him with a phone call and said, 'Here I am. I have a trout reservoir outfit with me. What about that sea trout trip?' True to his word, the following evening we were off to a little tributary river of the Tweed, the Till, but he warned don't expect too much but you should catch a sea trout or two.

For anyone thinking of trying sea trouting at night, your reservoir fly rod coupled with a floating fly line is all you need. I fished with a two-fly leader of 8lb, an Orange Peter Ross on the point and a hackled Viva on the dropper.

There were several good pools to try and Gavin told me to familiarize myself with them before it got too dark. Concentrate on the head and tail of each run was his advice. Amazingly, my eyes acclimatized to the darkness to still see reasonably well and I was so pleased with myself at not getting one tangle and not turning the torch on once during the three-hour period. I landed three good sea trout and lost one; all were hooked in the tail of the pools, places you wouldn't bother to cast to in daytime. The takes were explosive and each fish jumped in the darkness three or four times. This is very exciting fishing and it had been six years since my last trip; I promised myself I would not leave it so long again.

As my friends will tell you, I would rather go hungry than eat a rainbow trout, but sea trout are something else. Wild and fresh from the sea their flesh is sweet and tender and the hotel chef cooked one expertly for me. If you get the opportunity you really must try sea trouting at night – it's a sport all of its own.

It was back in the 60s that the late Cyril Inwood and Frank Cutler introduced me to the River Conway in North Wales. This very exciting river is one of the best known for its very big fish. In those days both Cyril and Frank would take a family caravan holiday for a fortnight in the Betws-y-Coed area. Being selfish anglers, like most of us, they used to pray for a good heavy rain storm, for they knew this would bring plenty of new fish into the river.

Like most rivers the Conway can be bait fished during spate and they would catch a few salmon and sea trout by worming in the worst conditions, then spinning as it fined down. Then, by day two or three, the river would be clear and go back to normal once more, but with plenty of new sea trout to try for. Now they would get tickets for a night session because this was going to be the cream.

They always fly fished at night and this was the method that brought them many double-figure fish year after year. Cyril's best two in his career went 18lb and 16lb 7oz. Mostly these would fall for a very large fly that Cyril invented. A sort of Teal Blue and Silver variant with a badger hair wing.

In the years that followed I've fished many different rivers and lochs for sea trout and usually this has meant snatching the odd session. One thing I did find out and must pass on is that to get the best out of a night session it is a good idea to become very familiar with the pool you intend to fish.

It is usual to wade the shallows in thigh waders, casting across the river into the deeper run along the far bank. I use my ordinary 10ft reservoir rod and tackle, with either a WF No. 8 floater or the same in slow sinkers, although some pools need the faster lead-impregnated sinker. My favourite flies are Squirrel and Silver, Claret Mallard, Teal Blue and Silver, Black and Peacock and, when big fish are about, a Black Hairwing with a green fluorescent tail tag – this last mentioned is on a tube with size 10 or size 8 treble.

Get into the water well before dark, merely to get the length of casting to the far bank without forever fouling it. Hopefully, you will be able to drop the fly a foot or two away from the bank. The fly then swings round naturally with the current; in the case of a floating line a little mending of the slack will be necessary. The take is usually quite vicious and cannot be missed. After getting to know the situation of the pool, rest it until about one hour after dark before starting to fish seriously, and the darker the night the better. It's surprising how your eyes will become accustomed to the darkness, enabling you to see quite well. Torches are taboo and should only be used in emergencies, or well up on the bank. Then take care not to shine the light on the water. I admit to being a little out of practice now, but I used to be able to tie a tucked half blood to change my fly in total darkness. With practice it can be done.

Basically, my tactics after dark are very straightforward. If I am fishing a deep pool with plenty of flow, I use the sinking line. If on the other hand it is a tail shallow run, say up to 3ft or so, I use a floating line. Cast across the river at a one o'clock angle just slightly downstream. With the sinking line let the fly sweep from the far bank, until it is lying limp, straight downstream, then retrieve and repeat the cast. Mostly I have had my best results after dark on the sinker.

However, I do remember fishing just in evenings when on the Spey's main tributary, the Avon. When I was there this river was being fished only for salmon, therefore come early evening I had great stretches to myself. In this situation, when the sea trout are not scared they can be caught very well during the three hours up to dark. The method then is a floater; I did so well on a Black and Peacock lure, casting under the far-bank bushes. These sea trout of about 2½lb to 3lb were feeding, or seemingly so, on caterpillars that were dropping off the trees.

8
World Travel

Fly Fishing Travel Adventures

It's only in the last twenty-five years that I have travelled widely in search of top fly fishing. These trips have been mainly for all kinds of trout, but salmon, char, sea trout and bonefish have also made for some exciting fishing. In short, I've fished my way around the world both ways and here are some of the tales I can tell that will live in my memory.

First: something different – a fortnight in the Bahamas for bonefish. Going back to the late seventies, everyone was raving about it being the best fighting fish there was – pound for pound. After a little encouragement from Don Neish and Roy Marlow, who had both been before, Peter Dobbs and I thought we would give it a go. After a couple of nights in Nassau we took a short flight to the then un-commercialized island of Andros. You go out looking for bonefish on the flats, in a fast flat-bottomed skiff. Lanky Langford was our guide and each day we motored out sometimes as much as 15 miles. In the gin-clear water over coral we could easily spot huge manta rays and sting rays in the deeper connecting channels.

After finding a suitable looking area that the gentle tide had flooded to a depth of 2½ft or so, fishing would begin. We had our fly rods set up ready but, also, we were advised to bring a light bait-rod outfit. Lanky wanted us to use the bait rod, baiting the 1/0 hook with a freshly killed crab minus its shell.

Lanky would stand on the stern of the skiff and pole it along. Then he watched for the flash of sunlight mirrored off the tell-tale surface-protruding fin of a bonefish. He would say, 'Here they come man, cast there now.' Like as not, we would get the big rod-bender take and we hooked bonefish after bonefish. We stopped bait fishing and picked up the fly rods only to continue catching – in a couple of hours of our first morning we had twenty-five bonefish. Was this luck? We never found them difficult at all, and that went for the rest of the party as well.

While all this bonefish excitement was going on, every so often we would spot a big barracuda strike into the shoals with terrifying speed. Then there were the sharks, which forever cruised by seemingly paying little attention to things, some were as big as 12ft long. Both the barracuda and shark lived mainly in the deep channels, which eventually connected up with the deep drop off.

By day two we were already quite impatient and wanted to fish for the barracuda and, hopefully, shark, but Lanky was not keen and didn't want to know about the shark at all. By midday we were catching the bonefish quite easily yet again, then I hooked into a small barracuda on my fly rod; it came in just like a 3lb jack pike.

We could stand it no longer and we set up spinning rods with 12lb BS line and 6in spoons; the boat was anchored on the edge of a 15ft-deep channel. After boating a few medium-sized barracuda, Pete latched into a spectacular fish that sped through the water before giving one incredible leap; after that, all 30lb of it surrendered and it came in meekly. Really it was like summer piking with extra gravy on. 'Now what about the shark Lanky?' we asked. He complained about getting blood on his new boat, so we bribed him with a language he understood – money. He soon sensibly relented. The first thing he did was to slit the big barracuda's stomach from head to tail (these Northampton lads are all the same), put a rope through its gills and hung it over the side. The blood poured out downwind and in a few minutes our little boat was surrounded by nine various sized shark, and they looked mean and hungry.

I can tell you now, shallow-water shark fishing is probably one of the most exciting sports there is and, at times, more than a little dangerous. Dobbie put a longer trace on his spinning rod while I used a light beach caster, baits were half bonefish on 4/0 hooks. Again this was like piking but a thousand times more exciting. Pete had a take almost as his bait hit the water and on a Bruce & Walker salmon-spinning rod he was obviously in for some sport. I was soon into a lemon shark, then a big barracuda.

Pete was playing his shark for a while and getting the better of it when it made a mad dash onto the shallow receding tide flats and beached itself – about 50lb we estimated. This sort of thing continued on more occasions during the holiday and we caught four varieties including hammerhead, lemon shark, black tip shark, and sand shark. The best we did was around twenty fish in a session to around 100lb, but Roy Marlow and Rodney Pinches had a catch of thirty sharks off the point of a tiny Robinson Crusoe-type island. This was absolutely brilliant sport, which, according to the guides, no-one had ever taken advantage of before. The natives thought we were out of our minds for ignoring the highly rated bonefish, which the Yanks rave over. By the way, the majority of the shark were returned after we became skilled at handling and unhooking them.

Trolling the blue water from the big game boat called *Andros Angler*, which was moored at the original Captain Henry Morgan's Cove, was our alternative sport and this too proved to be very good fishing. The big game dolphin fish known as dorado (not to be confused with the mammal) were on their annual migration running the Tongue of the Ocean deep water. These fish were magnificent with their iridescent vivid green-blue colouration. They fought harder and longer than any fish I have ever known, on 30lb line class as well. Between us we caught sixty-six of these in the few trips made; my best went 43lb with Rodney's a shade heavier – both over halfway to a world record.

Various other fish came our way on the troll, like yellow fin tuna, wahoo, grouper, barracuda and the spectacular, extremely fast Atlantic sailfish. Peter had not been lucky with the big dolphin, but he was lucky enough to contact the first sailfish. We were out in a big wind and high wave action at the time, and this made the fight of boating the fish quite dramatic.

A heart-stopping moment came when a massive blue marlin came at my bait, which was only on a short troll. It showed itself to be several hundred pounds and had eyes as big as tennis balls. It stared at me and then at the mullet bait, which was skipping across the surface, but then refused the offering. Our boatman said it must have been hooked before and had escaped, which now made him wary. I would have dearly loved to have hooked that fish; perhaps next time.

The surf almost silently kissed the platinum-white coral sands no more than 50yd from our hotel chalet. This small American-owned twelve-chalet hotel was the only one in the area and we lived for much of the time on fresh seafood. Half-a-mile out from the beach was the more sinister reef edge (we are now on the opposite side of the island to the bonefish flats). The reef drop-off sharply shelves to an amazing 3.5 miles deep. We stayed on the shallow side and would anchor up about 100yd off the reef in the 14ft open boat where we caught the most exotic of fish, which carried every imaginable colour. In all we recorded over sixty different species. As well as the smaller marine fish that we could clearly observe in our glass-bottomed bucket, shark and big rays would move in from the reef edge and, for the most part, we were kept active.

We did not have too much time for shore fishing but, when we attempted it, something always turned up of interest. From shark at night off the jetty, where we would have been swimming only an hour or so earlier, to the snappers, which had the habit of being near impossible to hook as they stole bait after bait. The only audience we ever had was the ever present vultures hovering close by. On top of all this the jungle night life was pretty good, as you can well imagine, and we visited many a tin-shack bar in the middle of nowhere. Fortunately the natives are very friendly and very pro-British; they talk about King George as though he was still alive.

Tasmania

While retaining the world team fly fishing championship had to be the biggest thrill of our trip to Tasmania, I penned this comment for my local paper.

Wild and Wonderful – That's Tasmania

Although I've travelled extensively I've never seen a place like it. I thoroughly recommend it for a holiday, even if you are not an angler. The air is exhilarating, the scenery breathtaking, the flowers beautiful and the wildlife fascinating. I'm not after a job on TV's holiday programmes, but I reckon they should give Tasmania a try. Our guide, Noel Jetson, is a man of nature. He has his own log cabin high on the plateau where he has a golden touch with animals. After a day's fishing he would barbecue steaks for us and have wild possums coming into the cabin to take bread from his hands. We also saw four breeds of wallaby, wombats and deadly poisonous tiger snakes, which are 4ft long. If one of them decides to sink its fangs into your legs you had better be wearing tough waders. Not to mention Tasmanian Devil cats. And so on and so forth.

The plateau is just about the last unspoilt wilderness in the world, but the pure air does carry one nasty problem. Even though it wasn't sunny I suffered painful ultraviolet burns. Huge water blisters appeared on the back of my hands and when the blisters burst they left raw flesh. However, the pure air, which blows straight from the Antarctic, does wonders for the flowers which are incredibly colourful.

Incidentally, the locals are more like Norfolk or Fenland folk than Aussies. Their accent is remarkably similar. The gruelling flight to Tasmania took over thirty hours, but if you make it you won't be disappointed.

Our trip, remember, lasted for three weeks. There was little point in going all that way to the opposite side of the world for just a few days. There was plenty of time for exploring this beautiful unspoilt island. The trip, in fact, turned out to be the sort of adventure that I shall never forget, even if at times it was almost like a military operation and left me exhausted, but in a super-fit physical condition. Fly fishermen in this country would find the plentiful wild trout fishing of Tasmania totally enjoyable. The main expense is the return flight. A national fishing licence costs £13 a season, and that enables you to fish anywhere (except London Lakes, which are privately run by Jason Garrett from his superb country lodge).

Tasmania has 3,000 lakes of varying sizes, up to giants like Great Lake, some 20 miles long, and Pedder, the consistent 25lb-plus specimen brown trout water. On top of that, the sea trout fishing, with fish to 20lb, remains virtually untouched on a number of first-class rivers. From what I learned on my trip all this fishing has never been pushed as a tourist trade attraction. Those who know about it and fish there regularly are keen Aussie fly fishers from the mainland.

With chief fisheries officer Rob Sloane keeping a watchful eye on the way the future of the sport develops in Tasmania the locals can sleep peacefully. He is a young enthusiastic man who clearly knows his job inside out. I now realize why he had a little go in *Trout Fisherman* at our 'plastic' trout fishing when comparisons were made after his visit here.

During the championships I met most of the island's fishing guides, and these characters really look after you in style. We had Noel Jetson and his wife Lois, assisted by Craig Little, to look after the England team. They did a great job, taking us everywhere in their four-wheel-drive Toyota Land Cruisers. These vehicles are a must if you are to get to the best remote fishing places. Noel had the amazing ability to produce barbecue steaks, lamb or pork cutlets and numerous cups of tea miles from civilization.

Trout, of course, are not native to Tasmania but the environment there suits them better than almost anywhere else in the world. After a few failed attempts, trout and salmon ova were transported by the clipper sailing ship *Norfolk*. The ova were packed into pine boxes with perforated holes along the top, bottom and sides. These allowed water from packed ice to flow as it melted into the boxes and percolate through the moss-covered ova.

Francis Francis, the naturalist and writer, sent 2,000 brown trout ova from the Thames tributary, the Wey, while Frank Buckland sent another 1,000 Itchen stock. The main cargo of the experiment was made up from 100,000 Atlantic salmon ova and, on 21 January 1864, *Norfolk* sailed from London. After ninety-one days the eggs arrived at the salmon ponds in Tasmania and on 4 May the first young trout emerged. At the final count, 300 trout survived into breeding stock.

Rainbows followed from California in 1893 and the rest is history. The trout thrived and bred naturally everywhere they were introduced in Tasmania. Atlantic salmon never did establish reproducing populations. But today, more than a century later, every water course in Tasmania holds wild cunning trout.

Where the fishing was concerned, the normal local method of dry fly fishing, usually with a size 12 or 14 Red Tag and 4lb leader, was failing for us. So we turned to the English wet fly tactics with great success.

It wasn't until we had some free days following the world event that we easily spotted feeding trout as they foraged in the very shallow marginal waters. The main tactic for success is stealth. If you just stand very still these trout will swim virtually a rod length from you. One careless movement, though, and they are gone. I found a Black Pennell Nymph would tempt these fish. Really, you needed to be at the lake at first light to get the best action with tailing trout.

Noel took us to the isolated Western Lakes on the last day. It was sunny, ideal for the Polaroiding technique we had heard so much about from expert Jim Allen. The method can get into your blood I imagine, for Jim seemed to love it more than anything else. At his bar, Jim's photo looks down on you and he displays a brace of double-figure browns caught in one day on the Western Lakes with this method.

Noel at last did some fishing and soon he spotted two fish. He flicked his Red Tag with deadly accuracy into one of their paths and hooked a good brown that he released. He found another fish for our new World Champion John Pawson, who caught it and proudly announced to the rest of us, 'I've now done the lot.' He had, too.

Canada – the Big Country

A three-week trip to Canada's British Columbia, which is nearly as big as Europe, was very enjoyable. We flew into Vancouver before driving through magnificent scenery to Kamloops. This is the home of the famous strain of rainbow trout that is now found all over the world. We imported the Kamloops rainbow into England just over 100 years ago and in the last forty years it's been the major part of our sport under the rapidly building interest in fly fishing for trout.

Our base was the Roche Lake resort about 20 miles from Kamloops city. We chose this as there were a number of trout lakes close at hand: Horseshoe Lake, Black Lake, Peterhope Lake, Knouff Lake, White Lake and Roche itself. Comfortable cabins with modern facilities, owned and run by Ray Adams, surround part of Roche Lake. There's also a bar, shop and restaurant. We fished in May and June when the aquatic life over there is very similar to our own. Damselflies and midges were abundant, while the lake beds were crawling with leeches and shrimps. Hanging in mid-water were vast clouds of daphnia. And I can tell you that stillwater rainbows behave the same the world over.

Fishing from boats at anchor with simple flies like a Flashabou Buzzer, Olive Tinhead, marabou-tailed Leech and the Welsh Daiwl Bach brought us 530 trout, mostly rainbows to 9½lb with some brook trout to 4lb, over seventeen days. Canadian law insists you use only one fly at a time. Because of the great variations in depth, the right choice of fly line was crucial. On some lakes, the Hi-D was most effective. On others it was the Wetcel 2 or slime lines.

Double anchoring the boat on the edge of a drop-off in depth was the key to intercepting fish cruising along the shelf. In White Lake the water was so clear you could see the fish in 20ft of water as they swam over the white marl bottom. If you sat quietly in the boat you could present your nymph just right and actually see the take – very exciting stuff with rainbows from 2 to 4lb.

The key to catching even the larger rainbows was the buzzer. At Peterhope Lake, Chris Howitt and Brian Thomas spotted fair numbers of big fish patrolling a shallow spit. Eventually Chris hooked one on a 4lb leader and size 14 Olive Buzzer that weighed 7¼lb. Not to be outdone, Dave Grove caught an even bigger rainbow of 9lb 8oz on a size 12 Buzzer, one of the best-looking fish I've ever seen.

There's a lot more to angling in Canada than just catching fish. Ospreys shared the lakes with us while bald eagles and red-tailed hawks soared overhead. Every lake had its resident pair of loons with their eerie howling call. But perhaps the most memorable occasion was when a black bear wandered along the bank where I was fishing. At first I froze in horror, but a quick waggle with the rod showed the bear was more scared than I was as it disappeared back into the forest.

I suppose we all liked to fish at White Lake best because of the incredible clarity of the water. Sitting and nymphing at close range was, indeed, very different from our normal reservoir boat fishing. The tactic was to use a weighted size 10 Buzzer Nymph, in colours black or olive, then cast a very short line. You needed to concentrate on where your nymph had reached bottom and, when a trout came into the area, give the rod-top a slight lift. You could see the fish change direction to take the nymph and have the opportunity to time your strike perfectly. I had several between 3lb and 4lb on this method – magic sport indeed.

Finally, the England Commonwealth team travelled another 400 miles north to Nimpo Lake. Here there were no towns for 200 miles. We had a leisurely two-day journey travelling north into British Colombia, now on the Caribou trail. We stopped over at Williams Lake before continuing to our destination where the road runs out at Nimpo Lake. This is where we would fish the Commonwealth competition; there would be no practice, single fly and barbless hooks, and they were all wild rainbows.

Staying in a cabin close by was the famous Country and Western singer the late John Denver; he loved the fishing in this area. So he joined us and it was a private camp fire singsong of 'Rocky Mountain High' and 'Annie's Song' with the barbeque during the evening. Everything was perfect apart from the mosquitoes.

With Canada, New Zealand and Australia putting their best professionals in their teams, we knew we were in for a battle. There was no practice on the lake but, by the second of the four three-hour sessions, we had found fish on the 6-mile lake. Instead of the anchoring tactics for so long favoured, the English team opted to drift-fish in the traditional manner over shallow bays. This was a very brave move, giving us the winning bag of fifty-four trout. Team positions were: Dennis Buck (third); Charles Jardine (fifth); Bob Church (seventh); Chris Howitt (ninth) and Dave Grove (fourteenth) – a very consistent performance. New Zealand came second with (keeping it in the family) Wales third, Scotland fourth.

Iceland – the Land of Ice and Game Fish

With the years beginning to roll by, whenever I get the opportunity of what appears to be a good trip to a top game fishing country I accept and find the time. As they say 'you're a long time dead' and as this trip to Iceland turned out, it was the fishing adventure of a lifetime.

Imagine a country as big as England and Wales but with only a quarter of a million people living there. It's full of rivers and lakes that have never known the words 'pollution' or 'algae'. Every river we looked at held lots of salmon, sea-run char, brown trout and sea trout. We, Peter Gathercole, John Beer and I, caught all these species in good numbers on our four-wheel-drive tour of Iceland. We were guests of the Angling Club of Reykjavik. Basically, we were on a fact-finding trip just to see how good the game fishing really was, and also how much it would all cost. The first surprise was that the flight only took two and three-quarter hours, so Iceland is much closer than most would imagine.

The planned fishing was perfect. First we joined up with Jon and Freddie to fish the river Sog for salmon. The main run of summer grilse was just beginning here and we all hooked these except for Freddie, who landed a magnificent fifteen pounder. This took him fifty-two minutes to play and net on his single-handed trout rod, great sport indeed. The next day we moved back to Reykjavik and we fished a crystal-clear river that runs through the city, full of grilse (salmon between 4lb and 7lb). These fish give the best sport when fished for on light tackle, the type we normally use for trout. The flies used were tiny size 14 or 12 trebles with a Blue Charm or Peter Dean's Red Shrimp the best. This river also held some big wild brown trout, which we tried for with Goldhead Nymphs; both Peter Gathercole and I caught them – weight up to 3½lb.

It was about 8pm when we met up with our new guides, Jimmy and Oli. The club chairman, Fredrik, also joined us. We drove some 200 miles in two four-wheel-drive vehicles, crossing the black desert-like sands that are the remains of the massive discharges of volcanic ash. There is very little grass, no trees at all, but lots of lovely flowering alpine plants. We were heading for Veidivotn, or the fishing lakes; these are mainly water-filled volcanic craters and they hold a good head of big brownies. In the end we didn't do much fishing due to sightseeing, but we did catch a few and a local had a beauty of 4½lb on a fish bait. There are big char in these lakes but we didn't see any.

Of course, during Iceland's summer it is permanently daylight and because of this we had very little sleep for three days. Sleeping in cabins way out in the wild has its appeal I suppose, but I didn't see a razor or a mirror for three days and the end product was not a pretty sight.

Before leaving the area we were taken to look at the Stora-Laxa River, which has bright-green glacier-fed water and runs spectacularly through a narrow gorge. Two large salmon were caught by club members – 16lb by Fredrik and the heaviest, 17lb, to Jimmy's son Siggi.

We then took a long drive to a luxury cabin on the Hitara River where everything was just perfect for us. As we ate breakfast we looked out of a window to see a river full of leaping salmon; we could hardly wait. It was here we were to experience our best sport, catching lots of salmon and the lovely sea-run char (in total over thirty). Peter even managed the first recorded sea trout of the year, a fine six pounder, to a dry fly. Our new guide, Steinar, was well impressed. I used a 9ft Fenwick Ironfeather rod with a size 10 sink-tip line; this American-style approach gave me more mobility than when using traditional double-handed salmon rods. Certainly I shall use these sporting tactics more often when I next go to Scotland.

Iceland is not used much by us Brits for fishing holidays and, after experiencing what I did in just one week, this amazes me. I have been to all the top game-fishing countries in the world to fish, but I had never seen so many game fish that have been fairly straightforward to catch. It turned out one of the best fishing holidays I have ever had, catching plenty of salmon every day. There are not many places you can catch and release with Atlantic salmon, are there? Usually they are so difficult to catch you always keep them for eating. I did have seven grilse on my first run down the pool. On my sink-tip, of course.

The fishing can be expensive, but their lower-class rivers, which are much cheaper, are better than most of our best. The only real shock I had was on the final night back in the airport hotel at Reykjavik. I ordered two halves of lager for Peter and myself, and when I worked out the Krona Monopoly-style money back into sterling the bill had been £9.50! Ah well, you can't win them all. I shall definitely be going back to Iceland, as the game fishing there is so unbeatable.

Iceland's more recent record fish list:

Brown Trout	29lb	1960
Char	22lb	1987
Sea Trout	23lb	1989
Salmon	43lb	1992

Gourmet Food – Steelhead Trout on a French Mountain

Each early May I used to journey across to France to fish in the first round of the European Grand Slam. This is held at a mature landscaped ex-gravel pit at Dreux, some 60 miles south of Paris. This year I was invited to fish at another of France's growing still-water trout fisheries and what a fantastic place it was. The idea was to leave a few days earlier and take in some fishing at 'Le Lac de la Landie', a lake about the size of Ravensthorpe reservoir, but perched 4,000ft up a mountain. My travelling party was my wife and Mike Childs and Val.

Lac de la Landie stretches out on the plateau d'Artense, in the heart of the nature reserve of Haute Auvergne volcanoes. This lake was created thousands of years ago by the successive action of volcanoes and glaciers. Pottery dating back to the Iron Age has been found on its shores and nothing seems to have been changed since these distant times. Round the lake you will find hardwood forests and secret peat bogs sheltering some seventy rare species of plants. The miniature wild daffodils and numerous cowslips were out in full bloom during our visit. The hillside meadows looked so healthy, as cattle grazed with a chorus of cowbells. In a six-cottage village nearby, the famous St Nectaine cheese is made to ancient methods.

As you must now be aware, Mike and I dropped in on a real ecological gem protected from the adverse effects of civilization. North of this exceptional site is the Massif Central Reaches, with its highest point of close on 6,000ft – Pay de Sancy – this reflects itself in the lake's waters. There were about twenty French fly fishers tackling up or taking breakfast in the well-fitted fishing lodge. Owner Jean Bernard Cohendet, a retired surgeon from Paris, greeted us and said, 'Go and enjoy some fishing'. This was from bank or boat, and each of the ten ample boats was fitted with an electric motor.

We were told the species possible were pure Kamloops rainbows, steelheads, jumper trout (these are apparently a cross between a char and a brook trout), marbled trout and finally grayling. We agreed that this would be enough to keep us happy. Not being too sure of the best approach, we set up two rods each, one carrying a floating-line set up and the other a medium to fast sinker.

Drifting loch style seemed to be a good idea, as only a light breeze was blowing. We both had a very good morning's sport, catching twelve or so fish a piece, with the heaviest up to 4lb – these being ordinary rainbows as we know them. Some were a little on the lean side as, being so high up, the lake had only been free of ice for about one month. The food chain was only just awakening after winter, even the buds on the bankside trees and bushes were only just breaking through. No wonder the trout were hungry to take our flies in the gin-clear water.

We had been told to come in for lunch at about 1.00pm and this we did. What followed seemed quite normal to all the French anglers; do they know how to eat! I am not exaggerating when I say we had a ten-course meal, plenty of champagne and the best red wine. Before we realized it, it was 5.00pm by the time the sweet and coffee was consumed.

Jean Bernard announced that it was time to go fishing again and his wife asked that if anyone caught a big steelhead would they please bring it back to the lodge, they would cook it up for supper. Eating again was farthest from my thoughts but I did rather fancy catching one of his steelheads, as none had been caught during the morning session by the whole party of rods.

We casually motored out about 100yd from the boat jetty and cut the motor, as a few fish were beginning to rise. I was using a size 10 black Tinhead with a green-painted head on the point, a Hares Ear Nymph in the middle and a Soldier Palmer for a top dropper. The morning session had brought me fish to all of the flies on this cast while using a floating line. It was long casting and slow retrieving.

Almost like fate, the time now 6.00pm, my very first cast of that evening session and I was into what was obviously one of his huge steelheads. It ran 60yd of line and jumped a full six times, sometimes as high as 4ft from the water. It was a great fight, so fast and exciting, but he was hooked well and I slid the net under this bright silver well-proportioned fish. I wanted to ask so many questions. Where did such a fish come from? How come it was in such perfect condition, almost as you would expect such a fish to run a Canadian river? Such thoughts were baffling me, but I would try to get to the bottom of the story later. I had a twinge of conscience but I kept the fish as Michelle had asked.

The fishing remained very good and naturally suited Mike and my reservoir background – this water was made for us. Again rainbows to 4lb and we had a few of the jumpers and marbled trout. I did get another steelhead of around 5½lb but I slipped him back. Those fish did fight far harder than the other trout and it wasn't just because of their size.

With a sigh and the light now fading, we decided to go in and face supper, I wondered how much more we could eat. However, the French have got it right where food is concerned. They always take their time over the numerous courses and because of this you don't seem to get too full.

First, the gutting and the cleaning of the steelhead; in its stomach were five 7in-long rudd, no wonder their fish are in such good condition. I would normally expect them not to do so well in such a high altitude lake, but because of the large amounts of roach, rudd and minnows they are obviously thriving very well indeed.

Room for thought here on waters like Grafham and Rutland. I believe Dr Purdom did briefly experiment with similar fish at Grafham a few years ago, but no report was ever made public. Seems strange Grafham produced its first few double-figure rainbows after the experiment. I wonder?

Mike and I did manage our supper and we both agreed this normally quiet skiing resort had so much to offer the trout fly fisherman. We were told that the fish density is maintained with good stocking policies. All the fish stocked come from the leading fish farm in France, from a man who likes to experiment. Here he has found a water with strong inlet and outlet streams that do his fish justice.

As I mentioned earlier, it is the ideal place to go for a holiday. Taking your own car on the ferry from Dover to Calais, it is then a four-hour drive beyond Paris. It is mostly motorway and you make for Clermont Ferrand, after that a further 20 miles through little villages and climbing all the time. Day tickets are £35 with boat.

Sweden's Morrum the Magnificent

I've had a couple of trips to the south of Sweden to fish the famous river Morrum. At the time of my visits, first in 1992 and a return in 1995, the fishery was managed by Curt Johansson. As I found, he was the most knowledgeable salmon and sea trout scientist, and game river manager I had ever come across. His methods had restored the ailing salmon and sea trout stocks in this river to their very best. The actual size of Morrum fish is really amazing. The first two fish I saw being weighed in at the fishing lodge on the river Morrum were sea trout both larger than the British record. I was just about speechless but none of the locals seemed too bothered, as 20lb sea trout here are pretty normal. The salmon in the river are also massive and it needs to be 40lb to raise an eyebrow.

It was a trip of fishing here and there, but really there were just far too many lakes, which seldom see an angler, to choose from. Along with Martin Founds we were pioneering the fishing potential around Karlshamn in the south of Sweden right on the Baltic coast. The Baltic in many areas is just brackish water, so when we fished it in some quiet inlet bays we found pike and perch plentiful. It seems strange to catch freshwater fish amongst migrating jellyfish but that's what happened.

A trip to an angling camp, which has twenty-two lakes and neat self-catering log cabins to stay in, left us wondering which one to fish. As some were for spin fishing we chose a fly-only lake that reputedly held some good rainbows. Surely these fish would never have seen sunken-line lure tactics, I assumed. It wasn't long before my same Grafham 'Light Bulb' fish-imitating white lure caught me a fish of around 5½lb and another of 6lb that I returned. Martin also landed a four pounder on a similar white lure. Our guide, Bengt Rosengren, was a real outdoor type who cooked us rainbow steaks over a camp fire, also a pan of wild forest mushrooms that looked just like poisonous toadstools to me. After watching him tuck into them the least I could do was try them out; they were good and I lived to tell the tale.

There was a special river close by that was a series of cascade pools stretching for over a mile. This river was kept at constant flow as water was pumped up from the lake below. It was a put-and-take lake fishery where the fishing was relatively easy; we only spent a couple of hours here. After all, we were trying to escape from stock fish, but the river with a continuous strong flow was a sound idea. To be honest, it was those big sea trout and salmon in the river Morrum that had me drooling. I just had to spend a few sessions fishing for them. Curt Johansson, the director of the very impressive House of Salmon fishing lodge, kindly arranged some fishing for us.

Because the river had been so low all summer, a single-hook fly or tube was the ruling. This, of course, helps to avoid the accidental foul-hooking of fish as they rest in their lies waiting for more water. I soon found out that few fish were being caught but those that did get landed were exceptionally large. I hooked three fish in three short sessions, but never landed one of them. One was a sea trout of around 7 to 8lb that jumped and came off. The second, a salmon that was smallish at around 25lb, also came off after a couple of minutes. But, on the final evening with the river rising a little after rain, I connected with something the like of which I have never done before in freshwater.

I was tackled up properly for such a fish: my powerful boron 10½ft rod, a WF8 Wet Cell 2 line and 20lb breaking-strain leader with a tube fly and size 2 thick wire hook. The fish came towards me after I had hooked it while wading at my maximum depth; just 3in separated the water from the top of my chest waders. I then had full view of this giant salmon at 3yd range as it came right out of the water in its first bid for freedom. It then rushed across the full width of the river with me hanging on and applying maximum pressure, knowing the tackle was up to it. The fish then decided to go upstream some 40yd keeping under the far bank. It was then I realized all was not well, the fish was still on OK but I was not in direct contact. My line was attached to some obstacle in the middle of the river, but the line was running freely through it every time the salmon moved.

My guide, Isaac, risked life and limb to wade right across the river at a shallower point further upstream. The idea was for him to free the trapped line so I could continue the fight. Instead of entering the water well downstream of the fish, which was attempting to go upstream, he got into the river close to where the unseen fish was lying. As he began to wade out to where the line was caught, his feet touched the line between obstacle and fish. He bent down and his hand grasped the leader, which was only 3yd from the fish. Despite the 20lb breaking-strain line the salmon broke this like cotton, leaving me with just another fishing story. As it was, I would have returned the fish anyway; however, it would have been nice to have unhooked and admired such a fish of at least 45lb. I can honestly say I was so impressed with the brief fishing as I saw it. The twenty-four-hour crossing on the large Scandinavian Seaways ferry is more like a mini cruise than a ferry crossing.

For my second trip I organized a small party of like-minded friends, who I had told of the massive magnificent Morrum fish. This time it would be a full week just fishing the river and its thirty beats. Most are fly-only pools, a few long pools are fly or fly spin, because these are awkward to traditionally fly fish. A fishing guide can be booked for British parties and we had a very good one named 'Isaac', to be precise Isaacs Kristian.

I soon realized September was the time for the big sea trout, which were in good condition, but the salmon, although massive, were dark and well past their best.

On this trip we had eighteen fish between us. Fifteen salmon averaging well over 20lb with two about 35lb – all were returned – and three sea trout all in the 12lb class. It was during this September session that I realized my next visit must be in late May or June when the big spring salmon are in their peak of condition. September is obviously too late for salmon on the Morrum despite their size, although it is still the best time for the ultimate big sea trout.

One of our party was Carol Neal, who was a member of the England Ladies Fishing Team. On one of her sessions fly fishing Beat Four she had a big dark cock fish of about 25lb, which she duly returned. The German angler next to her was amazed and quite shocked at this. But when fifteen minutes later she hooked one of about 35lb and then she returned that, it was more than our German neighbour could stand – he stormed off chuntering to himself.

Curt tells me he would like to welcome more English fly fishers to the Morrum fishery. 'We don't see enough of them,' he said. 'We are very proud of our fishery, which produced 1,100 salmon and sea trout in 1994 with a total weight of 8.75 tons.' A further good number were returned. In the top ten list no fish weighed less than 20kg (around 45lb), with the biggest at 25.1 kilos (55lb) caught by a Dane, Ejgel Nederg, fishing the fly on 26 July. It is likely that no other Atlantic salmon river can show such a high figure. The top ten sea trout list is also impressive and all these went over 20lb with the general average around 10lb.

As I mentioned earlier, salmon and sea trout tactics are similar whether you are in Scotland, Ireland or Sweden. So for this reason I will not try and tell you how to fish the Morrum as it is the same as anywhere else, except for two things. Use much stronger leaders and tie up some old 'Allsuck' flies on big singles, doubles, trebles and tubes. There is no doubt that is the deadly pattern there. It's really a type of shrimp fly pattern.

Curt and I talked over a beer one evening and he said to me, 'Bob, I cannot understand why your river authorities have allowed the Hampshire Avon and Herefordshire Wye rivers to continue to deteriorate so badly.' The once common big spring fish that ran both rivers, around 20lb to 45lb, are now virtually extinct, purely because no one has bothered to get a grip of the situation. The Morrum was heading for a similar situation until Curt was given the job of returning it to its former glory. I bear witness to the fact he did a good job.

It means helping nature on its way, by netting a few of the largest hen fish still running, taking their eggs and matching with a suitable handsome cock fish and then rearing the fry on to smolt size before releasing them back into the river. After three years of continuously doing this, the situation will be coming back to good fishing. Also, every spawning stream and favoured salmon area should be raked out and cleared of all silt, leaving just the healthy clean bottom for the fish to lay her eggs. The last I heard was that Morrum fish were spawning naturally and successfully once again, meaning less help needed from Curt.

When you think about it, we are very slow on the uptake where salmon are concerned. Obviously the Avon and Wye fish could still be saved. Call Curt in as a consultant; I know I would.

Allsuck Fly Tying
HOOK: 2–4–6. Single, double, or tube
THREAD: Black
BODY: Black silk
TAIL: Scarlet hackle fibres with a few fibres from a golden pheasant rump feather
BODY HACKLE: Medium brown cock
HEAD HACKLE: Medium brown cock
REAR WING: A mixture of orange and pearl crystal fibres, tied thinly

Fishing in Finland – Lapland

To say that Finland is a fisherman's paradise would be stretching the truth. Yes, the river fishing for trout and grayling is outstanding, but the fierce, biting midges can make it all a nightmare if you are not prepared.

Taking the internal flight up-country from Helsinki in a prop aircraft, as opposed to a jet, allowed me to get a good look at the countryside. It altered very little all the way north to Kuusamo. There were thousands of lakes and the land was covered in barren pine and silver birch forests. I decided to check the records; there are 187,888 lakes in Finland, and some are very large.

The two rivers that we were to fish were the River Kuusinki and the River Kitka, both of which run out of Finland into Russia. We were given a top local guide to look after us. His name was John Vainio. He took us to fish a stretch on the Kuusinki that is well known for its run of Russian brown trout. These browns are bred in the headwaters of the river, they then move downstream over the border into Russia where they live in the massive Lake Paanajarvi for thirty months. They then return to the rivers as wild browns of great size – rather like migratory sea trout, except they never enter salt water. The most memorable morning's fishing was when we caught four magnificent Russian browns. Chris Ogborne and Brian Leadbetter both tempted fish around 6lb, then our Finnish guide John, using a weighted

Olive Sedge Nymph on a size 10 longshank hook, decided he would join in the fishing. We must have brought him some luck as he connected with his largest ever Russian brown – a specimen of 8lb 8oz.

I had been fishing all morning with heavy tackle, because of the size of these big browns, but without any success except for a grayling. I decided to change to a lighter outfit with a 5lb leader, a size 12 weighted Hare's Ear variant on the point and a size 12 Zulu on a dropper, then I walked half a mile from the rest of the party. I started fishing a whitewater rapid, which was quite shallow and rocky. I had waded a third of the way across the river and no sooner had I cast my nymph into a flat mini-pool than a big fish took and I was into one of the best fights I can remember. The first leap was a magnificent four-footer, and I immediately thought I would never land this fish. I was on my own and without a net, as we had been returning everything.

My luck was in, however, for after several dazzling runs I was still keeping a steady, even pressure. At the same time I was keeping my rod very high, because I didn't want my dropper fly to catch one of the many rocks the trout was zigzagging past. The trout kept looking for an escape route, but the hook held firm and after about fifteen minutes the trout was getting closer. I had slowly backed up and was near to the bank. The fish made yet another leap as it raced into very shallow water and, on falling back, it stunned itself on the rocky bottom. Without any hesitation, I leapt in and pushed it up on to the bank. I was overjoyed and this was the only fish out of 200 that I kept during my two weeks' fishing in Finland. It was a magnificent specimen of 7lb 6oz. It made a good meal for our party back at the hotel, and was a welcome change from reindeer meat.

Each year some 500 Russian browns, going up to 20lb in weight, are caught in the Kuusinki. After these fish return to the river they behave more like salmon than trout and you have to tempt them by fluttering a fly or lure across their path, which they take as if it were an intruder to their resting position.

Apart from the migratory brown trout, the river held large grayling stocks, as well as a good head of whitefish. We caught plenty of them all. I also caught unwanted perch, pike and ide all on fly. The ide looks just like a roach but it has a record weight in Finland of 11lb. My best catch of grayling was fifty-one, between 25 and 28cm, in a three-hour session whilst fishing on the River Kitka. The best whitefish catch came one evening when Chris Howitt joined me to fish an area where the river ran into a lake. Whitefish were queuing up to take our flies, which, at first, were weighted caddis or sedge larvae patterns. I had especially designed these flies for this trip, after Oliver Edwards had prompted the idea. As the evening progressed, I began to take whitefish on a dry USD (upside-down) sedge pattern and over thirty fish were caught and released – the best about 3lb plus.

I imagine that you may be interested in Finnish fish records, so let me list some of them for you: pike of 52lb, sea trout over 40lb, brown trout over 32lb, grayling over 14lb, Atlantic salmon over 88lb, bream over 24lb and burbot, which is now extinct in Britain, over 33lb. So, you can see that Finland has great potential for all kinds of fishermen.

The staple diet at our hotel meant that all our party lost weight except for one Yorkshire man, Mike Mee, as he ate reindeer meat for breakfast, lunch and dinner – and loved it. With every meal being reindeer in one form or another, or raw fish, coupled with lots of walking in chest-waders in temperatures of 86–88°F I simply melted away. I lost nearly a stone in two weeks. Another major hazard were the giant midges, which were present in their billions. They even managed to bite through layers of jumpers on top of shirts and thick moleskin trousers. In the end, we sprayed one set of clothes with three or four bottles of repellent and wore these same clothes everyday. Also, a midge net worn over your hat was very essential.

A trip to Kussamo in early July will coincide with the run of the Russian browns. There is no doubt that these unique fish are well worth a trip. There is no human population by the Kuusinki river, so it is possible to wander freely along both banks – it could be termed as a wilderness river. Grayling over 2lb are regularly caught from deeper pockets in the rapids or from the large slower pools. And because there is plenty of fill-in sport with other species, plenty of action is guaranteed. It's just a pity about the reindeer meat and midges – but if you are willing to pay the price. . .

How I Catch Grayling

Traditionally regarded as being little more than a food thief to be persecuted at every chance, the grayling is at last beginning to be regarded as ranking equal to its game-fish cousins. Grayling are still culled on the lordly Test and other southern chalk streams where the trout is king, but now it's being done with care. The sad days of the piles of beautiful fish left to rot have thankfully gone. Grayling are far more widely distributed than many anglers realize. I doubt that many Midlands fly fishers who spend their summers on the stocked stillwaters are aware that nearby Derbyshire has no less than half a dozen rivers holding large shoals of grayling.

Obeying a different spawning calendar from the trout, the grayling are in peak condition in wintertime. Grayling are eager feeders and are suckers for a maggot or worm trotted carefully down into their haunts but, for me, I feel that they deserve better than that and my own plans revolve around nymphs, bugs and the dry fly, fishing close to the surface in the dead of winter. Believe me, it pays to keep an eye out for hatches of small olives, especially for that brief time around noon when the weather is as warm as it's going to get. The rise may last no more than twenty minutes and so you must be ready for it. Linger too long before switching to the dry fly and the opportunity will be lost.

I was fishing the Yorkshire Ure with host Mike Mee. It was a freezing cold December day and it seemed sensible to scour the bottom with leaded bugs and the like – and then the rise started. Mike, an experienced grayling hand, had his second fly rod ready mounted. Sacrificing his own chance of sport, he handed me the rod armed with a Partridge and Orange, Waterhen Bloa, and a Snipe and Purple on the point. That last fly was the most thinly tied fly I have ever seen, being just a wrapping of purple thread halfway up the shank and no more than half a dozen fibres of snipe feather for a long hackle. Any doubts that it would even be given anything more than a second glance by the grayling, by now feeding hard on the little olives, were forgotten as I took half a dozen from the shoal in less than twenty minutes. Locked into the efficiency of the little spider patterns, I now fix one on a dropper 2ft up from the point, even when fishing deep with weighted bugs.

Choose, if you can, a swim where the water races into the pool or where the pool tail lifts up into about 4 or 5ft of water. Casting just slightly upstream and allowing the flies to wander around with the current until they are below you will bring plenty of fish. On these days everything works, but as always with any kind of fishing, it isn't always like that. I learned a great deal about grayling fishing in Finland. One method I picked up is quite deadly. You go out in chest waders and stop when you're in the centre of a run. The cast is made upstream and then a small loop of fly line is flicked downstream. This allows the nymphs or bug time to sink down. If no takes are forthcoming, let the line go past you and pay out a bit of slack line. This stops the flies from lifting up in the water – just like trotting with a bait if you like.

New Zealand – the Most Impressive

We had driven past lake after lake, river after river, and all looked great places to fish. Suddenly I said to my car passengers, Dennis Buck and Jeanette Taylor (now Church), 'I am going to stop the car right here and try this lake out. I want to catch a New Zealand trout.' Setting up quickly with an intermediate fly line, with a mini Cat's Whisker on the point and a Damsel Nymph on a single dropper, I slipped into my chest waders and off I waded into the gin-clear shallow lake. Later on I knew it to be Lake Rotoma.

The sun blazed down from a clear blue sky and I admit my chances looked slim. Dennis and Jeanette commented, 'You have little chance here, it's too shallow and clear.' I tended to agree with them, but I kept casting and taking a few paces. Then after only five minutes or so, 'wham', a take so hard it could have broken me, but I was in luck. Then followed another ten minutes of a screaming reel and at least six high jumps from the angry cock rainbow of just over 6lb.

I played him into the shallows, removed my Cat's Whisker fly, a quick pose for a picture and off he swam none the worse for taking that funny English fly pattern. So it began; three weeks of incredible fly fishing with which I was so impressed. True, I have had some spectacular fishing holidays in my life, but I have to admit that my New Zealand trip in November 1991 was one of the best. Everything about it was as Zane Grey had said, 'The Fisherman's El Dorado'. So many pure crystal-clean rivers running over white pumice stone through unspoilt native bush was but one feature. The trout in these rivers, both rainbows and browns, went up to about 6lb, with 2lb to 3½lb common. Because it was only the spring season, by far the best method to catch these river fish was with various weighted nymphs.

Really, the giant trout of the large nutrient-rich lakes was such a mouth-watering prospect this was going to take much of our time. The only problem we were faced with from our home base of thermally active Rotorua was that there were too many good places to go and fish with fourteen nearby lakes in all. The lakes offered no easy fishing, as they do in autumn when all the fish come into the feeder stream areas to spawn. At this time of the year they have regained prime condition and migrated back into the massive lakes and, of course, they could be anywhere.

It pays to have a good fishing mate who owns a decent boat and luckily I knew just the man: Pat Neville who lives in Rotorua. Pat was stationed in London when he was in the New Zealand Air Force and during that period I shared a boat with him on Rutland Water. Pat said to look him up if ever I made the long forty-one-hour journey and I am glad I did. First, Pat took me on a tour of all the best lakes so I could make up my own mind where to fish. As it happened, I chose his favourite water, Lake Tarawera. It was a most exciting place to fish, not only for the large rainbows to be caught there, but also for its dramatic and tragic recent history.

Mount Taramera now has a flattened top to it, because in 1886, with little warning, there was a violent volcanic eruption. The Maori village of Te Wairoa was buried in rock, mud and ash. The whole affected area was 10 miles long, 2 miles wide and over 500ft deep. This then formed a new lake, Rotomahana, which now occupies the site of the original thermal basin. In all, 153 people lost their lives and 5,000 square miles had been destroyed. Today the native bush has regrown, and the lakes are placid and so rich in the right minerals for growing an abundant food chain on which trout grow fat, not least crayfish.

Pat's boat, like all New Zealanders' lake boats, was fitted with a sophisticated depth sounder. The method of catching fish most favoured at this time of year was what is known as 'harling'. We would call it trolling fly lures on motor. I wanted to try something different. 'Can I use standard English early season reservoir tactics and see if they work here?' I asked Pat. We duly found a depth of 15ft, where the anchor was dropped. I could then cast my fast-sinking line and white Tinhead lure way out over the drop-off ledge into 18 to 20ft of water. In theory this should be a holding spot and, yes, I hit the jackpot straight away again.

Our whole party killed very few trout on this whole trip, but Pat said that if I should get a few fish he would like them for smoking. They would be the first of his new season. After a few minutes I caught my first fish, 6lb 10oz, then two of 5½lb. I lost one and had another follow-up from another big fish, all in less than half an hour. Pat commented, 'I think we ought to move on, there's too many standard-sized eighteen-month-old fish about here.' As you might guess we never found a better place. Those fish were full of big crayfish and lots of smelt, which my Tinhead imitated well. The next day we returned and it was Jeanette Taylor's (now Church) turn to get into the action with some rainbows of 4½lb to 5½lb.

The famed Rangitaiki river was running high for the whole trip, but before it became heavily fished by practising competitors we did manage a couple of good catches. My best effort was seven fish, which came by fishing a sinking line and heavily weighted Stickfly with a Black and Peacock Spider on the dropper. These I allowed to swing into my near undercut bank, where the trout were laying out of the heavy current. Most trout were rainbows in the 1½lb to 2½lb weight bracket.

After we had been in Rotorua a week and a half, mostly using our own hired car, Jeanette, Dennis and I teamed up, while Paul Canning, Brian Thomas and Peter Cockwill had a second vehicle. We really got into the adventurous spirit of our travels. It was most interesting to note how all the creatures and plants brought in by the early settlers had thrived beyond all belief. Chaffinches, blackbirds, sparrows and thrushes are everywhere, and so too are wild turkeys. I made a friend of one of the native birds called the Tuis. They are very good mimics; by whistling to them they gradually come closer and closer to you, copying whatever tune you whistle. I even had one copy 'Pop Goes the Weasel', which left Jeanette quite amazed. The forests are full of wild deer, both sika and red, and also wild pig. I mustn't forget the quail, which is quite common. There was so much to see and do; if you were not careful, fishing times would suffer. Really, what I am trying to say is that New Zealand is a lovely, exciting place to visit.

Now came our lucky break – we were issued with the two top guides in the region to look after us for our final week's stay. Our man was Lindsey Lyons and his four-wheel drive would take us anywhere. First the Whirinake river, high in native bush, where I met a Maori with the unlikely name of James fishing from horseback with telescopic rod and worm tackle. He had caught nothing all morning, while I was banging out three pounders all morning on Hares Ear Nymphs. I even caught him his dinner.

Lindsey insisted we fished the local Lake Rotorua itself, for it is the most prolific trout lake in the area. Covering 79 square kilometres it is also the largest. It was just Dennis and me out on this trip and first of all we tried 'harling'. This produced fish after fish on the incredible trolling gear. This consisted of 100m of Led impregnated backing that was attached to a 770-grain Deep Water Express shooting head. Then the leader was about 30ft in length carrying two fly lures. Their method for attaching the lures is not on droppers as we would, they tie a second length direct on to the hook bend of the first lure. In practice this worked well and not many takes were missed. After a couple of hours we were back fly fishing and, although we had a few, results were not so good. Our catch: twelve rainbows from 3lb to 5lb in three hours. A boat nearby had a lovely 6lb brownie.

Next Lindsey took us to Lake Okataina; it had steep-sided native forest right to the water's edge. Access was limited and there was no sign of any human habitation. Again it was mixed fly fishing and 'harling', with Dennis getting a seven pounder and Brian one of 7½lb. Paul Canning saved his face after catching a couple on the 'harl' by taking a four-and-a-half pounder off the top, 'loch' styling. We did hear the best fish came from here a week before we arrived, an 18lb wild rainbow. One of our party, Ray Burt, took a 10lb-plus fish, which he returned, on a sinking line and buoyant Ethafoam fly pattern, fished as we do Booby-style.

Lindsey saved his best trip of all for our last day with him. It was to his favourite Waipa River in King Country of the Central North Island. It rained heavily all the way on the long drive but my first fish, a 3½lb rainbow, took my leaded nymph. Dennis took a rainbow and Jeanette a good brownie but, as we feared, the river was colouring up. Within half an hour the river rose a foot and was running bright rust-red and impossible; we had no alternative but to pack up.

Lindsey made matters worse on the drive back to Rotorua. He kept sighing, 'I saved the best to last, because this is where all the 5lb to 6lb browns are.' Can you imagine what we would pay for river fishing like that in this country. In New Zealand it's free, except for a rod licence.

Was the long journey really worth it? Well after forty hours, stopping at San Francisco, Honolulu, Fiji and finally Auckland, then a three-hour bus ride, I somehow made it. Yes, I had a long sleep still fully clothed. Yes, I had jet lag for three days but, yes, it really was worth it. I shall go back. Prices were not outrageous, Air fare return was £800, perhaps £1000 now with United, but you will gain with the price of food and drink, which is very cheap. Believe me, after going to Tasmania and now New Zealand, the world seems a much smaller place.

9

The West of Ireland – the Place for Me

Although I have fished in virtually every top game fishing country throughout the world, it is to the West of Ireland I still head for most. It is my all-time favourite place. Everything about the West (Co. Mayo and Co. Galway) suits me; four massive wild limestone loughs, plenty of wild rivers, smaller loughs for salmon and sea trout – it's endless. The other great attraction for me is that time doesn't matter and the people are great. Their hospitality is the best there is. In short, I love Ireland; I have always felt completely at home there. For many of my early adventures I was staying at Robbie and Nan O'Grady's guest house in the little town of Ballinrobe, where time seems to stand still. When staying with Robbie I would always concentrate on the 21,000-acre Lough Mask and the really lovely 4,000-acre and shallow Lough Carra.

When fishing at Lough Conn, 12,876 acres, I stayed at the Pontoon Bridge Hotel where Brendan and Anne Geary were hosts – but now run very ably by son John, who was just a young boy on our first trips. Lough Corrib is so big it pays to explore a number of guest houses around its massive shore-line; at 41,617 acres it is very, very big. The wild brown trout fishing here is a challenge for any angler and a good catch gives the greatest satisfaction. On occasions I widen my horizons to fish one of the smaller loughs that has a run of migratory fish. Waters like Innagh, Kylemore Abbey, Beltra, Ballynahinch, Costello, and two others at the Burrishoole fishery loughs, Furnace and Feeagh. The sea trout fishing (pre-salmon-rearing cages in estuaries time) was magnificent and the salmon fishing from the drifting boats has always been difficult but OK. So the salmon food trade has a lot to answer for. I am not going into the reasons, as most know them because the same thing happened to the West of Scotland sea trout stocks. However, let's get on to the good things.

Let's look at Lough Conn first. To get there in the fastest time, fly from Birmingham to Knock, then hire a car and you can walk into Pontoon Bridge Hotel two hours after stepping on the plane.

Irish tourist board UK fishing manager Paul Harris and I were going to do an exploratory fishing trip on a couple of waters. Following a good breakfast, all Paul and I had to do was load our fly tackle into the waiting boat in the hotel's own little harbour.

Paul and I were lucky to have a top ghillie in Keiron Connolly. Keiron was always out on Conn before moving to England to work, but he returns for his six weeks' holiday each summer and where do you find him? – out on the lough. He told me he gets more pleasure ghillying, and helping visitors have good sport, than actually fishing himself these days. It was 10.30am. Total number of anglers in sight, just two, Paul and myself. A typical Irish laid-back approach to the day. As we tackled up we saw the odd mayfly fluttering around in the shelter of the hotel. This is not unusual, as on all four loughs you will see a few mayfly, even in September. What was unusual was to become apparent as we motored across the lough and into the first little bay. Here it was, 6 August, and we were witnessing the best mayfly hatch I have ever seen in Ireland. By the time we packed up at tea time, we had caught twenty-three takeable-sized trout to 2½lb, keeping ten for the hotel.

Our three fly floating line cast was to fish a size 14 Black Spider on the point, a size 12 Green Peter in the middle and a size 10 mixed Yellow-And-Olive Hackled Mayfly on the top dropper. The fish didn't come too easy at first and it wasn't until I sprayed the Mayfly well with floatant, so that it fished proud on the surface, that the main action began. The wave was light and Keiron skilfully manoeuvred the boat's drift, using the back oar occasionally, to keep us on the edge of the shallows close to the rocks and islands, and sometimes the natural shoreline. If you allow the boat to drift too far out over the very deep black water your chances became much less. About 10 to 15m out was the right distance. We possibly rose over 100 trout to catch the twenty-three – it was that kind of day – and needless to say it was the Mayfly that was the most effective pattern.

The secret of fishing Conn is not to cover the same drift twice. Apart from the fish being put down, there is so much water to choose from, so why waste it? Now, I have to stress, to those of you who have filled in your apprenticeship with rainbows at the small fisheries and the reservoirs – this fishing is for you. The ultimate challenge awaits you here.

As well as my normal holidays to the West I used to put in a few extras with *Trout Fisherman* magazine editor Chris Dawn – we had worked together a lot over the years, as previously he was features editor at *Angling Times*. Chris always liked to go off on a fishing adventure when the job allowed and he had been invited to do Conn. He knew I was familiar with the place so I was asked to make up the fishing side. Chris is as good a feature writer as any of the greats and I remember reading his story in *Trout Fisherman* on our trip a month later. This is how he opened the piece: 'A black cloud wrapped itself in sinister fashion around the 2,646ft peak of Nephin Beg mountain, heralding the storm to follow. Above us the elements joined in battle as the unusual clear blue skies were quickly blotted out by heavy banks of cumulus from the west.'

Chris, that was a great opener. I would have probably said, 'As we headed out the skies looked stormy and we could expect a downpour very soon'. I remember that session well, because Dessy Burke was our ghillie. We had a slow start but eventually 'Dessy' put us on a new drift to come down the Colmans Shallows. The waves looked scary as they sprayed across the shallow rocks, but it was here that the brown trout were prepared to rise up and take the top dropper bob fly. By expertly pushing and pulling on the back oar only, Des drifted us through the most productive areas. As we came to the end of the drift, I had boated four good trout to 2½lb; all came to my own-tied slimline version of the famed Green Peter.

Of course, salmon run through the lough and lots of grilse are taken on wet fly by trout fishers. This peaks during June time. Bob Morey, who was out in another boat, was broken on a salmon on this day. His boatman, the experienced Martin Crawley, had already taken six salmon amongst his trout by June. The short stretch of the River Moy that joins Conn to the little Lough Cullin, which is very shallow, is also good for salmon. It had produced fish to 18½lb and an individual catch of nine salmon on the best day. As Martin put it, 'A terrible year for hay means a good year for salmon.'

There are lots of stories about Conn I can tell. The day Jeanette and I were out on Conn we had an excellent catch on a mayfly pattern called the Yellow Humpy – it's an American tying. Jeanette had fish to just over 4lb while my best went 3½lb. Then I did an Irish television film on Conn with Jack Charlton prior to the World Cup when Ireland got to the last eight to be beaten on penalties. The film was good and I had a good banter with Jack on fishing and football. If you get to Conn yourself, my old pal Alan Pearson lives close to Pontoon and he takes anglers out on the lough, then out-drinks them in the bar afterwards – how he has done this for ten years I don't know; I envy him. Look him up for a good day out.

Lough Carra

Before we go on to the big loughs, let's go to the smallest of the four – Lough Carra. Mind you, it's still as big as our largest, Rutland, with Pitsford added on. I've spent a lot of time on this beautiful lough, much with my old mate Frank Cutler who I miss so much when I now go to Ireland – but he did reach eighty years of age. I can remember fishing here in a boat with Jeremy Herrmann when I caught a lovely three-and-a-half pounder on a dry Daddy-Long-Legs. I fished with Peter Thomas, Robbie O'Grady, Mal Parrott and, of course, Jeanette; always, there would be some kind of rise during the day.

Carra is very consistent and you will always get half a dozen fish; I have had a dozen or more on perfect days. The olive fishing is very good, then, when the mayfly arrives, it hangs around on and off until September. There will always be fish to rise up to you as the whole lake is very shallow. There is a passage through the reeds for you to get into the upper lake, and this fishes very well as it doesn't get fished so regularly. Successful flies are Delicate Dry Mayfly, Sooty Olive, Golden Olive, Olive Quill, the old traditional Greenwells Glory, Daddy-Long-Legs and the fly invented by some Scottish friends, the Peter Hog. They had some superb catches of big fish to 4½lb on the muddler-style Wake Fly.

Carra is a unique water, for the first impression I got when arriving for my boat at Brownstown was that of a coral reef. All of the shorelines were packed with white snail shells and the water is unbelievably clear. The white chalky bottom can be seen at all times, even when drifting far out in a boat. The very high pH content grows a good mixed food chain and the trout thrive accordingly.

There is another fly that does well on Carra in mid-summer and that is a size 10 Goats Toe tied with the blue peacock breast feather. I had ten fish to 2½lb while fishing with Peter Thomas when the trout were feeding on natural damsel flies that day. Remember that, next time you see lots of mating damsels that mainly fall on to the water where they are sipped under by feeding trout. Often, we all tend to fish with damsel nymphs when confronted with this situation. As I proved on a number of occasions, the Goats Toe is a sound artificial at this time.

Lough Mask

This 21,000-acre giant is wild, moody and dangerous, but quite exciting to fish. I first fished on Lough Mask back in the late seventies with Paul Harris, Frank Cutler and Alan Pearson. We stayed that first time with Robbie and Nan O'Grady and I was to partner Frank in the boat sessions.

That was a baptism of fire for us all. To say the weather was bad was an understatement, for each day we suffered very strong, squally cold winds. This set up some really big waves roaring down the lough. The safety angle is so important. We hit one rough wave that I am sure was 8ft high – and remember, I am used to big waters. Robbie insisted we did the wise thing and fish in close to the many islands. One of the largest is called Devenish and has a herd of wild goats on it. Frank and I started wet fly, traditional style short-line fishing, as even in such a blow there were a few flies hatching in the shelter of the island. Our first drift produced three good trout. I had one which Robbie called a 'Gillaroo'. He pointed out a double bulge in its stomach – apparently they have developed over thousands of years of evolution. It looked just like a fatter, more spotted brown trout to me.

We were too early for the mayfly hatch, when fishing is incredibly good. But there were hatches of early, small dark sedges and lake olives. These were imitated with a favourite Irish tying called the Sooty Olive. I found Teal and Black, Mallard and Claret, Golden Olive and Invicta very good. But, as

Frank discovered, in the largest waves it was a Soldier Palmer on the dropper which made the fish rise – even if they did take one of the other flies. Even in these poor conditions I found Mask trout very free rising, and when hooked they fought and jumped more times than our Grafham rainbows. The average size is about 1½lb but the fly takes trout to 5 or 6lb.

We caught plenty of fish during the week, mainly lough-style wet fly fishing, but we also had several fish on nymphs. I took them mostly on a Black Buzzer. Strange as it may seem, with the limited amount of sunken-lure fishing we tried, none of us even had a take. But we did so well at the wet fly fishing that we were asked to return to the lough during the first week of August to take part in a World Cup Open Professional or Amateur competition. Fly fishers from all over the world travel to Ireland to fish in this match, which takes five days to complete. We didn't need inviting twice; we came back for this superb fly fishing festival. There are always 600 to 700 anglers entered and the knockout heat system of around 150 anglers a day when 20 per cent each day go through to fish the final.

At breakfast in the guest house Robbie would greet us. 'To be sure, there's going to be a bit of a breeze on the lough today lads,' he would smirk with a wry grin. 'I've just heard the weather and they're forecasting a Force Nine. Don't forget those life jackets now.'

It's all part of Robbie's kiddology. The ominous forecast has the desired effect of striking fear into the breasts of his rivals, all striving to qualify for the final of the prestigious World Cup Wet Fly Championships. Robbie knows the score. He's the only man to have won the event twice already and he's looking for a hat-trick. But first – like the rest of us – he's got to qualify. And under the appalling weather conditions that had lashed Ireland all summer, that was no easy task.

This is the twenty-first World Cup on Lough Mask – that frightening sheet of water that separates the mountains of County Mayo from the meadows and peat bogs that stretch inland to the Shannon. Large enough to swallow seven Rutland Waters, Mask has a reputation for sorting the men from the boys. Three drownings the previous year (1978) just confirmed the dangers of the great limestone lough. Advised not to venture out in an unsuitable boat, the trio paid for their mistake with their lives. Mask employs more full-time boatmen than any other Irish lough and to venture forth without one is simply courting disaster.

Lough Mask's dangers lie in its reefs of pointed, hull-tearing rocks that reach up from the bottom to within a few inches of the surface. In a big wave – and on Mask that can mean 5 or 6ft – they can become uncovered for long enough to rip out the bottom of the most carefully motored boat. This is where the skill of the ghillie ensures that you arrive back safely. For over years of working the lough, each man has built up a mental picture of where the hull-crunching rocks lie. So he skilfully manoeuvres the 19ft craft through the hazardous areas. Not that they still don't scrape the occasional rock. This past summer's incessant rain raised the lough's level by several feet, concealing many rocks beneath the surface and calling for even more vigilance on the part of the boatmen.

Secretly, even Robbie O'Grady is concerned about this forecast. He's fished the lough man and boy as a professional ghillie, and understands her many moods. But this is the worst weather he can remember for twenty-five years. It speaks volumes for the experience and safety of the boatmen that no-one has yet had to be rescued. All Mask boatmen carry provisions to cope with a shipwrecked night on an island if their motor fails and they are driven ashore. Escape from drowning may be one thing, death from exposure is another.

Despite weather that seems to have been conceived by an Atlantic hurricane and dispersed across the ocean on the wings of a storm to Mayo's wet and windy shores, the little market town of Ballinrobe is bustling with the excitement of the World Cup. Not too much happens in Ballinrobe. It's one of those anonymous little West of Ireland towns that you might drive through without a second glance. Yet for World Cup week it really comes alive.

Try and squeeze into Art O'Neil's Bar at eleven o'clock and you'll be lucky to find elbow room. A heady mixture of tobacco smoke and Guinness does nothing for the fishing to follow. And if you can twang a guitar or banjo then rest assured you'll be joining the impromptu ceilidhs that keep the town swinging until the early hours. But talk of the fishing is never far away. The day's results are posted up in every bar in town, while you can pay for a handful of Green Peters, Murroughs or yellow-hackled Mayflies with your beer. Art will also give you odds on winning if you're a betting man. And what Irishman isn't?

Today the final chance to qualify for the Bank Holiday Monday final. And every Irish wet-fly crack seems to have been drawn to compete on this day. Our English contingent is guardedly optimistic. A practice two days ago brought fish for everyone, but with a new 12in limit many of the trout were undersized. Choice of fly on these limestone loughs is usually limited to a dozen tried and tested patterns. You must have a yellow wet Mayfly somewhere on your cast – the mayfly stays longer on Mask than on other Irish waters. Then a green-bodied sedge like the Green Peter in one of its many tying forms. The other great favourite is the big dark Murrough Sedge. Local Ballinrobe angler Jo Jennings was to win this big event. It was a difficult low weight day, but Jo did the trick with two fish for 6lb 12oz. Jo only had one small fish of 1lb 7oz with twenty minutes to go when he hooked a specimen brown of 5lb 5oz to give him victory.

I've been entering this World Wet Fly Competition now for twenty-odd years but there is just one problem with having this week's fishing holiday –

you need another week to get over it! It's all fishing, eating, drinking, socializing and partying, with very little sleeping. I am afraid now I am much older I cannot keep it up like I did, so it is everything in moderation these days.

I've had some great days afloat with Robbie as boatman; he tells a good tale and is very funny. He sings Frank Sinatra songs, either to you in the boat or to everyone in the pub at night. Robbie has won the World Cup twice and a few years ago nearly made it three when he came a close runner up. I can tell you that takes a bit of doing with 700 top anglers all trying to win it. My best performance was a close second when I lost by 1½oz to a German, Kurt Menrad. In that final I also lost a fish of about 1½lb at the net when the fly pulled out.

I have always looked upon the competition as the ultimate challenge; a kind of pilgrimage to the fearsome Mask. I think the element of danger felt on those big wind days helps to spice up what is normally considered a tranquil sport. When I was younger, the rougher it was the better I liked it, as I have never been afraid of water. After experiencing a rough day on Mask with all those dangerous hidden rocks, Rutland Water will seem like a goldfish pond. Where the World Cup is concerned, there is always another year.

So To Corrib

Lough Corrib is, at 44,000 acres, by far the largest of these loughs and for variety and quality it has to be looked upon as the best. Of course, it's my new favourite after those giant ferox browns I caught in the summer of 2001. The early season duck fly or buzzer fishing here is also the best of all the loughs.

An early trip with the *Trout Fisherman* magazine crew saw us target the early season buzzer fishing in the first few days of April when the hatches peak. Our two boatmen for the day are the Malloys, Martin and John, although they are not related, it's a common name around Corribside. They pick us up from the jetty at Currarevagh Bay, below the magnificent western shore of the lough above Oughterard. Often they'll troll on their way to and from the various marks in the hope of a bonus salmon or big brownie. With the winter rains making the lough extra high at the start of this season, the commercial trollers were able to rake the shallows with up to six rods at a time and cull a number of quality browns before the flyfishers had a crack at them. 'Shall we be taking the brickeens, sur?' asked Martin. These were a can of minnows, as used by locals by tradition for many years as an accepted way of catching a few trout and salmon for family food; we politely declined.

But there is now a growing number of local anglers based around Galway who are developing new flies and methods for Corrib. Out are the thick leaders and fat bushy wets of the past. In their place are English-style ideas of long, fine leaders of double-strength line, and fly patterns more representative of the hatching duckfly in all its various stages. Armed with these new imitative Irish patterns, and some of our own, we head north towards the mountains of Connemara and the remote Doorus peninsula, where traditionally the best of the fly fishing is to be found.

We've heard many reasons why the big black chironomid is called the duckfly, but our boatman Martin has the most sensible reason as he points out a party of baby mallard. The fly hatches at the same time as the wild duck, whose young greedily gobble them up from the water surface. Hence the name.

Our first drifts – if you can call them that – are in the area of Bob's Island off the Doorus Peninsula. Unfortunately, the light wind has now ceased to exist and we are becalmed in 10 to 12ft of crystal-clear water. Looking over the side of the boat, I can examine every lime-encrusted rock and pebble on the bottom. The rising sun has now burnt away the last vestige of cloud and we are greeted by a day more in keeping with the Mediterranean than the rain-lashed Ireland we are used to. Apparently, Irish summers are changing too, greenhouse effect or not.

Trout are rising in the flat calm but, despite all our efforts to creep up on them, they keep their distance. Then a light ripple spreads across the lake and we start to drift, with our boatmen expertly working the back oar to take us past any little spits or other fish-holding areas. We search out the 'black holes' – the name given to those tempting deeper areas of calm water in the shelter of the islands where the duckfly hatch and trout feed. Massive boulders, which lie on the bottom as if thrown there by some giant, suddenly give way to darker, deeper areas of water that hold the trout.

Photographer Peter Gathercole (Chris Dawn's boat partner) is the first to score as his True-to-Life Buzzer imitation is gently taken by a 2lb brownie. Like most wild browns, the fish stays deep at first, fighting under the boat before launching itself airwards in series of spectacular leaps. You just don't catch small browns on Corrib, where the average fish is around 1½lb. But the ripple dies away as quickly as it appears and, with no sign of clouds or breeze, we make for land and the traditional boatman's brew-up.

Just to prove that Corrib water is among the cleanest in Europe, the kettle is filled from the margins while we hunt for stationary chironomids among the blazing gorse for Peter to photograph. Great black clouds of the midge dance in the air above our heads as we relax in scenery unchanged for centuries. A grey bank of cloud from the north-east sends me and Paul Harris, hurrying back on the water. And our confidence is justified as a fresh drift off Cassidy's Bay on the other side of the Doorus Peninsula produces us a fish apiece to sparsely-dressed Bibios.

Chris hooks a fine brownie close to the boat on the local tying of the Hatching Duckfly with its pearl body, and moves another. Flies that represent the duckfly are legion but traditional black and red patterns like the Bibio and Zulu are effective early in the season. Peter Ross, Watson's Fancy, Sooty Olive, Connemara Black, Black Pennell, and Black and Peacock Spider are other local favourites.

Again the wind dies down to nothing and we are left becalmed over water where you could get out and walk. Yet just a few yards away a 'black hole' drops away to the depths. The sun is now so bright that our floating lines cast a shadow across the bottom. The only answer is to long cast and intercept individual rising fish.

Peter sticks to his buzzer pattern, and a purposeful draw across the path of a moving fish produces a smash take and a curly end to his fine-diameter, double-strength leader, which has become kinked in casting with no wind to straighten it out. Paul and I are into fish and we call across to the others; our killing flies are now Black and Silver Spider, and a similar Delphi Spider with its jungle cock tail. Again it's long casting to rising fish that brings results. Peter's enthusiasm hooks and loses him another fish on the Spider pattern, while Chris resorts to pushing the rod tip beneath the surface to sink the line a few inches and stop any wake in the flat calm. The response is immediate from a near two pounder that grabs the middle-droppered Watson's Fancy. Then it's time for a few more drifts off Bob's Island before we have to head for home. But the fish here are shy and we hook a couple only to lose them.

The fishing has not been easy due to the unseasonable weather, but every trout hooked has fought like the leopard whose spots it seems to have borrowed. That evening we are to see a magnificent catch of fish to 5½lb, caught on buzzer patterns from 5pm onwards by a local angler with his own boat. Certainly Corrib gives you the chance of big fish in water that, although clear, is invariably sheltered enough to let you get afloat on most winds. And if you can persuade the ghillie to stay out after five then your chances are improved.

A drift on Corrib is something every trout angler ought to experience at least once in his life. But if you do go and try it, you will come back time and time again as I do.

Since that first trip I've fished Corrib at olive time with Jeremy Herrmann; this a terrific time to be on the lough. Just pre-mayfly we do OK on normal olive patterns but Jeremy cracked it one day when it was very hard to get a take. The lough was flat with almost the tiniest of breezes. Jeremy kitted up with a very slow-sink neutral-density fly line, 4lb sub-surface nylon leader and a couple of well spaced-out Olive Nymphs, one size 12 and the point size 14. Typically, Jeremy cleaned up with six good browns with everyone else blanking or getting ones or twos. A good tip that.

As time has past, of course the skinny buzzer and 'bung' method of fishing them has caught on well on Corrib. Basil Shields, the very experienced ghillie, soon cottoned on to the successful English reservoir technique and used it with exceptional success on Corrib.

Our friend, top London fly fisher Micky Bewick, took a holiday on Lough Corrib during the month of May last year expecting good Mayfly fishing sport. Mick said, 'In the sunny calm conditions I cast out three dry Mayflies and then realized how ridiculous they looked. As there were a few buzzers hatching I decided to set up a 20ft fluorocarbon leader and then fish three Buzzer Nymphs at varying depths.' The flies fished totally static and the takes were easily spotted as the floating line sailed off at a different angle. In four successive sessions, some just half days, Micky took at least four browns with an average weight exceeding 3lb; that is quality sport and the locals were still talking about it on my visit. It proved that methods developed on the English stocked reservoirs would work equally as effectively on Ireland's largest wild brown-trout lough.

Micky returned this season; he started his first Corrib session at gone 11am; by 2.30pm, he had trout of 3lb 14oz, 3lb 5oz, 3lb 4oz and 3lb, and this is how it went on. Micky used olive or black lightly dressed seal's fur buzzer patterns, ribbed with plastic nymph glass. As he pointed out, they sink very quickly on the fluorocarbon leader and this is an important part of their success.

Basil told me this story about Micky, who I know very well of course. Basil is not one for passing new ideas by, so he was trying the same method himself this year, going one step further and trying the skinny all-varnished body buzzers. Catches have been excellent and the average size of the fish is up by a very high margin. It is important to concentrate this buzzer fishing on Corrib's weedy shallow bays (some bays are as big as Grafham) where the natural insects hatch in abundance. This is also where the bigger trout live, close to these easy food items.

My fishing companions this trip was Carol Neal and Kevin Garn and they had already been out with Basil for a few days before I arrived. They had caught on a mixture of tactics, the buzzer was still working even though it was getting late for them. However, although traditional wet fly lough style did work, another English method was working even better, that of Hopper dry fly fishing, again this was static. Kevin and Carol managed the best catch of eleven trout, up to 3lb in weight. While Kevin and I scored well on the dries as well, one beautiful spotted fish I had took a size 14 all-black Hopper.

The other waters I fish in and around these loughs, all in Co. Mayo and Co. Galway, are Lough Furnace and Feeagh for salmon and sea trout. This is known as the Burrishoole fishery. I have observed and fished there under the management of Chris Mills, Ken Whelan and now Pat Hughes.

When fishing short-line wet fly tactics it's worth remembering that the method that kills the plentiful sea trout, a very fast retrieve, misses out on the salmon. On the other hand, the very slow salmon-style of retrieve, dropping the rod on the take and so on, misses out on the sea trout. We lost five salmon this day, all taking on the fast retrieve but of course not being hooked properly. All were summer grilse of around the 6lb or 7lb mark. Trout anglers are well-known for losing salmon, because they always strike too quickly. You must allow a salmon to turn down on the fly, pausing long enough for him to be pulling off line before you strike. This is something that is far easier to do when you are fishing a river and are after salmon only.

To sum up, I have introduced this area of Ireland to a number of friends over the years. To a man, each enjoyed the fishing and good company (the 'crack') so much that they return as often as possible.

On one occasion a business pal of mine, Dave Whitrun, was there to pick me up and drive me to Newport House Hotel. This is a fine traditional sporting hotel and life there revolves around the game-fishing guests. Newport House has the Newport River to fish for sea trout, salmon and brown trout. The famous Lough Beltra is also available and it was my idea to spend some time on this lough when I booked the trip with Paul Harris. However, fate was about to take a hand in the matter as I was in for one of the biggest surprises in my angling life.

I recognized Paul's car parked on the verge by the river as we were almost into the little town of Newport, so I asked Dave to pull over. I called to Paul, 'What's the fishing like?' The beam on his face meant something good. 'I am just warming up,' he said. 'Only been here an hour or so but I have had six over 3lb.'

By now, I thought he was winding me up, because nobody catches six specimen sea trout during midday in bright sunny conditions. He stopped fishing and emptied his bass bag. There in the grass were six fine rainbows of around 3lb apiece, all carrying sea lice. I was speechless but, as Paul stressed, 'I don't know what's happened, but let's make the most of it'.

I checked into the hotel, put on my fishing gear, including chest waders, and set up an IM6 rod, No. 7 floating line and 6lb leader with one dropper. As I arrived back at the river Paul had packed up and it had begun to rain heavily. 'I'll ghillie for you, sir,' Paul joked in his best Irish accent. 'The top pool is just below the weir and this is affected by the back-up of the tide. It is, in fact, the last spot where the tide influences this little river.'

I waded out into the centre of the tree-lined stream, where I needed to Spey cast to drop my flies – size 12 Golden Olive on the dropper and Bibio on the point – close to the far bank. With my fifth cast I had a fat 3½lb rainbow, which fought much harder than any sea trout would at the same weight. This was soon followed by another three pounder – both took the Golden Olive. By now we had begun to call these fish 'poor man's steelheads'. Steelheads are an American sea-run rainbow. Yet Paul and I had never heard of such behaviour before, either in the UK or Ireland. We realized that the fish were escapees from sea-rearing cages.

Back in the foyer of the hotel the fish were laid out in traditional manner, and caused quite a stir among other guests. As it turned out, each tide brought fresh fish but we soon tired of them as the novelty wore off. However, I did manage a lovely 4½lb specimen which fought more like a fresh salmon. The hotel guests had a great time catching these rainbows, which certainly made up for the lack of sea trout, which are usually prolific in September. Poor sea trout fishing was the story throughout the whole of the West of Ireland last summer. An in-depth survey into the problem is being carried out right now. By comparison the salmon fishing in the region has been better then ever, with the famous Moy system producing over 1,000 fish every week throughout the summer and autumn.

We did, of course, get on to Lough Beltra for a day. But it was the only day the sun shone and this spoiled our chances. I rose a salmon that refused my artificial Daddy at the last second and, on the day, all of us needed to get our sport from small brown trout. It was better later on.

Let me quickly run through other places where I have caught salmon and/or sea trout or both. Lough Carrowmore is very good in May and June. I also like the fishing as Ballynahinch Castle and the hotel is superb. Costello fisheries' sea trout are back in big numbers; on my last day there we had twenty-seven and all were returned. Kylemore Abbey lake and Lough Innagh along the Connemara Pass are both good. I feel I have not seen the best of Kylemore yet. We caught some fine sea trout one evening in the upper lough. Jeanette had the largest at 4½lb.

The Corrib weir outflow forms a short river to the sea and the Galway salmon fishery is a place I love a day at when I am anywhere near the city. Then, of course, you have the most prolific grilse river on these islands, the River Moy. The Ridge Pool and Cathedral Beats at Ballina produce massive catches. So too, it is good at Mount Falcon Castle beat; one afternoon a party of us caught eleven grilse there. It is where Jeremy Herrmann caught his first ever grilse that day. While I think of it there are a few other loughs I've fished for brown trout; they are Lough Owel, Lough Arrow, Lough Melvin and they were, for international competitors, good. A couple of trips to Lough Allen for pike proved very good for specimens. Alan Pearson had an estimated thirty pounder on the troll, while Frank Cutler had a 22lb fish and Jeanette and I had fifteen pounders. During the next trip, Paul Harris and I had lots of fish in double figures with the best a twenty-two pounder to Paul.

Going back all those years to 1968, when I first visited Ireland, I remember flying in an old Dakota plane from Birmingham airport to Dublin. From there I went to the town of Boyle where I fished the river for bream. I also caught pike in Lough Key. Thirty-five years have come and gone since then and I've been back so many times. I hope for a few more years yet – I'll just take things more slowly.

10
More River Fishing

River Fishing with Fly

The English rivers I fly fish are, of course, the Test, Kennet, Itchen, Derbyshire Wye and that's about it. The other river I like is the Welsh Dee downstream from Lake Bala on to Llangollen. This fishing is dry and nymph for trout and grayling.

On a River Test visit many years ago Barry Welham taught me the real fishing ethics of how to approach the river for trout in high summer. It's a discipline I have passed on to others over the years and on this trip my son, Stephen, would learn about this leisurely art. The slow start of purchasing more kit from the tackle shop in Stockbridge, the riverside lunch, the chat and anticipation while eating, is all part of the build up to put you in the right frame of mind. When you reach your river beat there is no need to rush because it's all yours for the day.

The secret is to tackle up a light outfit. Mine was my own Chalkstream 8½ft rod, with a DT5 floating-line; this had a finely tapered hollow braided leader 1m in length attached and from this was another metre of 4lb low-diameter nylon. At this stage you do not tie on a fly until you find out what is hatching.

So now you put on your Polaroids and hat to walk slowly upstream, fish-spotting and looking for any rising trout. You will certainly see some fish but not necessarily any rises, so you sit on one of the many riverside seats and wait. Resisting the urge to just begin fishing is all part of the gentleman's handicap.

For sure, sooner or later there will be a hatch. After determining which natural fly it is, tie on your own tiny dry artificial version. Then by slowly moving and casting upstream you will cover the persistent 'riser' and, more often than not, a good cast means he is yours. It's real stalking, cat and mouse style, which leaves you in a world all of your own and far away from the rat race of reservoir competition fly fishing. It's a welcome change of style, which makes you think tactics every bit as much. Also, there is something very special about fly fishing in a good quality river.

There were a few little black gnats and sedges about and it would appear the odd rises were coming to these, but there was no proper hatch at the moment. So I began by tying on a size 16 Black Gnat and covered my first rise with it. The fish, a brownie, rose and refused my fly. I soon realized why; I had not degreased my leader nylon enough and it stuck out like a sore thumb on the surface. Casting very accurately upstream is easily done, because of my braided tapered leader and short nylon length; turnover of the little dry fly is perfect. The very next cast up the same brown came again and I was into a lively 2½lb fish. With this type of mobile fishing I always carry a small flick-up landing net, which is kept in a holster on the left side of my belt. As the trout is played out I just reach for the net, give it a flick to erect and then press the button to release the spring-loaded extension handle. The landing is then easily carried out.

As early evening approached a good hatch of iron blue duns (*Baetis niger*) began and now there were more rises to cast to. Steve soon got the hang of it as we tied on the correct artificial pattern. We had some nice rainbows up to 3lb and three grayling of 1½lb, plus a couple more similar-sized browns. We joined up with our host, Ron, who also had a good mix of rainbows and browns. All in all it had been a great day's sport and I was content in the thought that I had trodden the path of many great anglers long past. For it was here that F.M. Halford and Marryat learned their dry fly styles, which were passed on to be a common approach today. Fishing days can be booked from various locations up the Test valley. It really is worth treating yourself to a day that you will picture in your memory forever.

These days I fish the Test at Longparish with a great friend, Geoff Clarkson and also a few days as Ron Randell's guest on the Leckford beat. I must, though, finish with a tale of my very first Test trip as I told it to my *Angling Times*' readers almost thirty years ago.

Test Match Drawn

Who would ever have guessed it? There was I, the original lure bottom scraper of the reservoirs, all tackled up on the banks of the famous River Test. I had a prototype carbon fibre dry fly rod, a No. 5 DT fly line carrying a 3½lb leader and a tiny No. 16 nymph on the end.

On top of all this, my most generous host – Dermot Wilson of Nether Wallop – had provided me with a real luxury, a ghillie. Trout fishing ghillies are a rarity these days but in Nick Mitchell I had a very good one. He not only knew the particular beat well, but also the lies of some big fish that had refused to be tempted by anglers' patterns all season.

I was pleased to be fishing a river again, especially England's finest for trout. The beat did not vary much, except that the weed beds were thicker in places. These created stronger currents through narrow runs where trout waited patiently for food. The main feature of the stretch was a deep gin-clear pool, and here the water was fast and turbulent as it came rushing through the tunnel of a wide road bridge.

Nick told me that any pattern within reason was allowed – in this pool only – and would I like to try some of my reservoir nymphs as an experiment? To be honest, I didn't really. But he seemed keen to see if they would work on the aristocratic Test trout.

Green fluorescent has proved to be a very successful attractor colour with reservoir rainbows in recent years, and I had a few of this colour nymph with me. They were slightly weighted, and tied up especially to try on those Avington fish.

I put one on, dropped my fly on the water and as it sank a few feet there was a flash and I was broken. Of course, No. 8 short shank was too big a hook for such a delicate leader. I changed to a 5lb BS tip and on went another fluorescent green nymph. In the next hour I believe I caught seven rainbows.

The thing that amazed us both was how well the fish reacted to my 'induced take' type of retrieve. As well as the fish I caught, others came out of their secure hidey-holes and behaved in a very excited manner. The bright lights of colour had certainly stirred them up.

A return to the hut for some lunch and some liquid refreshment stored at river temperature went down well. This was followed by a serious hour of nymphing with imitative patterns on the main stretch. I managed another good fish, as the sun shone brightly, which took a shrimp twitched along between the weeds.

Really, I was looking forward to the evening and hoping for a good rise to fish at. I went back to the 3½lb leader and tied on a No. 14 Lunns Particular in readiness. Nick took me to the downstream end of the stretch and a few fish began to rise as we walked.

One fish on the far bank took the eye, for it was a most persistent riser, showing every few seconds. I covered him from a slightly downstream position and several times my fly almost touched his nose. But he didn't want to know.

There were a few small sedge about, but Nick reckoned it was a Pale Watery that he was taking. This was tried with equal failure.

Even though I say it myself, my casting was pretty good as far as accuracy and presentation were concerned, and I tried several more patterns, like Sherry Spinners, Caenis, White Moth, Olives and so on – all no joy.

The thing that amazed me at this point, half-hour or more later, was that the fish were rising more confidently than ever.

Nick then laughed and said he was just trying me out. Apparently he knew this fish well. It was between 4lb and 4½lb, had been in this spot all summer and lots of anglers had tried to catch it.

My first thoughts were to try for some other easier fish, as several were now rising up and down the river. I didn't want these though, for it was a matter of pride. I felt I must stick with this one while he continued to rise so tantalizingly.

'Try finer tackle and a more sparsely dressed dry fly,' Nick advised. This gave the fish a well-earned rest for he obviously knew all about anglers, me especially. A 2¼lb leader was really pushing it, but on it went, with a No 14 Hornsby Pheasant Tail.

My first cast was short but the second was spot on, and he took. In a split second I hooked him, rolled him over on the surface and was broken. I doubt if the fish felt much of the impact, because the line broke like cotton. Just to prove what a superior fish he was, within a few minutes he was rising again.

It had taken a good hour to tempt him and Nick was full of congratulations. He knew the important thing was not necessarily to land this fish but to just fool him. It had happened to me and many before.

It was now dark and I felt quite good after my battle of wits with such a Test fish. As I walked back to the car with a brace of fish, I realized the truth of the old saying, 'There is more to fishing than the catching of fish'. Deep down I know that trout will die with old age.

Nowadays it's upstream only and I do love the dry Mayfly. Jeanette and I have some great days together at mayfly time. I've got lots of river fly fishing stories, but I want to go back now to my local river, the Great Ouse, where I learned my water craft with chub fishing all those years ago.

Barbel in the Great Ouse

I had been chub fishing the Great Ouse on my local Northampton Club card since the mid-fifties. My old friend, the late Frank Wright, used to meet up there with me at Turvey, where the chub was always our passion. We did get a few of 5lb plus, but in the main the chub were smaller then – so many of 4lb to 4½lb and a few five pounders – however, it was still good. Both of us used to holiday down south at Christchurch, to fish at the Royalty Avon Fishery for barbel. Also we would go to the nearby River Stour at Throop Fishery, again for the barbel, which was an exciting treat for us.

First Double-Figure Barbel?

In 1966 I took a week's summer holiday at the Royalty Fishery on the Hampshire Avon. There I used to meet up with my old friend Peter Wheat and, being a local, he would always give me good advice on swim and the like. Even in those days there was a bit of a rat race for popular swims and the Pipe Slack on Green Banks was supposed to be pole position. Anyway, I managed to muscle my way in somehow and although anglers to my left and right were very close I decided I would stick them out and see who gave in first.

Not much happened in the morning so it thinned out a little. I then fed about half a gallon of maggots into the slack and just on the edge of the current. This I did over the afternoon period. I was using a split-cane Richard Walker MkIV rod, 5lb breaking-strain nylon, a three swan-shot link leger and a size 12 hook. Bait was my favourite sandwich of two maggots and nip of fresh bread flake on the hook shank.

I had a 5lb barbel then an eight pounder with someone else's hook in its mouth. It was from a guy fishing some 20yd upstream; he had been broken in the morning and came and checked, and it was his hook alright. As the light faded just before packing up time, I had a serious bite while touch legering. It took a fair while to land that barbel but it was quite big. With only one major angler left, he came to look at my fish. I weighed it in a light mesh piece of netting and it took my 10lb-maximum little Samson scales down with a bump. He was no help, he had no scales either, so I shall never know, but at least I got a picture. (Do you like Brylcreem? *See* black and white photo section.)

The stocking of the River Severn with barbel in 1962 is one of the greatest gambles ever to pay off in modern-day fishery management. The fish have found the Severn very much to their liking and so the reproduction has been high. Every angler who fishes the river has benefited from this. Match weights have been boosted considerably since the barbel began to show up in numbers, while specimen hunters and casual anglers have made impressive catches. In fact, everyone who visits the Severn these days is secretly after the barbel. All this has triggered off anglers in my locality asking, 'Why can't we have some barbel in the Great Ouse?' Well, I can tell them this idea is nothing new.

The Northampton Nene AC own much of the fishing rights from Olney downstream to Carlton. Some eight years ago the question of stocking club water at Newton Blossomville and Turvey was brought up at the annual meeting when it was suggested that barbel would be at home in these lengths. They would I am sure, breed easily giving good sport to both matchmen and specimen hunter. Frank Wright and I pushed this point.

The meeting was in favour of pursuing the matter further but, after looking into it, they found that barbel stock was impossible to obtain. That was eight years ago. The situation could well have changed now and I believe our club president, Ray Edgely, is keeping his ears open. With the roach still very short on the stretches mentioned and the bream only rarely co-operating, the barbel, I am sure, would fill the gap handsomely. Yes, I do know barbel are already present in small numbers on some stretches of the Great Ouse, but in the main these come from well downstream of Bedford.

In the mid-1960s a few barbel were caught at Hemmingford Grey, in a weirpool. My good friend Ian Howcroft of Luton discovered this spot, but it would be true to say the fish are few and far between, even if their smallish size does prove some successful breeding. Many years earlier Dick Walker caught six fine barbel between 6lb and 9lb from Offord weirpool, but little has been heard of such fish coming from that area since.

That barbel are terrific fighters and one of the most exciting of our freshwater species to hook and play is true. Northern and southern England have fine barbel rivers, which many Midland anglers travel big mileage to fish. It would be so nice, though, to have such a barbel river on our doorstep and I think this could be achieved, if a fair stocking of fish were put in the right place.

After looking at the Ouse over the years (almost from the source to where it enters the sea) I was confident in the 1960s that the gravelly shallows, complete with streamer weed at Turvey and Newton Blossomville, would suit barbel so much that they would reproduce in much larger numbers. This would trigger off a more general stocking of the river as some fish dropped downstream from time to time. The stumbling block is where to get the barbel, and getting support from the river authority – mind you they did give us permission to stock eight years before but we failed to obtain any barbel.

As I said earlier, the situation today is quite different. I am sure the head of fishery officers of the various river authorities must be acquainted with each other. With the River Severn absolutely teeming with small barbel I am sure an arrangement could be considered, whereby, say, 100 fish could be transferred to the Ouse. It would be a very small loss to the Severn, but could well be the making of great things to come for the Ouse!

In fact, in the 1970s, Des Kelsall of the Severn and Trent Water Authority gave the Northampton club sixty barbel of 1½lb to 2½lb from the river Severn and they went into the Great Ouse at Lavenden. Those fish have now (2003) bred so well they have populated the whole river down to Bedford. The fish at Great Linford and Adams Mill upstream of this area were a different stocking. From such small beginnings, then and thirty years later, the Great Ouse is classed as the best barbel river in England and still they are growing bigger. I would go as far as to say the river itself is also in better condition now than it was in the fifties. Certainly, on average, most species of fish grow larger; that is true of chub and those incredible perch, even the pike went to 33lb last winter. The river is very clean and clear just now.

As many of you know I drifted big time into stillwater trout fishing and so my trips to the Ouse were neglected. I put this right two years ago when John Emerson and I decided we would seriously try for the river's big barbel. Re-discovering our old favourite spots, which were once chub swims, we found they now held barbel and we began to catch a few to around the 8lb mark. Gradually the barbel bug was getting us.

I began to do a lot more fish location spotting as well as fishing; certainly this helps in plotting the downfall of a really big fish. This is really for the summer and early autumn when the Ouse is low and gin clear for much of the time. Then in winter, when the river is higher and coloured and spotting is no longer an option, at least you have a good mental picture of where they will be laying. One thing for sure is there are barbel-holding pools where they live and do not often feed. Then there are swims they move into purely to feed, then move out again. This is well proven with many of the Ouse's bigger fish.

With specimen chub mixed in here and there with the barbel, it is natural to take advantage of the situation you sometimes come across, especially when exploring new stretches. In fact, it was chub I was doing best with at the start. I came across a shallow swim with three good chub in and one looked well over 5lb. This was at Harrold. Not rushing to fish for them straight away, I sat back behind some rushes and watched their behaviour. They were taking the odd morsel as it came into the little pool from a fast streamy run-in. I helped nature on its way by flicking a few grains of corn in. As they seemed suspicious of these I soon changed to flicking sinking trout pellets in. Very soon their heads were down feeding as I introduced more and more pellets and now there were seven chub in my swim, one of which was 6lb plus.

Because of the very shallow nature of the swim, I knew it was going to be one cast and one fish before I would spook the rest in the landing operation, there was no way to avoid this. So a two swan-shot link leger and a size 12 delicate hair rig hook carrying two trout pellets was flicked out quietly in the direction of the better fish. As it happened the bite was instantaneous and I couldn't miss it, so confident were those chub feeding. It turned out that I had hooked the second biggest fish from the now disappearing shoal, but at 5½lb I was very pleased because it was in prime condition.

In this period I caught a lot of good chub between 4½lb and 5½lb, but the barbel had stopped at 8lb 12oz and I was looking for my first Ouse double. By now I had met up with my old pals Phil Smith and Stef Horak and they gave me plenty of encouragement. I was impressed with Stef's great air of confidence and so it was I changed to feeder maggot and dropped the pellets and soft pellet boilies that had worked well in summer.

Fishing up the river at Turvey, John had caught three doubles topped by a December-caught fourteen pounder. In November I paid the ultimate price for stupidity; whilst turning my back on my rod to pour a flask of tea, the big barbel bite came – in short I lost this very powerful fish, a mistake never to be repeated. In January I again hooked a big fish on the maggot and at 12lb 12oz I was both pleased and relieved – at last a double. My first Adams Mill barbel.

So far I found out that Ouse barbel were fairly straightforward to catch where they are plentiful and of all sizes. However, where they are much larger, but in fewer numbers and extensively fished for, to say they were difficult was an understatement (for instance, Adams Mill). Two of the most successful barbel fishers, Graham Attwood and Trevor Wilson, seemed to be catching more than others and they were known to be very good on baits – in short, special paste baits. Naturally, as friendly as they were, they kept no secrets other than their baits.

Trevor (bless him) said to me one day near the seasons end, 'Have you ever thought of trying a sweeter bait as opposed to savoury?' That was enough information for me to prepare for the next season. During the river's close season (God forbid it will never change) I contacted well-respected bait maker John Baker and talked through the situation, telling him roughly what I wanted and asking him to come up with a special Bob Church bait for me to use for Great Ouse barbel. He never let me down; I purchased a bulk 10kg load of frozen boilies and also enough dry mix to make my special paste for the rest of the season. I chose my old favourite caramel flavour for this.

I caught quite a lot of good barbel up to 14lb 4oz from different stretches of the river on the boilies. I even threaded two of them on Gareth's over-long hair rig for him to hook his massive 17lb 5½oz fish on – will I ever learn? So, my tip here is have your own bait that is a bit different. Some shops are really specializing in barbel tackle and Leslies of Luton have even developed their own complete section. Just as the carp boom began, there are signs that barbel are moving into second place in the popular-species league.

Although keen barbel hunters travel all over the country to fish many famous rivers, the Great Ouse upstream of Bedford does take some beating. For those who don't know, for just over £100 in total you can join four angling clubs. They are the Northampton Nene Angling Club, Newport Pagnell Angling Club, Milton Keynes Angling Club and the Vauxhall Club. All these clubs' waters have produced many big barbel to well over 14lb, so there is plenty of riverbank to choose from. I am also positive there are some stretches holding big barbel that are still unknown – why not try to find them with me?

In the first chapter, I covered the year 2001, so let's move on to 2002 when Ray Walton made a video of the regulars fishing here. Adams Mill is probably the home of the most well known stretch of river anywhere in this country. That includes all the top salmon fishing. I admit to being completely absorbed in the place and I can enjoy a session there just walking, talking and socializing and, very importantly, fish spotting, studying their general behaviour.

This stretch is just twenty minutes drive for me so I am rather lucky. I was never more pleased than when I knew I had been accepted as one of the new syndicate there, which began on 16 June. I would add that it's the only syndicate I have ever belonged to in sixty years of fishing. But as fate played its hand, it had to be.

In the last week of September, in very low gin-clear water, there was only Paul Thompson and myself at the mill. Beneath the bridge, in clear view, was: a British record barbel and another very close to it; a solitary massive roach of well over 4lb, probably another national record; five chub over 5lb with one monster of about 7½lb; and finally a perch of around 3½lb. Oh, by the way, don't just take my word for this, as most anglers who go there have seen them and collectively assessed these weights. They have resided there for two months now.

Paul started to fish, while I was going to watch the fishes' reaction with just my head sticking over the bridge. He went as light as he dared and fished a natural bait, 'lobs' instead of the normal boilies. The bait at times dropped within a couple of feet from the roach but it never even looked at it. The two big barbel would drop back downstream a few metres before moving forward close to the lobworm where they merely looked at it. Even the big perch was having none of it and the chub ignored everything. He did catch five perch, with the best close to 2lb. I watched this for around two hours and it was quite fascinating.

Mark Ward has built up a reputation for catching the first Adams Mill barbel of the season and he did it again this June, on the 16th, with a fine 13lb 7oz fish from 'two trees' swim. He made it a double P.B. when he also landed a big chub of 6lb 4oz later in the morning.

I had a decent chub on opening day of 5lb 3oz, and to date the chub fishing was excellent, as I've caught others of 5lb 12oz, 5lb 9oz, 5lb 7oz, 5lb 5oz, two of 4lb 14oz, 4lb 10oz and several others over 4lb. Quite a few members have targeted the massive chub which we all see regularly, but cannot catch; it appears to be at least 7½lb now.

There was a period in July when Adams was invaded by large pike, which must have come up from the deeper water downstream. Unfortunately, they had an appetite for big chub that rather shocked us. We caught a few fish with pike slashes on their flanks. John Pawlowski was playing a 4½lb chub when a pike came from the weeds to take it across its jaws. John managed to manoeuvre the fish so the pike let go – the chub barely survived. That's minor to the amazing sight that Tim Gillard from Milton Keynes witnessed, one July evening. Tim quotes:

I first saw a flash of silver in the clear pool as the pike hit the chub. The pool then erupted as the pike had the chub held across its jaws. Now it was shaking and turning the huge chub to swallow it. Scales the size of 50-pence pieces were flying like confetti and then the pike sank into the depths out of view.

Enter Ray House the bailiff, who had loaned a small spinner and trace from my bag. He tied it on his rod, cast blind across the pool and started reeling. It was then he got lucky and foul-hooked the pike, which he soon brought to the landing net. To all our amazement there was just a massive tail and about 6in of the rear end of the chub protruding from the pike's throat. The pike went around 15lb but, wait for it, when Ray pulled the still just alive but savagely lacerated chub out it weighed 5lb 10oz, a true specimen size. The chub died and we moved the pike to deeper water above the weir where we put the other big ones.

Graham King has worked quite hard to keep the flow going during the long low-water period. He has been in, complete with wet suit, to remove a large bed of rushes above the weir, which was causing a dam effect, slowing down the flow. Once removed, the flow increased and tumbled the weir faster creating more oxygen for the fish. He also cleared all the nasty obstacles from beneath the flood raft so no hooked fish would be tethered if it ran under it. Having just played a good fighting twelve-pounder that went right under the raft during the fight, I can vouch he did a good job.

Graham is a top carp man and a well-travelled fisher, taking big sailfish, wahoo, and tarpon on the fly. However, he began his Adams Mill barbel career with twenty-eight blanks two and a half years ago. He was very determined to succeed and, to his credit, began to get a fish or two most times he fished. This all built up to an amazing catch he took on 11 July, when he caught six double-figure barbel. The river had risen about a foot or more and was dropping back to normal. Conditions were good and the catch came from four different swims as only a couple of anglers were about. Here is the catch in order: 14lb 8oz, 13lb 2oz, 12lb 4oz, 11lb 8oz, 13lb 8oz and 14lb 1oz, which I was there to photograph. The daytime catch went 78lb 15oz, which to our knowledge is a national record. Graham has been the most successful angler for barbel at Adams so far this year.

The two largest barbel caught so far came in July. John Pawlowski caught 'Red Belly' at 16lb 13oz, which was about right for the record breaker's early summer weight. Steve Curtin also had a fish of 16lb 6oz, known as 'Stumpy'. This fish had not been caught since Stuart Morgan landed it lower down the river at Kickles Farm. One and a half years ago, it briefly became the record at 17lb 14oz – who said these fish were easy?

As we go to press, the news is that 'Red Belly', the current record fish, has died. Found very freshly dead it weighed 19½lb; it was put into a deep freeze by syndicate member Steve Fisher. Certainly, a couple of days earlier I had been watching these two fish swimming together, as they have since last July when they were both caught. It was noticeable when 'Red Belly' came out the last couple of times it had developed cataracts on both eyes. As Ray Walton said, 'It was probably over twenty years old.'

Although the current record, to Steve Curtin in October 2001, is 19lb 6½oz, it was always slightly smaller than the fish known as the 'Pope'. This was last caught in September 2001 at its lower weight of 18lb 4oz. I feel, had this fish been caught last February–March it would have broken 20lb plus, and that goes for this season too.

11

At Last a Taste for Carp

I have fished for everything that swims – well, almost. From roach in the Nene, to sailfish in the Bahamas and a lot in between. The incredible thing though, in all these past years of specimen hunting, the one and only fish I have never spent serious time after is our most popular fish, the carp.

Why this should be, is hard to track down but, when I was young, actual results at carp fishing in my locality were pretty poor. There was Billing Aquadrome, which produced blank seasons for angling acquaintances, so I did not want any of that. I was more into tench, eels, chub and pike and of course there was always those trout, as there are six major reservoirs from ten minutes to forty minutes' drive away.

I suddenly realized I had this huge gap in my lifetime angling c.v. so I decided this year, in the barbel close season, I would try and put the carp on my decent specimens caught list. I had, of course, dabbled for carp over the years, catching quite a few doubles up to 16lb or so. But I had never done the job properly. I had plenty of expert advisers from the Northampton Specimen Group, Tony Gibson, Chris Berry and Gavin Walding, and from the Adams Mill crowd, Steve Curtin and Graham King. How could I fail? I filled two extra spools on my small 5000 Shimano bait runners with 15lb Catana line and dug out a couple of 11ft 2.5 test Bob Church Carp/Pike rods. I was advised to keep my hook rigs simple, which I did.

This year I have been doing my own boilies and pop ups to the trade, so bait was freely available in quite a variety of flavours. In April and May the tench had taken a great liking to the Wild Strawberry Isotonic Boilies. I had as many as twelve in a session at a Fenland pit. At this water, every so often, I hooked a wild carp and they were so fast and strong, taking me into the tall reeds where they had a knack of depositing the hook. So first of all the stronger tackle was tried out here and, I was pleased to say, with a reasonable degree of success. I could now apply instant maximum pressure and keep the carp from getting into those reeds, which were growing in 5ft of water.

I started to try different boilies and it seemed these wildies liked the yellow-coloured Burnt Scopex baits best of all. Gareth Hancock and I were getting wildies of 6lb to 7lb and over 8lb. They were lovely sleek fish, but we wanted the 20lb-plus jobs that it seemed lots of other anglers were catching up and down the country. Gareth did, in fact, lose a good common in the 24lb class a year earlier; he had stalked it, then got it feeding on sweetcorn before hooking it on that bait, with three grains on a No. 10 hook hair rig. Gareth had to hold on pretty tight as the rushes, reed and lilies were so thick, but the hook hold slipped – to his great disappointment. However, we did realize after this incident that there were some larger fish amongst the smaller wildies and well worth catching.

I had now stopped fishing the lighter tench tackle, concentrating solely on catching a big carp here. I definitely wanted one over 20lb. When I have switched on my determination button in the past, it has meant a P.B. is on the cards. I was determined to get a big carp without bivvying up, because I have so many backaches and pains, I did not want to aggravate this situation – but dawn till dusk was OK.

We baited up a new swim in a shallow gravel pit, which ran out some 30yd into the 20-acre pit, using all sorts of old broken boilies, corn and new 'Beanies'. This was early on in the day; we then went and fished elsewhere only to return here as the light faded to twilight. After about ten minutes I had a screaming take on my Spicey Crab beanies (two) and I was in to a powerful fast-fighting fish. Even on the 15lb breaking-strain line it was going well. Then, as I played it closer to us, we could see it to be a long fish, and there was another of similar size swimming with it. Gareth confidently said, 'You have got your twenty', and I thought so too, right up to the landing net. It was not to be, but I had caught the most beautiful wildie I am ever likely to catch. It weighed 14lb only, but the colours and its length made it a special fish. I was happy and at least they were getting bigger.

National barbel record holder Steve Curtin is a very experienced carp angler, but over the last three seasons he has switched to barbel. We have become good fishing mates during this time so he decided to lend a hand and help me with my carp quest. We spent a day at a big gravel pit near his home, one that holds some very big carp. 'Your tackle is fine,' said Steve. 'Just keep it simple and sit back and wait.'

A 22lb fish had been caught at first light by an angler bivvied up and we were fishing by 6am. We both had good looking swims casting across to an island. Lunch time arrived without a bite and then we heard a 29lb mirror had been landed right round the opposite side of the pit. As we were told there were a lot of carp gathering there for spawning, we decided to change our swims and drive round.

The fish were spawning alright, as they were crashing about violently across a narrow channel towards another island. Steve gave me the choice of spots but all I had was a line bite, while he kept up his good form by landing a mirror of 22lb 6oz and a lovely well-marked young eight pounder. He genuinely said at packing up time, 'I wished you had that twenty pounder.' I said, 'Steve, it's better if my big carp does not come too easy, as I will respect it more when I get one.'

Then I had a good stroke of luck. Every season I spend a couple of days trout fishing with Ron Randall. He takes me down south to fish dry fly on the River Test and I return the compliment on a trout reservoir. Ron had been saying for some time, 'You must come and try my syndicate carp lake, I am able to take a guest.' For some reason I had never got round to it, but my new carp interest and quest had changed all that. It is a very old 6-acre landscaped lake.

So, on the day England played Argentina in the World Cup, I was at the lakeside to meet Ron at 5.30am. He had pre-baited one corner of the lake with my new isotonic boilies; these were a mix of four varieties, as I was using up some that had been damaged in their package in transit. So there was no set flavour to put on as bait. It was absolutely pouring with rain and in my eagerness to get started I never put my over-trousers on. I got under the brolly and put out my rods. Strawberry boilies on one and the nice smelling Burnt Scopex on the other. The first two hours brought me two jolting line bites, as the rods nearly pulled off their rests.

Then I reeled in the Strawberry rod and put on my new pineapple-flavoured fluorescent-pink 'pop-up'. This I set to fish 3in off the bottom. I cast out to the same spot, wound down to my lead, set the free spool baitrunner and before I could sit down it was away with a confident run. I knew it was a big fish as soon as I struck the hook home, as at first it was slow moving but very, very heavy. I took my time and gradually played the big fish across the neck of the lake. In the dark-coloured water I got a glimpse of the fish and could see it was a big common. Ron was on hand to net it and at 31lb it was a new lake record. I was completely soaked because of the weighing, photography and so on and so forth.

I couldn't wait to cast out again quick enough, so I stayed wet. I was soon in for another surprise that was to give me a red letter day I would not forget in a hurry. This time, an hour later, it was the Burnt Scopex bottom-bait rod that went, again a good long fight before landing a longer but leaner common carp. It turned the scales at 28lb and I was one happy angler.

We stopped fishing at 12 noon, I changed my clothing and generally dried out. A fine lunch and a glass or two of wine, then England stuffed Argentina as we watched the match on television. This was doing things in style. I wondered, would we catch any more fish in the afternoon session?

As it happened we did, Ron had a 'wildie' of 9lb while I had another nice wildie of 12lb. At 6pm we packed up and it was still raining. I think I had actually arrived as a proper carp fisherman. Three fish for a total of over 70lb, not a bad day's sport in anyone's book. Interestingly, the 6-acre lake had risen 6in during the course of the day, such was the continuous downpour.

I've done quite a lot of other specimen hunting with perch to 3½lb, roach to 2lb 6oz, rudd to 2lb 12oz, zander 10lb 8oz. I've even had a crack at sea fishing round our shores from a boat. I once caught a British record small-eyed ray of 12lb, when the record was 11½lb. I've taken blue shark from Cornwall, and lost a giant porbeagle shark off the Isle of Wight. It's not often I talk about the ones that get away, but I must tell you this one.

Back in May when the sea had hardly warmed up, I was trying for my first porbeagle shark. Again I was in luck and had the only take of the day. I allowed it plenty of line, – he was on and well hooked. At this stage the shark was some 100yd from the boat. I steadily pumped it back; this took about fifteen minutes. I felt the sweat trickling down my back and could hardly believe that any fish could be so strong, especially as the line breaking-strain was 130lb.

Everything was going well, I applied more pressure and the skipper was holding the gaff in readiness. Then it happened, a sudden burst of speed and strength from the shark, the power was fantastic. The reel screamed off 50yd or so of line on maximum drag and I was pulled to the side of the boat. Then suddenly the drag stopped slipping, everything pulled tight, the fish never looked like turning and 'ping' went the line. The skipper let off some violent curses, I momentarily sat in disbelief. Even now it is hard to forget, for the fish was an estimated 200lb-plus porbeagle.

What made things worse, it would have been the first shark caught off the island since 1971. The breakage was caused by the reel jamming when the slipping drag was losing line at maximum speed. This all happened while fishing out from St Catherine's Point on Dick Down's boat *Zane Grey*.

I want to end this book by mentioning some of the big-name stars of show business and sport who I've fished with for the day. First and never to be forgotten, Eric Morecambe; Bernard Cribbins, Chris Tarrant and I do lots of fishing charity days – these two are very good all-round anglers and would be considered expert fishers. Geoffrey Palmer, Frankie Vaughan, Sir Michael Hordern, Jenny Handley, Jack Charlton, Emelyn Hughes, Jimmy Greaves, Gareth Edwards, Bobby George, Bob Anderson, Ian Oglive, Malcolm Fraser (ex-Australian PM), Anton Rodgers and John Denver the Country and Western singer.

All of the sporting and show-business stars I have fished with have one thing in common – they love the total escapism fishing gives them.

I fished with Vinnie Jones in a boat on Rutland Water when he was nearing the end of his football career. He is a good fly-fisher and on the difficult day, he caught three nice trout on a Hawthorn Dry fly. He then was guest of honour at our Bob Church Classic competition. He made a humorous speech and presented the prizes. I think it was one of his first big after-dinner speeches and he went down very well. I cracked to him afterwards, when you finish with football you could earn yourself an income doing this sort of thing. Little did we both realize he would soon be a Hollywood superstar!

The lovely Eric Morecambe never failed to make me laugh so much when on television. So when we met at a special fishing day at Patshull Park and he knew me as a top fly-fisherman, I was very flattered. But he was quite an able fly-fisher, as was Frankie Vaughan, and they were drawn to fish together in this particular charity competition. Everyone had caught a few trout that day and were all queuing to weigh in. Eric had about ten trout in his bag as did others, but Eric's catch was far the heaviest. This was thanks to a bronze heavy replica trout; he weighed in with his other rainbows.

The glamorous Jenny Handley was the compère of *Magpie*, the long-running kids' programme. I was asked to take Jenny and the crew to Fenland to catch some pike. This we did successfully and it was filmed the following day on television. At the end of the programme, Jenny did a competition for the juniors to see who could catch the heaviest pike. The winner would be presented with a Bob Church Pike rod and reel. This would be at the Thames Television studio during her 'live' *Magpie* show. Jenny told me to come down to London on the train to Euston, where I would be picked up by the TV chauffeur. I was certainly given the VIP treatment, as Jenny was there to meet me and take me to lunch in the Thames restaurant. She arranged for me to sit in between Diana Dors and Sir Harry Secombe over dinner and I was well entertained as the old 'Goon fan' I had always been. Later I got through the live show fine and the Terry Thomas broadcasting tuition and experience helped by giving me the confidence needed on such occasions.

Welsh rugby wizard Gareth Edwards and England's football World Cup winner Jack Charlton were trout and salmon fly-fishing fanatics. On a day spent with Gareth we shared a catch of twenty-five trout of over 2lb each at a fishery called Westward Park. Jack and I got to know each other very well and fished several times together. We made two very good videos, one on Rutland Water when we both caught our limit of eight fish, and one on Lough Conn when Jack was manager of the Ireland football team.

I have known both Bernard Cribbins and Chris Tarrant as fishing mates for over twenty-five years. Both are very good all-round anglers and fish for most species as I do. I did witness Bernard catch a super sixteen-pounder from Aveley lakes in Essex. He is always very consistent, even winning a competition on Grafham Water. Chris was a mad keen carp fisher in his younger days – pre-*Tiswas*. He caught 30lb+ carp when fish of that size were very rare. He has a list of large specimen weights of most species including salmon over 20lb, pike over 20lb, brown trout over 10lb, etc; etc: at present Chris is trying for a giant barbel from the Great Ouse.

So I end it all in a bit of a hurry, but 80,000 words is my maximum. I hope you have enjoyed reading about my travels and experiences. When it comes to it, though, my local fishing takes some beating. In that respect, I have and always will be very lucky. Tight Lines!

Index